Woodturning
A Foundation Course

Woodturning
A Foundation Course

NEW EDITION

Keith Rowley

Photography by Tony Boase

With a foreword by Bert Marsh

Foreword to the new edition by Ray Key

Guild of Master Craftsman Publications

This edition first published 2015 by
Guild of Master Craftsman Publications Ltd
Castle Place, 166 High Street,
Lewes, East Sussex BN7 1XU

Reprinted 2016, 2018

First published 1990
First edition reprinted 1991, 1992, 1993, 1994, 1995, 1996, 1998

Second edition published 1999
Second edition reprinted 2000, 2001, 2002, 2004,
2005 (twice), 2006, 2007, 2008, 2009, 2011, 2012

ISBN: 978-1-78494-063-8
(ISBN 0 946819 20 3 1st edition / 978-1-86108-114-8 2nd edition)

The publishers and author can accept no legal responsibility for any
consequences arising from the application of information, advice
or instructions given in this publication.

A catalogue record for this book is available from the British Library.

Publisher: Jonathan Bailey
Production Manager: Jim Bulley
Managing Editor: Gerrie Purcell
Managing Art Editor: Gilda Pacitti
Designer: Fineline Studios
Cover Design: Rob Wheele at Wheelhouse Design, Cornwall
Set in Rotis Semisans
Colour origination by Viscan Graphics (Singapore)
Printed in China

Contents

Dedication

This book is dedicated to the memory of my late father who taught me to appreciate the beauty of trees and wood and persuaded me to follow a trade working with them. Also to my wife, Jean, who has always provided unfailing support and encouragement in both the professions I have followed.

Acknowledgements

I would like to thank Geoff Ford, who has spent many hours in my workshop preparing all the excellent line drawings for both editions of this book, in addition to undertaking all the photographs for the first edition. He is extremely talented in his field, and I have come to regard him as a good friend. Thank you very much, Geoff!

To Tony Boase, a talented turner in his own right, I express my thanks for the pleasurable few days he spent in my workshop, patiently and professionally undertaking the coloured photography in this new edition. The quality of his photography speaks for itself.

A big thank you is also offered to a neighbour, close friend and valuable workshop assistant, Robert Ollerenshaw. Bob is a retired engineer, and he has rendered valued opinions and assistance with certain aspects of both editions.

A special thank you is extended to Axminster Power Tools Centre. They went to great trouble to provide the Woodfast lathe that has been used for all the sequence photographs in the new edition. Nothing seems too much trouble for this company, and their response to any request is efficient and prompt.

The following companies have also provided tools and equipment, and my sincere thanks are extended to all of them: Art Veneers Co. Ltd; Ashley Iles Ltd; Craft Supplies Ltd; Crown Tools; Multistar Machine and Tool Ltd; C. & M. O'Donnell; Record Power PLC; Robert Sorby Tools; Henry Taylor (Tools) Ltd.

Last, but by no means least, I am most grateful to all the staff, past and present, at GMC Publications who have given me help and encouragement in producing this book, in particular Liz Inman and Stephen Haynes.

Important note

Readers are strongly recommended to read the section on safety, pages 169–70, before attempting any of the practical work in this book.

Metric and imperial measurements

Although care has been taken to ensure that metric measurements are true and accurate, they are only conversions from imperial. They have been rounded up or down to the nearest whole millimetre, or to the nearest convenient equivalent in cases where the imperial measurements themselves are only approximate. When following the projects, it is important to use either the metric or the imperial measurements consistently; do not mix units.

Foreword to the new edition

I was delighted to be asked to write the foreword for this new edition of *Woodturning: A Foundation Course*. Since its publication in 1990 it has been rightfully acknowledged as one of the standard classics on the subject in recent times. It is directed in the main at those just starting to turn, but there is much in it that many a seasoned pro could learn from.

The title of this book was an inspired choice: there can be no doubt that if you put Keith Rowley's advice into practice you will indeed have a secure foundation in the craft. Written in a clear, no-nonsense style, it shows you how to do things correctly, while also making you aware of what can go wrong. This is teaching at its best – not easy to do in print, but Keith manages it wonderfully. Exercises and projects are progressively structured to build up the reader's skills.

Much of the text remains essentially unaltered from the original edition – and rightly so, as it all makes such good sense. But its publication in full colour adds another dimension, while the totally updated account of equipment now on the market, and the addition of a number of new projects, make this a book you will want to own even if you have the original.

I have known Keith for a number of years and know something of his competitive spirit – you have only to challenge him to a game of pool or golf to find that out. In some ways, writing a book on woodturning, when there so many on the market these days, requires that kind of spirit.

Keith Rowley is one of the true gentlemen of the woodturning world, and in writing this book he has done a great service to those just starting out.

Ray Key
Evesham, 1999

Foreword to the first edition

People may argue the reasons why, but no one can disagree that recently there has been a great upsurge in interest in woodturning. Numerous enthusiasts with a thirst for knowledge have been watching demonstrations, attending seminars and courses and initially being inspired, but becoming frustrated when finding themselves alone in their workshop. This is often because the proper groundwork has not been laid down, and this book will, I am sure, help to encourage the development of the necessary basic skills, which will lead to both greater satisfaction and enjoyment in woodturning.

It is especially good to see someone writing a book from the depth of their experience, rather than regurgitating recently read or discovered facts. Keith, a professional woodturner who, to use his own words, 'Had a life-long love affair with woodturning', has succeeded especially in writing a book which provides a safe basis for beginners. The title, *Woodturning: A Foundation Course*, describes the book exactly. A foundation is a firm base to build on, and I am sure that this is what the book will provide for many readers, who by following its advice will go on to become accomplished turners.

I remember talking to Keith soon after he had set out to write this book. He was very pleased to tell me he had moved into the twentieth century, the era of technology. 'I bought myself one of those computer, word processor things,' he said. Then he proceeded to tell me how, after reading the instruction manual, he quickly set about enthusiastically on the first chapter. After a time, very pleased with his efforts – a screen full of text – he pressed the button to print. Oh dear – wrong button! The script disappeared for ever. With a gleam in his eye, he said, 'That was the best thing I have ever written.' This may be the case, but somehow I doubt it, and thank goodness the urge to push that particular button was overcome.

With the text finished, and the addition of a considerable number of excellent photographs and very well produced drawings, this is a book to be valued and referred to by amateur and professional woodturners alike for many years to come.

Certainly I am sure that many turners and would-be turners will be most grateful that Keith got the buttons right on his computer.

Bert Marsh
Brighton, 1990

Preface to the new edition

In the nine years since this book was first published, the popularity of woodturning has continued on an upward curve. More and more people are appreciating the joys of working with wood, and woodturning in particular. Because of this increased interest, lathe, accessory and tool manufacturers are constantly striving to improve the range and quality of their products to meet the demand.

In essence, the main objective of this new edition remains the same – that is, to impart a thorough understanding of the basic, safe and correct techniques. However, it was thought necessary to update certain parts of the book, to make the reader aware of some of the improved lathes and accessories available at the present time. Additionally, it was considered appropriate to include and briefly describe two items of ancillary equipment which are of great benefit and

practical use to the woodturner: the pillar drill and the bandsaw.

To create added interest, six new projects have been included. All are capable of being undertaken by the newcomer to the craft after the main thrust of the book has been carefully studied and the recommended exercises diligently practised.

Perhaps the most striking change from the first edition is that all the photography has been undertaken in colour, and this, I hope, will add to the appeal.

Finally, I take this opportunity to thank all those readers of my first edition who have personally congratulated me on how much the book has helped them with all aspects of their woodturning. I very much appreciate your comments; perhaps you will find enough appeal and additional information in this new edition to tempt you into purchasing a copy.

Keith Rowley
Nottingham, 1999

Introduction

Being born into a mining community in south Derbyshire, where on leaving school most of the lads went to work in the mines, I was destined to work for 'the company' in some capacity.

My father, a miner too, was equally determined I was not going to follow in his footsteps and insisted that I learn a trade. His advice went something like, 'Get a trade behind thee, lad, it will always stand thee in good stead. In any case it's worth five quid a week to see the sunshine and the crows fly over. You don't want to be stuck down the pit.' (£5 was an awful lot of money in those days.)

Thus I went into the joiners' shop to serve my time, working on projects such as ventilation doors for the mines, pit-pony shafts and carts, wheels, general joinery, and furniture making and restoration for the company offices and estate houses.

Most of all I liked to use the huge woodturning lathe in the corner of the workshop. Perhaps this was understandable when you consider we had very few woodworking machines and the majority of dimensioning, mortising, moulding, etc. had to be done by hand. While such labours developed my wrists and forearms to blacksmith proportions, the hard physical labour was in marked contrast to the ease (after instruction and much practice of course) with which I was able to fashion newels, balusters, chair and table legs, and so on, using gouges and chisels on the lathe.

My 'love affair' with woodturning therefore started very early, and my father, being very proud of the fact that I had followed his advice, bought a new 8 x 6ft shed and an early model Coronet lathe for me to practise on at home.

The demise of the coal industry in the Erewash Valley of south Derbyshire came in the late fifties and meant I was faced with the choice of moving to another National Coal Board area, or seeking alternative employment. By this time I was a married man with a family, and a millstone called a mortgage hanging round my neck. I therefore plumped for a secure job and joined the Nottingham City Police.

Almost 20 years of my service was spent in the Criminal Investigation Department, and the ability to commit often extremely complicated cases to paper in a chronological, easy-to-understand manner was a vital part of the business. I took advantage of the early retirement facility in 1982 and I have been woodturning professionally ever since, combining commercial turnery with the private courses of instruction I offer.

Travelling up and down the country and demonstrating at the various woodworking shows has brought me into contact with hundreds of aspiring woodturners. I enjoy talking to them immensely, and the dialogue invariably gets round to the difficulties and problems encountered with turning, and the same queries are raised over and over again. I hope that now I can suggest causes of and remedies for these common problems and incorporate them into my teaching methods and general approach.

I have described my background and experience in order to inspire confidence in my methods, and hopefully to persuade you that I am a practical man who understands the difficulties beginners face. Additionally, my 20 years' experience of 'putting it on paper' leaves me with no excuses for making other than a fair job of the script!

This book is written for the relative newcomer to the craft, the purpose being to impart a thorough understanding of its basic, safe and correct techniques. If the beginner can lay solid foundations, he will be able to build on them with confidence and develop into a proficient woodturner.

While there is no better way of learning a trade or craft than actually being shown by a competent craftsman/teacher, a good deal can be learned from a well-written textbook if the student is sufficiently enthusiastic, determined and diligent.

If after reading the book I have convinced you that 'you too can become a competent woodturner', and gone some way to firing your enthusiasm for what is a very satisfying and relaxing hobby, then I shall have achieved what I set out to do.

Chapter 1
Trees and Wood

Our Debt to the Forest

Trees are surely among the best chosen gifts of nature to man. From rain and from the scorching sun they afford shelter, whilst from the pressure of the blast they protect our homes and our gardens.

They provide the matchstick from which we procure a light and the log that blazes in our grate. They give us the door by which we enter our dwelling, the beam and rafter that support our roof, the floor on which we tread.

For our meals they give us the table, for our rest the bed. For our house-hold and farm tools the handle, for our travel the boat; for our evening smoke the pipe, for our worship the church pew.

At life's beginning they present us with the cradle, at our journey's end the coffin.

Music is in their leaves, nourishment in their fruits. Whether in vast forests, in woodlands, in stately avenues, in parks and gardens, or standing in solitary grace, they furnish almost a third part of the whole world's beauty.

(Anon.)

My love of nature was probably inherited from my father. For most miners, the countryside and fresh air were a means of escape from the dark, dusty and dangerous environment in which they spent almost a quarter of their lives.

Some of my earliest and fondest recollections are of exploring with my father the extensive countryside and woods near my childhood home. It was on such excursions that I was first made to appreciate that 'The best things any mortal hath are those which every mortal shares.'

My nature education therefore started very early. My father taught me how to identify wild flowers, wild animals and birds by their call, colour, flight and song.

And then there were the *trees*.

One has only to reflect for a short time to realize what an important part they play in our lives, and to appreciate why they are regarded as amongst the best chosen gifts of nature to man. In their natural state they adorn the landscape and perform an important ecological function. They vary considerably in shape and outline, and when fully clad in leaf, spike or needle, they vary even more in shades of colour.

Trees are things of beauty, and have inspired writers, poets and artists over the centuries. One of the saddest sights the countryside holds for me is the demise of the magnificent English elm. Once very common, its numbers have been devastated by Dutch elm disease, and in many districts all that remains is their skeletal, ghostly forms silhouetted against the skyline.

While for many the fascination of trees lies in their sheer beauty, it is in their converted state that they serve man more than any other living organism. When felled and sawn, timber varies tremendously in colour, grain and texture. It also varies in the uses it can be best put to, some humbler varieties being used for rough carpentry and firewood. Others, with rich grain and texture, are used for the highest grades of cabinetmaking.

It is incumbent upon all of us to play our part, not only in conserving this most precious gift of nature, but also in applying our very best endeavours in every project we undertake with wood.

It is also incumbent on every woodworker to be able to identify as many different varieties of timber as possible, and to know their properties so as to be able to put them to their best uses.

Timbers suitable for woodturning

While almost every species of wood can be turned, some are eminently more suitable than others. More and more turners are realizing that although some varieties of the foreign exotic hardwoods are beyond compare for certain types of turning, some home-grown species are not far beyond in their general appeal.

The following list is by no means exhaustive, but it should provide the beginner with sufficient information to be able to identify and be aware of the properties of the most useful species. Fifteen of the species described here are displayed in Fig 1.1.

Native timbers (UK)

Ash A large, elegant tree, and after the oak probably the most useful native timber in the UK. Recognition is easy. The pale grey bark is smooth when young but in maturity develops a network of ridges and furrows. The winged seeds, green at first, turn to brown and often stay on the tree all winter. It is easily worked, yet very tough and elastic, qualities which make it the ideal timber for such things as handles for tools, garden and farm implements, and for sporting equipment. In the past, it was also a timber frequently used by the wheelwright and carriage builder, and in toughness and resistance to shock, ash can only be equalled by hickory.

It is now used extensively in furniture making, high-class joinery and shop-fitting. The timber is pale in colour but often tinged with pink, and the heartwood is generally light brown. Ash turns very well despite its coarse texture, and I consider it underestimated as a turnery timber.

Olive ash/ripple ash These are two unusual characteristics normally found in more mature parkland trees which have had a chance to develop fully in girth rather than height. The 'ripple' effect runs at right angles to the grain and is combined with the grey-brown streaks running along the length of the grain. These very attractive features make this variety of ash much prized by all woodturners, which is reflected in the price you have to pay for it.

Beech A tall, stately tree which with good reason has been referred to as the 'queen of the forest'. Its silver-grey bole and branches make it one of the easiest trees to identify, and its huge domed crown forms a great circle of shade when in full leaf.

The timber is hard and close-grained, and has a fine, even texture. There is no marked difference between the spring and summer wood and the colour is generally pinkish-buff. Beech turns particularly well and was the timber predominantly used by the Chiltern pole-lathe turners. While not possessing the elastic qualities of ash, it does lend itself to

Fig 1.1 Samples of 15 of the timbers referred to in the text. *Top row, left to right:* **Brazilian mahogany, ash, English yew, Scots pine, walnut;** *middle row:* **beech, cherry, sycamore, plum, English oak;** *bottom row:* **bubinga, sweet chestnut, ebony, elm, burr elm. (Samples by courtesy of Art Veneers Co., Mildenhall, Suffolk)**

steam-bending and for this reason was used extensively in the furniture trade.

Spalted beech Again, much prized by woodturners. The 'spalted' effect is obtained from logs which have lain on the ground for some time after felling and are affected by a fungus which causes the attractive black lines and spots.

Chestnut (sweet) A large, handsome tree which develops a deeply fissured, spiralling bark. There is no mistaking this tree when it bears the prickly green husks which protect the golden-brown nuts. The timber bears a strong resemblance to oak, although it does not show the medullary rays that give oak its 'silver grain' when quarter-sawn. This timber is increasingly being used for high-quality work and is very suitable for turnery.

Elm (English) A magnificent, tall and stately tree which has been the victim of the most disastrous setback to native hardwoods in recent times – Dutch Elm disease. While by no means as valuable as ash or oak, elm was indispensable for many reasons. Village carpenters and wheelwrights appreciated its qualities of strength, durability and resistance to splitting, features which make it an ideal timber for chair seats, wooden pumps, wheel hubs and felloes, etc. In colour it varies from the yellowish-white of its sapwood to the light brown of its heartwood. Its wild, irregular grain makes it, for me, one of the most attractive of timbers.

Although the coarse and irregular grain means it is not the easiest of timbers on which to achieve a good finish, patience, sharp tools and a good turning technique will reward the user with beautiful results. It is particularly suited to bowl-turning in both 'green' and seasoned states.

Elm (wych) In outline a much smaller and more rounded tree than the English elm, but with very similar properties. Many examples have distinctive green streaks running through them which enhance their appeal and look well on bowl work.

Elm burr Burrs occur on several species of tree and are formed by a curious wart-like growth which, in the case of the elm, is usually towards the base of the trunk. They are caused by the stunted growth of a number of buds and when cut through, the burr reveals the characteristically large number of closely grouped miniature knots. Such burrs are indeed beautiful and make extremely attractive bowls and platters.

Hornbeam A smallish tree with silver-grey bark. The boles of the more mature trees tend to become deeply fluted and twisted. It is not in great supply, but is one of my favourite timbers for turning, and is particularly suited to long-stemmed and translucent goblets. The timber, yellowish-white in colour, is strong, tough and difficult to split, qualities which make it ideal for such things as cogs, plane stocks, skittles and mallets.

Oak Very few Englishmen are unable to identify the most revered of our native trees. It is one of the latest trees to leaf and the unique shape of its leaves, together with the acorns, makes it impossible to confuse with other species. Its properties are well known. For durability and strength, it is beyond compare. The possibilities with oak are seemingly endless, and it has been used for centuries for such things as ecclesiastical woodwork, furniture, roof supports and trusses, wheelwrighting, agricultural implements, timber-framed buildings, etc. But of course it is best known for the construction of sea-going vessels, the 'hearts of oak' which formed the British fleet.

Oak is by no means easy to turn to a good finish and demands a combination of very sharp tools and sound technique to achieve good results.

Sycamore A splendid and hardy tree. Its distinctive leaf form and yellow-green tassel-like flowers, followed by winged seeds, make identification easy. In its converted form, the timber is whitish, with a close fleck grain. Some logs have wonderful rippled markings across the grain and are in great demand, not only by woodturners but also for veneers and the bodywork of stringed instruments. (It is often referred to as 'fiddle-back sycamore'.)

'Sweet is sycamore as a nut' – a fact appreciated by the old rural woodturners, and it was extensively used for making dairy and kitchen implements such as churns, butter scoops, mashers, rolling pins and bowls. It is certainly a joy to turn!

Walnut A tree that might well be referred to as the 'aristocrat' of the woodlands because of its delicious nuts and the regal quality of the timber it yields. The leaves of the tree, late to show, are reddish-brown before changing to green. This characteristic, together with the unmistakable deeply fissured grey bark, again make identification easy.

The timber varies from a pale buff colour to dark brown and has a fine, even grain and texture. Besides being fairly hard and durable, walnut is capable of being worked to a smooth, lustrous finish. It possesses a beautifully attractive figure and occasionally throws up a 'ripple' effect such as occurs in sycamore. These qualities, together with its renowned stability, made it the favourite timber of the cabinetmakers of the Queen Anne period.

Supplies of this valuable timber are limited and if the woodturning beginner is fortunate enough to acquire some, I suggest that it should be saved until sufficient skill has been attained to do justice to it.

Yew One of our three native conifers, and although it is a softwood, its timber is very dense and harder than many hardwoods. The myths and legends surrounding the yew tree are endless, but it is without doubt best known for its use as in making longbows, as captured in the lines of Sir Arthur Conan Doyle: 'What of the bow? The bow was made in England, of true wood, of yew wood, the wood of English bows…'

Yew is the longest-living tree in Europe and some specimens are reputed to be as old as the churches in whose yards they stand. The leaves, bark and fruit are poisonous and children should be educated to identify the tree and to be aware of its dangers.

It is without doubt my favourite wood for turning. The colours vary tremendously from the whitish sapwood to the rich brown heartwood, which is often tinted with purple streaks and spots.

All the above are timbers of commerce, and are available, albeit some more easily than others, from sources which advertise regularly in the monthly woodworking magazines.

There are other, smaller, native timbers equally suitable for woodturning, which are not really 'timbers of commerce'. These smaller trees and shrubs, from gardens, orchards and hedgerows, are not generally on sale from timber merchants, although many turners feel they are most suitable for woodturning and prefer to work with them.

Furthermore, not only are such timbers suitable to turn, but many have beautiful grain and colour which can match even the most exotic of imported species, although the available sizes and sections are understandably small. Accordingly, contact with tree surgeons, park officials and local authorities may well prove a valuable source of varieties such as those listed below.

Apple Although a very difficult timber to season satisfactorily, it is well worth experimenting with. Despite being very hard and tough, it turns easily and provides a very pleasing reddish-brown coloured timber with attractive grain.

Blackthorn A common hedgerow bush that heralds the first signs of spring when its bare black twigs are covered in the familiar masses of pure white flowers. It yields tough, strong timber which has a very attractive reddish-brown heartwood and yellowish sapwood.

Cherry (wild and cultivars) Most desirable and beautiful timbers to turn. The wild cherry provides a slightly scented golden-brown timber which is much valued for high-class furniture, veneers and turnery. It is a tough, strong wood but easy to turn and polishes extremely well.

Holly A tree that is familiar and recognizable to everyone with its glossy, dark green prickly leaves. It yields a white timber which is very close-grained and turns easily. This makes it ideal for the 'green' turning of thin-walled bowls and platters, etc. for which many turners are now using it.

Laburnum There are few more welcome and striking springtime sights than the laburnum when it 'puts forth its gay blossom'. The timber it yields is equally beautiful and comes a close second to yew as my favourite timber to turn. It is hard and heavy, with a rich brown heartwood marked with golden flecks, contrasting strongly with the pale yellow sapwood. Do remember that all parts of the laburnum are highly poisonous.

Pear This is another of my favourites to turn. It is remarkably free from knots, hard and even-grained. Its pinkish, pale appearance is sometimes enhanced by the same 'ripple' effect found in sycamore.

Plum Very difficult to obtain in large sizes, but if you are fortunate enough to do so, be sure to make something special with it because the even-textured timber, which varies from a pale yellow to dark brown and purple, is absolutely beautiful.

In addition to the above non-commercial timbers, I suggest you experiment with others such as lilac, box, rowan, hawthorn and sumach (stagshorn – but note that one species of sumach is poisonous). You will be pleasantly surprised not only by the ease with which they turn, but also by the beauty they reveal in their grain and colour.

Scots pine A valuable commercial softwood, it is used extensively in the building and construction trade. You may have read that it is not suitable for turning, but I disagree. With the recent increased demand for pine bedroom and kitchen furniture, and the use of turned components, woodturners are realizing the full potential of this attractive timber. It matures to a rich honey colour when finished with clear lacquer.

Pine is an ideal timber to practise on. When you can get a good finish on pine straight off the tools, then you can consider yourself accomplished. I use it a great deal when demonstrating to convince people it is a suitable timber to turn, and that a good finish is possible without recourse to heavy sanding.

An important advantage of using this timber, particularly for practice, is that you can often acquire suitable off-cuts fairly cheaply, and additionally the workshop is filled with the pleasant aroma of pine shavings.

Imported and exotic timbers

I will not discuss the imported and exotic timbers in any great detail here, as I consider them unsuitable for novice woodturners, until a fair degree of proficiency has been attained. Mistakes on projects made in these exotics can be very costly indeed. Moreover, the sight of an expensive piece of timber whirling round on the lathe can make the operator too cautious and inhibited when he should be aiming for a relaxed attitude and fluency in tool use.

Havng said that, here is a simple list of a number of exotics which have proved to be ideal for turnery.

Amarello Origin: South America. A dense yellow-cream timber.

Blackwood Origin: Africa. A hard, dense and extremely heavy timber. The heartwood is black in colour, as you would expect.

Bubinga Origin: West Africa. It is purplish-brown in colour, sometimes having a mottled effect in deeper tints.

Cocobolo Origin: South America. This is one of my favourites. A rosewood species, it provides an extremely attractive colour variation ranging from purple to yellow and black markings.

Ebony Origin: India and the Far East. It is not always black, as many believe, but may be medium to dark brown. A fine, even texture and extremely dense.

Olivewood Origin: Europe, and another of my personal favourites. It is yellowish-brown in colour, with variegated darker streaks, and affords a fine, lustrous finish.

Rosewoods Origin: Central and South America, and India. There are many varieties of rosewood and all are suitable for turnery. They are all very expensive, but the timber is absolutely beautiful.

Ziricote Origin: Central America and West Indies. An exceptionally beautiful, hard and heavy timber with a fine, close grain. It is a dark grey colour with irregular black lines and comes up to a smooth lustrous finish.

There are now dozens of varieties of exotic timbers coming on to the market, and those who are interested in buying such woods should study the woodworking magazines to find reliable suppliers.

Finally, as regards timber species, even a brief account of tropical trees cannot omit:

Mahogany The excellence of this timber was recognized as long ago as the Spanish colonization of the New World – in fact some of the vessels of the Spanish Armada were made of mahogany.

For over a century it was the favourite wood of the cabinetmaker. This was because of its dimensional stability, the ease with which it could be worked by hand tools, and its beautiful, rich appearance.

Brazilian mahogany Widely used by woodturners and cabinetmakers and still available in very wide boards up to about 30in (760mm) wide. It is ideal for reproduction wine tables, dumb waiters, Victorian-style tea tables, etc., where dimensional stability is absolutely vital.

Some ecologically minded woodturners feel guilty about pursuing a craft that might be seen to encourage damage to world environments by indiscriminate deforestation. Such feelings should be dispelled, as many of the major timber suppliers only trade with sources which have embarked on policies to manage forests as a renewable cash crop. Such policies can in fact improve the environment and generate wealth in deprived countries.

With a little understanding

Understanding all the peculiarities and the unpredictability of timber demands a lifetime's study. The only real way to begin to understand is to work with it. However, it is desirable for any woodworker to have a basic understanding of the growth, structure, seasoning, shrinkage and defects of the timber tree. Such knowledge will enable him to choose the best species for a particular job and anticipate its problems.

Structure of a tree

Fig 1.2 shows a section of an oak tree, illustrating the internal structure common to most trees.

The **pith** is the original seedling, sometimes hardly visible. It remains soft and is commercially useless. It should be cut out.

The **heart** represents the first few years of growth in the young tree. This part dries up and is cut away during conversion, since it is unsuitable for constructional work.

Heartwood is the most durable timber and is the part of the tree between the heart and the sapwood.

Sapwood is the later growth of the tree and is quite porous. It is not suitable for constructional woodwork, but a mixture of heartwood and sapwood in 'green' bowl turning is very popular and produces spectacular variations of colour.

Annual rings, each indicating one year's growth, give an accurate indication of the tree's age and are formed by differing rates of growth in spring and summer.

The **cambium layer** consists of living cells which form new wood on one side and bark on the other side.

Bark acts as a protective covering.

Medullary rays radiate from the centre of the tree and are found in all woods, though they are discernible in few. They are very distinct in woods such as oak (silver-fleck grain), beech and plane.

Fig 1.2 Section of an oak tree

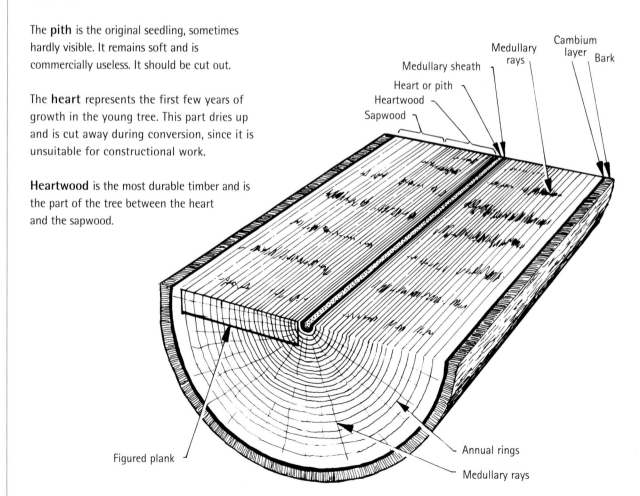

Medullary sheath
Heart or pith
Heartwood
Sapwood
Medullary rays
Cambium layer
Bark

Figured plank

Annual rings

Medullary rays

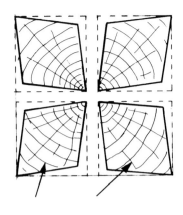

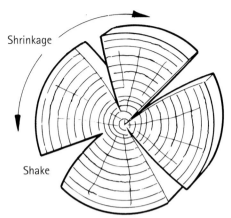

Fig 1.3 Shrinkage leads to converted sections warping

Shrinkage

Shake

Seasoning

The object of seasoning is to remove the sap and moisture which are present when the tree is felled. If this were not done, timber used for constructional work would shrink considerably, causing warping and open joints and a consequent loss of strength.

The two most common methods of seasoning are:

Natural seasoning This is without doubt the best method but can take many years. The planks, boards, logs, etc. are stacked in the open air but protected from direct sunlight and water by a roof. Laths or skids placed between the layers ensure a free circulation of air. The rule of thumb calculation for seasoning time is one year for each inch (25mm) of timber. Thus a plank 3in (76mm) thick would take approximately three years to season.

Kiln drying Timber is placed in a closed chamber through which hot air is circulated, which speeds up the seasoning process. Inevitably, it makes the timber more costly. It is also very much an exact science, and timber which is incorrectly kilned loses its elasticity and tends to become brittle.

Unseasoned or 'green' turning is much in fashion these days, particularly for bowl work. Many examples can be seen where the blanks have been turned extremely thin and allowed to 'find their own shape' by distorting as they dry.

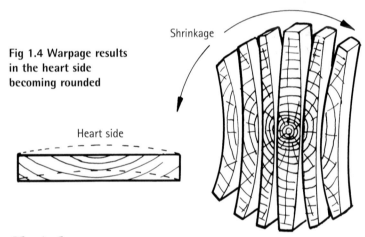

Fig 1.4 Warpage results in the heart side becoming rounded

Shrinkage

Heart side

Shrinkage

Shrinkage is caused by evaporation of the moisture in the wood. The unequal distribution of this moisture (the majority being located in the sapwood) means that shrinkage is not uniform. Thus in logs, shrinkage is obviously greater on the outside, and this causes cracks to occur on the outside first and run towards the centre (Fig 1.3).

Warpage

This unequal shrinkage causes planks and boards to become warped or 'dished'. It follows that the rounded side always appears on the heart side of the timber. Accordingly, allowances must always be made for such warpage in all branches of woodwork, including turning (Fig 1.4).

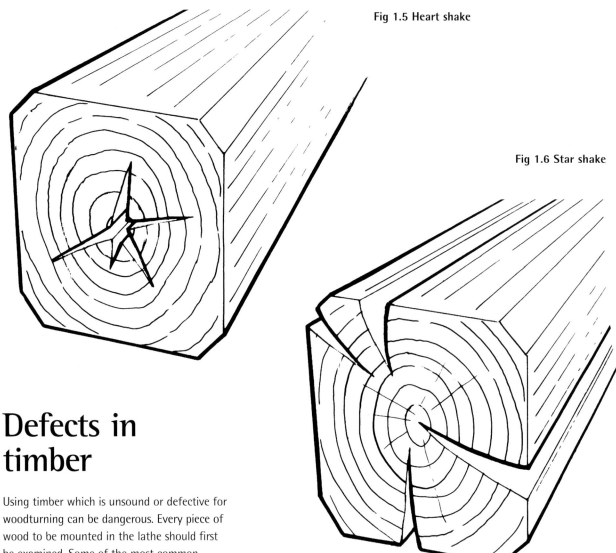

Fig 1.5 Heart shake

Fig 1.6 Star shake

Defects in timber

Using timber which is unsound or defective for woodturning can be dangerous. Every piece of wood to be mounted in the lathe should first be examined. Some of the most common defects are as follows:

Heart shake This develops if the heart of the tree decays, or the wood inside the growing tree shrinks.

Heart shakes radiate outwards from the pith and badly affected pieces should be discarded (Fig 1.5).

Star shake This begins on the outside of the stock and follows the medullary rays inwards. Star shakes are usually caused by unequal shrinkage, as outlined above. This type of shake can be extremely dangerous to the woodturner (Fig 1.6).

Cup or ring shake Cracks appear on the annual rings and are caused by a growth defect, probably as a result of high winds or of fungal or insect ravages. Again, they can be dangerous to the turner (Fig 1.7).

Knots There are many kinds. 'Sound' knots which are solid and hard, although not easy to cut, present no danger to the turner. 'Dead' or loose knots are a different matter and can cause injury to the turner if they 'fly'.

Hazardous timbers

There are a number of timbers, generally imported species, which can be harmful when being machined, turned or sanded. The fine dust from the mahoganies, rosewoods and many other exotic woods can cause irritation to the eyes, nose, throat and lungs. I adamantly refuse to work iroko, which badly affects me, even though I wear a protective mask and use an extractor. Makore, cocobolo, mansonia, padauk, guarea and partridge wood all affect me and prolonged exposure to dust from such timbers is obviously highly inadvisable.

Sources of timber

Timber is expensive, so the aspiring turner would be well advised to apply his thoughts to obtaining wood from cheap sources. As mentioned earlier, pine off-cuts can be obtained from most joinery manufacturers and are ideal for practice. Autumn is a good time to ask gardeners, park and local authority officials, tree surgeons, etc., for prunings and felled fruit trees.

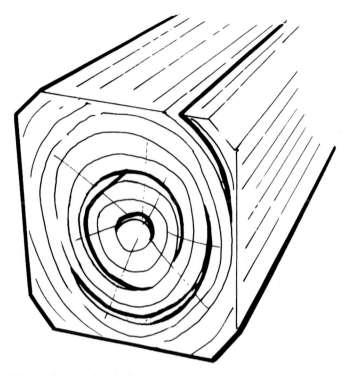

Fig 1.7 Cup or ring shake

SUMMARY

1 Teach yourself to be able to identify as many trees as possible, in both their natural and converted states.

2 While learning, make do with off-cuts, soft or hardwood, together with hedgerow, orchard and garden trees and shrubs.

3 Remember that green wood turns much more easily than seasoned timber and is comparatively cheap.

4 Beware of defects such as shakes in timber – they can be dangerous. Beware also of the dust from imported hardwoods and wear a dust mask when sanding.

Chapter 2

The Woodturning Lathe and Accessories

Brief history of the lathe

Indulgence in a little nostalgia may indeed be good for the soul, and certainly no book on woodturning would be complete without mentioning the history of the lathe.

Some early lathes consisted of sturdy wooden base frames with a lath or springy piece of wood conveniently positioned and secured to generate energy by reflex action. A piece of cord was fastened to the lath, wrapped twice around the wood and then tied with a loop hanging about 12in (300mm) from the ground.

The turner would insert his foot into the loop and depress the cord. This pulled the lath downwards and caused the wood to revolve. On releasing the downwards thrust, the lath would recoil or spring back to its original position, causing the wood to revolve in the opposite direction. Thus the wood was made to spin forwards and backwards, and the turner had to time the application of the tools to the work *only* on the revolutions towards him.

The 'loop' principle was eventually replaced by the more sophisticated treadle, and in the UK – particularly in the beech forests of the Chiltern Hills – pole lathes, which were very similar in concept to the more primitive types, were in everyday use until 50 years ago.

The turners, known as 'chair bodgers', produced chair components such as legs, stretchers and rails for assembly in the furniture centre of High Wycombe, established there because of the proximity of the beech forests.

The term 'bodge' is associated with inferior or shoddy workmanship today, but the chair bodgers certainly did not fit this description – they were highly skilled and industrious craftsmen. They hold a unique place in the history of woodturning in the UK. They set up their lathes in the woods and turned the timber almost *in situ*, rather than establish workshops in the towns or villages and have the timber carted to them. Simple and very often crude shelters were erected in the forest to house the turner and his pole lathe. The trees were selected, felled and then cross-cut to a suitable length for the various chair components.

With the aid of heavy mallets, axes and draw knives, the logs were cleft and rough-shaped before being mounted in the lathe and turned 'green'. The industry and speed with which the components were turned, bearing in mind the equipment being used, never fails to amaze. Many of the bodgers were capable of completing a chair leg in about two minutes, relying on a trained eye to a great extent to copy-turn. The illustration opposite gives some idea of what the shelter and pole lathe would have looked like.

Demonstrations on such lathes are regularly featured at the various woodworking shows, and witnessing them in action makes one realize how skilled the operators were, and how much physical effort was required.

In rural England virtually every village had its own craftsmen, including wheelwrights and carpenters. These craftsmen made use of lathes powered by an apprentice turning a handwheel or the more sophisticated treadle and flywheel. Such lathes were predominantly constructed of wood, metal fittings made by the village blacksmith being restricted to the 'drive' and 'dead' centres.

The Industrial Revolution heralded the introduction of heavy cast commercial lathes, several lathes often being powered by one electric motor through a system of pulleys, belts and shafts. Few people other than those earning a living from woodturning had access to a lathe. Techniques and methods were jealously guarded, which was understandable when you consider that the very livelihood of the turner was at stake.

Nowadays, with the increase in leisure time, there has been a tremendous resurgence of interest in the craft, on both a professional and a hobby basis. One has only to look through the various woodworking magazines to realize how great this interest is. Many companies are now producing lathes with electric motors which can be run off the domestic electricity supply.

Additionally, there is an increasing number of turning tools, lathe accessories and chucking devices available on the market. This can be extremely confusing to the newcomer to the craft, trying to determine what he requires in the way of basic tools and equipment to get started. The following goes some way towards clarifying the situation.

Fig 2.1 A recent model of the Graduate lathe, combining the old long-bed and short-bed models (Photograph by courtesy of Multico Ltd)

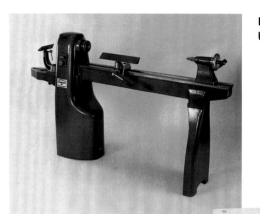

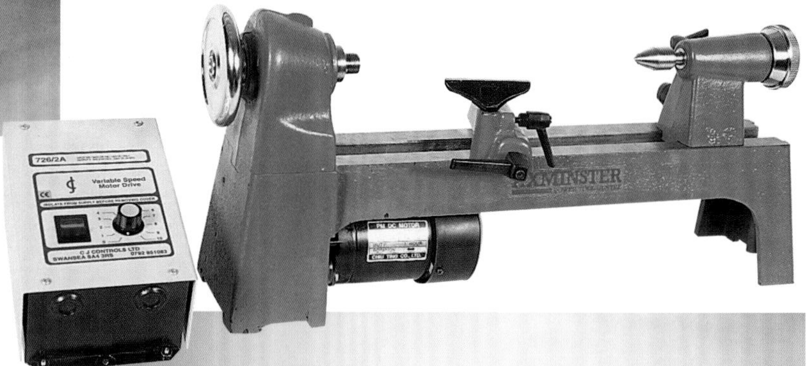

Fig 2.2 The Carbatec lathe (Photograph by courtesy of Axminster Power Tool Centre)

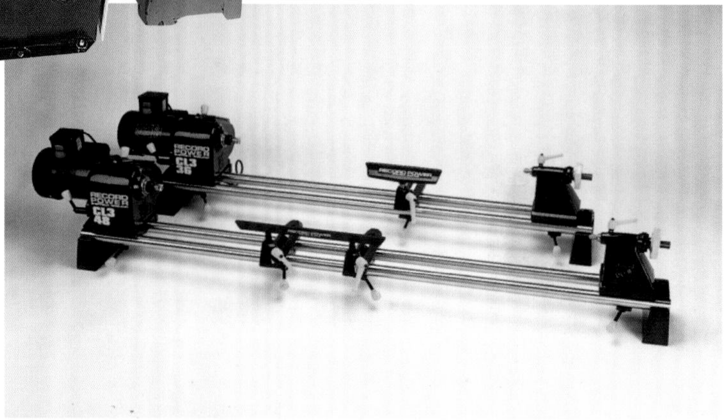

Fig 2.3 The Record CL3 lathe, available in lengths of 36 and 48in (914 and 1219mm) between centres (Photograph by courtesy of Record Power Ltd)

Types of modern lathe

Although woodturning lathes vary from manufacturer to manufacturer, the basic requirements of the lathe dictate that all must be quite similar. Broadly speaking there are two types of lathe.

Free-standing lathes

These are generally the heavy-duty variety used in the trade, and when rag-bolted into a concrete plinth are well able to cope with the sometimes extreme forces associated with large-section turnings. These lathes, with their heavy castings, are very expensive and it is not suggested that the novice rushes out to buy one. However, if, in the course of searching for a lathe, a reasonably priced second-hand model becomes available, then buy it *if* you have room.

Perhaps the best-known lathe of this type is the Graduate (formerly the Harrison Graduate), the design of which was influenced by the late Frank Pain, a renowned woodturner. These lathes are much sought-after in the second-hand market. I acquired a second-hand Graduate short-bed, which is ideal for turning table tops and large, heavy bowls. The current model (Fig 2.1) is a combination of the older long-bed and short-bed versions.

Bench-mounted lathes

Bench-mounted lathes vary considerably in size, weight and cost, the heavier models being suitable not only for the keen hobbyist but also for many professional turners and cabinetmakers.

One of the most popular of the smaller bench-mounted models is the Carbatec lathe (Fig 2.2). This is compact and made mainly of cast iron to provide smooth, vibration-free running. The most recent model is equipped with a variable-speed unit, giving full adjustment of speed and torque, and also incorporating an electronic clutch. This is not one of the cheapest of the smaller lathes, but it is certainly one of the best.

Record Power of Sheffield produce a wide range of bench-mounted lathes, from modestly priced small machines to their 'flagship' model CL3 (Fig 2.3). This is their heavy-duty lathe, and

Fig 2.4 The Robert Sorby lathe (Photographs by courtesy of Robert Sorby)

Fig 2.5 The Apollo Professional lathe, with (right) a detail of its swivelling headstock (Photographs by courtesy of Apollo Products)

many professional woodworkers and turners use it. To add to its versatility, a swivelling headstock is incorporated into the design, enabling large diameters to be worked. Various lengths of bed can also be obtained.

Robert Sorby of Sheffield, a long-standing manufacturer of woodturning and other edge tools, has now gone into lathe production (Fig 2.4). Their lathe is of heavy construction and available in lengths from 2 to 6ft between centres (610–1830mm). It can be supplied for bench mounting by the customer or, if preferred, a robust stand is available at extra cost. A maximum diameter of 13in (330mm) can be swung over the bed bars and, with the swivelling headstock facility, diameters of 30in (760mm) can be turned with the bowl-turning attachment. Cast iron is used extensively in the

construction and, in addition to the 5-speed poly-vee-drive model, Sorby have now introduced a variable-speed unit to provide greater flexibility of the speed range.

Apollo Products of Dereham, Norfolk provide a range of exceptionally high-quality lathes. Their smallest is the Chipmunk, which is ideally suited to the newcomer to the craft, being modestly priced for such a smooth-running and robust lathe.

Their middle-of-the-range Woodpecker model is a very popular lathe. It is available as a standard 4-speed model, or alternatively with an inverter for electronic speed control. The unique pull-out bed design allows a maximum 16in diameter (405mm) to be turned.

The largest model in the range is the Professional (Fig 2.5), which continues the

13

Fig 2.6 The Myford Mystro, mounted on the manufacturer's own stand (Photograph by courtesy of Myford Ltd)

Fig 2.7 The Woodfast M 910 vari-speed lathe (Photograph by courtesy of Axminster Power Tool Centre)

high-quality design and manufacturing approach of Apollo machines. The Professional comes complete with full inverter drive and 4-step pulley system, providing a constant high-torque performance throughout, from zero to 3000rpm. Incorporated into the headstock is a unique bowl-turning bed which utilizes the standard toolrest assembly; work can therefore be turned at 45 or 90°. A maximum of 16in (405mm) can be swung over the bed, and an impressive maximum of 25in (635mm) can be turned in the front position. Other valuable features include a 24-position indexing system and cam-lock-type locking handles. Anyone with a modicum of engineering knowledge will concur that this is a superb lathe, ideally suited to the professional woodturner.

Myford Engineering of Nottingham enjoys an international reputation for manufacturing precision grinding machines, metal-turning lathes and, of course, woodturning lathes. Their revered ML8 wood lathe sold in its thousands worldwide, and many turners formed their skills on this lathe during their schooldays.

The ML8 was superseded some years ago by the Mystro lathe (Fig 2.6), which, as is to be expected, is another example of their high-quality engineering. The standard version is equipped with a 5-speed pulley system, which provides a good range of speeds. Alternatively, a variable-speed model is available. This is equipped with a 3-phase electric motor, but the electronics that control the vari-speed also allow for it to be plugged directly into the single-phase domestic output. This, combined with the exceedingly high-quality headstock casting and proven bearing system, provides extremely smooth, quiet, vibration-free running. Both models come with a reversing facility, which is particularly useful for dealing with stubborn end grain in bowl turning.

The headstock can be swivelled and locked on its vertical axis at any angle between 0 and 180°. A plunger locking mechanism facilitates not only the easy removal of faceplates and chucks, but also the indexing of the spindle through 24 positions.

This lathe is probably the most user-friendly I have used, and oozes Myford quality. It can be supplied as a bench model, or with the manufacturer's own stand at extra cost. Fig 2.6 shows the Mystro on the manufacturer's stand.

The final lathe I shall discuss is the Woodfast M 910 (Fig 2.7). Woodfast lathes are manufactured in Australia and have earned worldwide repute. There is a wide range, including bench-mounted and free-standing models. I was fortunate enough to be supplied with the top-of-the-range M 910 variable-speed, free-standing model to use in the production of this book, which gave me the chance to test it thoroughly.

The heavy, one-piece, cast-iron bed supports an equally heavy cast headstock, which contains the large main spindle supported in three industrial sealed bearings. Using a tachometer attached to the motor, the vari-speed versions have a controller that monitors and adjusts the motor power output to the load, producing high torque at all speeds.

Some of the lathes described here may well be beyond the pocket of most beginners, and my advice is to buy a modestly priced lathe to get you started. If you find that woodturning is not for you, you will not have lost out a great deal after selling it on. If you really get the bug and want to progress to a bigger and better-quality lathe, go for the one best suited to your type of work, but buy the best you can afford.

Lathe terminology

At the beginning of your venture into the craft of woodturning, it is important, as it is when you buy a new car, to get to know your machine thoroughly and as quickly as possible. Knowledge breeds self-confidence and makes for a more assured approach. The purchasing of spares and accessories can be quite a painful and embarrassing experience if you are not familiar with the characteristics and specifications of your own lathe.

I have said that lathes vary from one manufacturer to another, but the names of the main components do not alter. Fig 2.8 shows an example of a bench-mounted lathe with the motor fixed underneath the lathe. (This is purely in the interests of clarity as the majority of this category of lathe have the motor mounted behind or to one side of the headstock.)

The 'business' end of the lathe is called the **headstock**, which on the better lathes is a casting of iron fixed to the bed at the left-hand side. The **mandrel** on to which drive pulleys are fixed is mounted in bearings, the quality of the bearings and distance between them being of paramount importance in smooth, vibration-free running.

Some mandrels are hollow to facilitate fittings being removed by tapping out with a round bar and hammer. The mandrel may be threaded on the inboard side only (as in the case of the swivelling headstock and sliding headstock types on pages 12–14), or on both the inboard and outboard, as shown in the drawing; the combined outboard and between-centres models such as the Graduate (page 12) have the latter arrangement.

The inboard side of the mandrel is nearly always bored out with a decreasing tapered hole called a **Morse taper**, into which fit corresponding tapered fittings such as pronged drives, Jacobs chucks, etc.

Fig 2.8 The components of the lathe

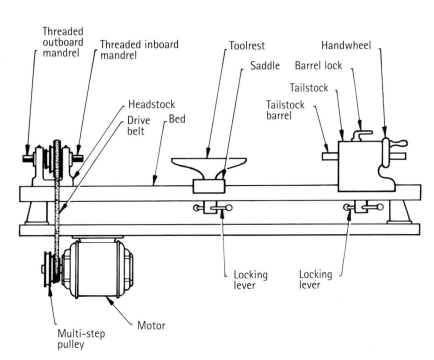

Threaded outboard mandrel
Threaded inboard mandrel
Toolrest
Handwheel
Saddle
Barrel lock
Tailstock
Tailstock barrel
Headstock
Drive belt
Bed
Locking lever
Locking lever
Multi-step pulley
Motor

The Morse tapers should be kept clean or they will not 'home in' correctly and this could result in 'chatter'. Check with your handbook and find out what size of Morse taper is fitted to your lathe. The sizes range from 1 to 3, although the majority of bench-model lathes come with the number 1 size.

Power to the mandrel is supplied by the electric motor and activated by the drive belt fixed to the **stepped pulleys** mounted on both the motor and mandrel. These stepped pulleys also determine the speed at which the lathe will run.

When turning between centres, the wood is fixed between the headstock and the **tailstock**, the latter also normally being bored out to take Morse taper fittings. It can be slid along the bed of the lathe to the desired position and secured in place by the **locking lever**.

Additional adjustment can be made on the tailstock by means of the **handwheel** and **threaded barrel**. It is important, particularly when boring holes using a Morse taper chuck in the tailstock, that there is at least 2in (50mm) of travel on the barrel, or it will be painfully slow to bore.

The term **swing over bed** means the largest possible diameter capable of being turned between centres. For example, if the height between the bed and the centre of the mandrel is 4½in (115mm), the 'swing' will be 9in (230mm). (Note, however, that the toolrest assembly will obviously reduce this maximum capability.)

Lathe beds are manufactured in a variety of sections, such as single round bars, double round bars, square bars, angle iron and pressed steel. The most important demands on them are for stability and strength to prevent flexing and distortion in use. Unfortunately some of the cheaper lathes fail this requirement. Additionally, the lathe bed should be accurately machined to ensure that the tailstock and toolrest assembly slide easily along it.

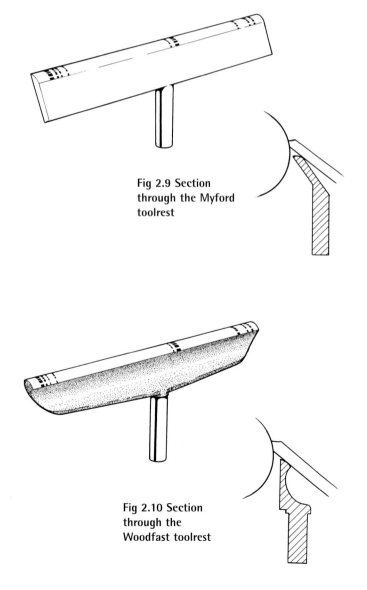

Fig 2.9 Section through the Myford toolrest

Fig 2.10 Section through the Woodfast toolrest

Basic fittings

Toolrests

These come in all shapes and lengths, but I consider that about 15in (380mm) is the maximum length that can be adequately supported by a single stem. Rests longer than this will require a double stem and the corresponding extra saddle.

The sections of some toolrests are abominations and make tool manipulation and control extremely difficult. The two profiles that come closest to my preference are the ones supplied with the Mystro and Woodfast lathes. Both afford smooth, unimpeded traversing cuts, which is of particular importance to the spindle turner. Fig 2.9 shows a section of the Myford toolrest, and Fig 2.10 shows the Woodfast.

Drive and tailstock centres

You will probably get a **four-prong drive centre** and a **dead centre** supplied with your lathe, the pronged variety being fitted to the headstock and the dead centre to the tailstock.

Drive centres are made with either two or four prongs and vary in width across the prongs from about ½in (13mm) to 1½in (38mm). Dead centres (which means they are static, the wood revolving round them) are normally conical in shape and can create problems such as burning, loosening of the wood and the consequent 'chatter'.

The desirable alternative to the dead centre is the **live or revolving centre** fitted with a bearing allowing the centre to revolve with the wood. This eliminates friction, burning, loosening and chatter. Beware, though, for there are some very poor examples on the market, fitted with extremely inadequate bearings with too much movement in them.

Faceplates

These come in a range of sizes and I think for general purposes a 4in (100mm) plate is the most useful. Traditionally, faceplates were the favourite method of many turners for bowl and platter work. Many now prefer the modern, sophisticated (and very expensive) specialist and multi-purpose chucks.

Faceplates are drilled to take a thick-shanked screw to allow them to be fastened to the workpiece. I use the largest sizes for turning table tops; they provide maximum support and prevent deflecting, which can cause a heavy dig-in.

Minimum accessory requirement

Generally speaking, a lathe comes with the basics such as a drive and a dead centre, one small toolrest and possibly a faceplate.

What then is the *minimum* requirement so far as accessories are concerned? First, if a faceplate is not included in the package, I would suggest you buy one.

Additionally, I suggest you buy a heavy-duty woodscrew chuck from one of the reputable accessory manufacturers.

Finally under this heading, I recommend you purchase a **Jacobs chuck**, which is a must for the many boring and drilling jobs on the lathe. It can be used in either the headstock or the tailstock by means of the Morse taper. However, in my opinion, the best type is the one where the Morse taper unscrews from the main body to enable it to be screwed on to the mandrel, so providing a much better hold when boring large holes. A few drills and bits can also be purchased to get you going.

The basic accessories shown in Fig 2.11 will enable you to carry out a wide variety of woodturning functions, and many turners

Fig 2.11 Basic accessories. *Top, left to right:* **arbor for Jacobs chuck, Jacobs chuck, woodscrew chuck;** *bottom, left to right:* **two drive centres, hollow ring centre (see pages 155–6), faceplate, live or revolving centre**

Fig 2.12, *left to right:* **dividers, internal callipers, external callipers;** *bottom, left to right:* **two machine wood augers, sawtooth machine bit, two engineer's twist bits, Vernier callipers**

derive a great deal of pleasure and satisfaction from making additional wooden chucking devices themselves.

Ancillary equipment

While in no way essential for mastering the techniques of woodturning, the following equipment will serve to speed up and simplify many operations:

- measuring instruments such as callipers, dividers, etc. (Fig 2.12)
- boring equipment such as drill bits.
- a long-hole-boring kit for the boring of holes in standard and table lamps, etc. (Fig 2.13). This equipment is described more fully in the table-lamp project on pages 155–9.

Modern chucking systems

There seems to be an absolute oversupply of chucking systems for woodturners. In my capacity as a demonstrator, I am often asked the question 'What chuck should I buy?' Before answering such queries I always enquire what brand or type of lathe the chuck is to be used on. Then I ascertain what type of work is

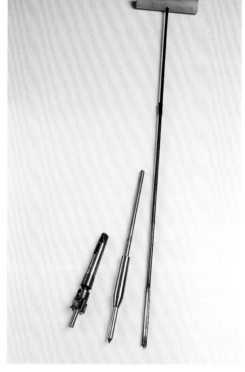

Fig 2.13 Long-hole-boring kit. *Left to right:* **counterbore tool, hollow ring centre with centre finder, long-hole-boring auger**

normally undertaken or aspired to. I am then in a position to offer advice.

It would be ridiculous to recommend a heavy-duty four-jaw scroll chuck for a cheap lathe with small bearings. It would probably ruin the lathe in no time. Therefore, the type of lathe dictates to a great extent what type of chuck is suitable. There are many quality chucking systems available, but I can only comment on the ones I have had a chance to use.

APTC (Axminster Power Tool Centre) four-jaw scroll chuck
For me this is the most outstanding heavy-duty scroll chuck available. Its weight, solid construction and projection off the mandrel make it suitable only for lathes with substantial headstocks and quality bearings. It is a favourite of mine and is permanently fitted to one of my

Mystro lathes. It is extremely adaptable, versatile and true-running. Changing from one mode of use to another is quick and simple. As you would expect, it is quite expensive. Fig 2.14 shows this chuck with some of the available accessories.

The scroll chuck has been used on metal-turning lathes for decades, but only comparatively recently has its value to woodturners been appreciated. A geared scroll forms part of the main chuck body, enabling key-operated matching jaws and accessories to be engaged in sequence. Many turners now prefer this type of chuck because it is quick and easy to use but, more importantly, because of its accuracy.

The following are some other chucks I have used and can recommend.

Craft Supplies Ltd Precision Combination Chuck (Fig 2.15)

This has been around for 14 years and thousands of owners will testify to its versatility, ease of use and many accessories. What is more, it is suitable for most types of lathe and is competitively priced.

Craft Supplies Ltd Maxi-Grip 2000 (Fig 2.16)

This is a relatively new chucking system, and with its 'easy to add on' features it is most versatile and easy to use. This chuck is also suitable for most lathes, and again not over-expensive.

Oneway four-jaw chuck (courtesy of Craft Supplies Ltd) (Fig 2.17)

This chuck is made in Canada to exacting standards and is suitable for all lathes other than light-duty machines. The self-centring

Fig 2.14 The APTC four-jaw scroll chuck and selected accessories

Fig 2.15 The Craft Supplies Precision Combination Chuck

Fig 2.16 The Craft Supplies Maxi-Grip 2000 chuck

Fig 2.17 The Oneway four-jaw chuck

Fig 2.18 The Multistar Duplex chucking system (Photograph by courtesy of Multistar Machine and Tool Ltd)

scroll allows speedy, accurate gripping in both contraction and expanding modes. It has an excellent range of accessories and I have been impressed with its ease of use.

Multistar chucks

This company manufactures a range of superb-quality chucking systems. I have used two of their chucks and the first thing that strikes you is their 'good looks' and quality of machining. Such excellent finishing usually means a quality product, and in this case it is certainly true.

Multistar Duplex chucking system (Fig 2.18)

This chuck has been on the market for some considerable time, and I have yet to hear anyone speak of it other than in glowing terms. Its versatility is second to none, and it is extremely accurate and durable. It has a most impressive range of accessories, including a universal carrier which takes Morse taper drive centres. This means that between-centres turning can be done without removing the chuck from the lathe, a feature which I find invaluable and time-saving. This chuck, which also has an in-built indexing facility, is suitable for virtually all types of lathe and is a joy to use.

Multistar Titan compact scroll chuck (Fig 2.19)

For those turners who prefer a scroll chuck, this takes some beating in the lighter-weight chucks. It is compact, as the name suggests, but with no compromise on holding power, performance or accuracy. The in-built indexing head is also a feature of this chuck, and the many available accessories extend its versatility to cater for most needs.

I am sure there are other quality chucks on the market and, depending on the type of turning you do and the depth of your pocket, you will certainly find something that suits you. It is a good idea to visit one of the major woodworking shows so that you are fully informed of the range available. You will be spoiled for choice, so shop around and buy the best you can afford that meets your requirements.

Considerations when buying a lathe

Ask yourself the following questions:

What kind of turning do I propose to do or aspire to?

How much space have I got to site the lathe? If space is limited, remember the swivelling-

Fig 2.19 The Multistar Titan compact scroll chuck

headstock type of lathe facilitates larger-diameter turning without having to stand and work at the end of the lathe.

How much money have I got to spend?

When you have the answers clear in your mind, you will need to compare the specifications of the lathes you are attracted to for such matters as:

- the required distance between centres and the swing over bed
- the range of speeds available (I consider you need no fewer than four different speeds, ranging from approximately 500 to 2000rpm)
- ease of adjustment to tailstock, speed-changing and toolrests.

Consider whether the manufacturers are reputable and well established, whether they offer a good range of accessories and spares, and how long a guarantee they give.

If you decide on a combined outboard and between-centres lathe, you must be prepared to spend extra on left- and right-hand attachments.

Getting the best out of your lathe

As with any other machine, thought has to be given to several factors to ensure you can use it to its full capability. Additionally, any machine needs to be well maintained and securely mounted.

If you take into account the factors listed below, you should ensure you derive maximum performance, comfort and satisfaction from your lathe.

Siting

Make sure you site the lathe so that you are left with enough room at the tailstock end to use such accessories as the long-hole-boring kit. Similarly, if your lathe is of the outboard or sliding-headstock type, you need at least 30in

(760mm) of extra space beyond the end of the lathe to work in.

Every turner needs the best possible light to work in, so it makes sense to position the lathe under a window. Daylight will of course need to be supplemented with perhaps strip lighting and/or a movable spotlight, which is particularly helpful when turning hollowware.

Maintenance

Bearings of the adjustable type need to be correctly set and lubricated in accordance with the manufacturer's instructions.

Drive belts need to be kept at the correct tension to provide adequate drive and to prevent 'belt slip'. This can also occur if the drive pulleys work loose, so check these too and tighten the securing grub screws with an Allen key.

Keep the toolrests in good order by occasionally running a file over the tool-bearing surface to remove any slight nicks. White spirit (mineral spirit) applied on a rag will remove oil and the resinous deposits which some timbers exude. It is a regular practice of mine to wipe a waxed cloth along the surface of the toolrest, and this certainly makes for ease of tool traversing, particularly on long, straight cylinders.

Keep the lathe bed clean by occasionally spraying it with something like WD40 and rubbing with a fine wire wool. The threads on all the fixtures also need regular lubrication, and don't forget to use a small file to keep the prongs of the drive centres sharp.

Morse taper fittings (male and female) need to be cleaned. I use paraffin and wire wool. Oil obviously cannot be used, or they will not 'bite'.

Time spent on cleaning and maintaining your lathe is well spent. Not only does it make for ease of use, but it also ensures the lathe keeps or even enhances its value.

Mounting

No matter how good a lathe is, you will not get the best results if it is incorrectly mounted. You should have stable, smooth running, otherwise you will encounter all kinds of problems.

Floor-standing lathes are generally rag-bolted into a concrete plinth and this,

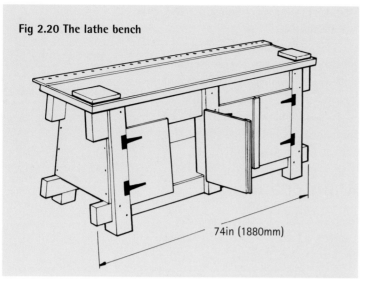

Fig 2.20 The lathe bench

74in (1880mm)

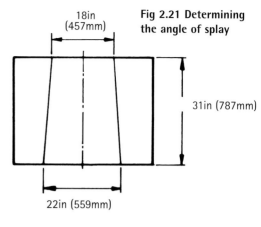

18in
(457mm)

Fig 2.21 Determining the angle of splay

31in (787mm)

22in (559mm)

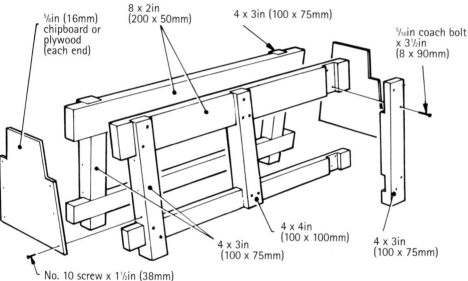

⁵⁄₈in (16mm)
chipboard or
plywood
(each end)

8 x 2in
(200 x 50mm)

4 x 3in (100 x 75mm)

⁵⁄₁₆in coach bolt
x 3½in
(8 x 90mm)

Fig 2.22 The construction of the bench frame

4 x 4in
(100 x 100mm)

4 x 3in
(100 x 75mm)

4 x 3in
(100 x 75mm)

No. 10 screw x 1½in (38mm)

combined with the very heavy weight of the lathe, provides for optimum performance and smoothness.

To get similar results from a bench-mounted lathe, the bench needs to be as heavy and robust as possible. Below is a description of how to make a wooden bench like the one I made for my Myford Mystro lathe; Fig 2.20 shows its general design.

The construction of the bench is well within the capabilities of most people and the cost is small. The length will obviously have to be arrived at according to your particular lathe, but the method of construction will remain the same.

In the interest of a comfortable working posture, the *height* of the lathe is very important. As a rough guide, the centre of the lathe mandrel needs to be approximately in line with the turner's elbow.

Method of construction

Set out the angles of splay on the bench ends by drawing out a section full size on a piece of plywood (Fig 2.21). Now set your adjustable bevel to the angle so determined. To work out the height of the bench:

- *Add together* the measurements of **(a)** distance between bottom of lathe foot and centre of mandrel and **(b)** any packing piece or cushion you choose to place under the lathe feet, both to give more space for the hands and to damp out any slight vibration. (I used pieces of 1½in-thick (38mm) plywood, and also pieces of ¼in-thick (6mm) rubber.)

- Now *subtract* this measurement from the other relevant measurement (from ground level to elbow height). This will give you the optimum bench height.

Set out the halving joints on the legs, top and bottom rails. These can be cut using a panel

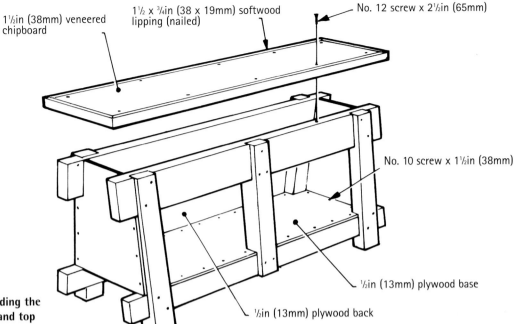

1½in (38mm) veneered chipboard

1½ x ¾in (38 x 19mm) softwood lipping (nailed)

No. 12 screw x 2½in (65mm)

No. 10 screw x 1½in (38mm)

½in (13mm) plywood base

½in (13mm) plywood back

Fig 2.23 Adding the base, back and top to the frame

saw and chopped out with mallet and chisel. Now cross-cut the rails and the legs to length. The legs at top and bottom will require cutting at the previously determined angle. The uppermost edges of all four rails will also need to be bevelled at the same angle along their full length with a hand plane. Glue and bolt the two main frames together (Fig 2.22).

Cut the end panels as determined by your full-size drawing, drill and countersink for the screws and then assemble. You may well need some assistance to keep the side frames steady while you screw up the end panels.

The bottom shelf now needs to be marked out, cut to fit around the protruding legs and

inserted from the top of the bench (Fig 2.23). Failure to do this before fitting the top will mean that you cannot get the shelf fitted in one piece. The shelf can be either nailed or screwed in position.

The top, which ideally should not be less than 1½in (38mm) thick, is then screwed to the frame and lipped if desired with some ½in-thick (13mm) material, either soft or hardwood. A toolrack can be added at the back (Fig 2.24). The plywood back should now be fixed, preferably with woodscrews.

The space under the bench is considerable and can be used to store all kinds of attachments and accessories. This will also help

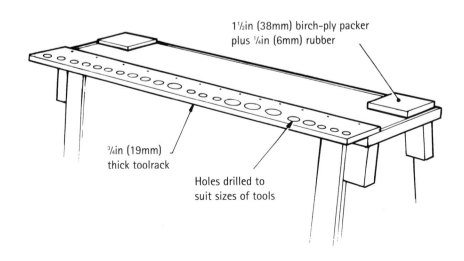

1½in (38mm) birch-ply packer plus ¼in (6mm) rubber

¾in (19mm) thick toolrack

Holes drilled to suit sizes of tools

Fig 2.24 Lathe packers and toolrack

Fig 2.25 The cupboard door

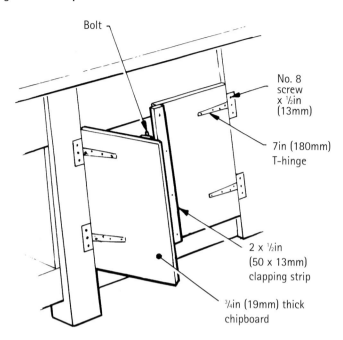

Bolt

No. 8 screw x ½in (13mm)

7in (180mm) T-hinge

2 x ½in (50 x 13mm) clapping strip

¾in (19mm) thick chipboard

gentle and far deeper cut than the circular saw with a much smaller electric motor. Another advantage is that the narrow kerf of the bandsaw blade results in much less waste. Finally, the cost of a bandsaw blade is only a fraction of the cost of a good-quality circular saw blade.

The cost of a new bandsaw varies considerably according to suitability (and quality) for heavy-, medium- or light-duty applications. For newcomers to woodturning, one of the smaller bench-model bandsaws should prove more than adequate. Fig 2.27 shows a Tyme model BS 200, which is an example of a good, reliable light-duty machine.

It is particularly important in the interests of safety and efficiency of operation to choose the correct width of blade for the job in hand, and to make sure that the blade is sharp and

to make the bench more solid and stable. The cupboard doors are simple to hang, making use of T-hinges. Bolts, catches and 'clapping strips' can be fitted if thought necessary (Fig 2.25).

Some types of lathe must be positioned on the bench at a specified distance from the front edge. If this is not done it may well mean, for instance, that the swivelling headstock cannot be swung through its intended arc. The handbook provided with the lathe should specify any such requirements.

Fig 2.26 shows my Mystro lathe mounted on the completed bench.

Other workshop machinery

Bandsaws

Next to the lathe and the bench grinder (discussed in the next chapter), the bandsaw is the most-used item of equipment in my everyday production work. It is extremely versatile and safe to operate, so long as common sense is used. A continuous band of cutting edge where the thrust is always downward makes it much safer than a circular saw. This arrangement has several other advantages, one being that it allows a more

Fig 2.26 (above) A Myford Mystro mounted on the completed bench

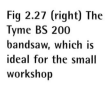

Fig 2.27 (right) The Tyme BS 200 bandsaw, which is ideal for the small workshop

correctly set up. Ripping is best achieved with as wide a blade as possible, and the feed rate should be slow and smooth. A push-stick must always be used, and eye protection is an absolute must.

When cutting discs, it is important that the correct width of blade is used. It is impossible to be precise about the smallest radius any given size of blade will cut, as much will depend on the species of wood being used and on the skill of the operator. Most manufacturers provide a handbook offering advice on this, in addition to the correct setting-up and safety precautions. These instructions should be carefully studied and complied with.

While a bandsaw is not an absolute essential for the newcomer to turning, it will certainly speed up many operations and remove the drudgery of preparing discs by arduous hand methods. Having made use of one for a short while will make you wonder how you managed without it.

Pillar drills

Accurate drilling is extremely difficult with hand-held tools, and the drill press or pillar drill not only does this, but also provides the means to hold the workpiece firmly. The essential features are:

- the motor, and a belt and range of pulleys that allow for a wide range of speeds
- the chuck that holds the drill and boring bits
- the table, which is height-adjustable
- the depth stops.

The bench-type pillar drill that I use is the Startrite Mercury (Fig 2.28), which is an engineering-quality machine and expensive. Please note that the belt and chuck guards have been removed for the photograph. These must always be fitted when the machine is in use. It is also important to clamp the work firmly when drilling anything but the smallest holes; a drill-press vice is essential for this.

Fortunately for the prospective buyer, there are many much cheaper brands of pillar drill on the market which are more than adequate for woodworking operations. As with the bandsaw, you will find that it is a very much used machine in the woodturner's workshop.

Fig 2.28 The Startrite Mercury pillar drill. Note that pulley and chuck guards have been removed for the purposes of the photograph only. A drill-press vice, in which many projects can be securely clamped for drilling, is also shown

SUMMARY

1 Choose the best lathe suited to your purposes, after taking into account the advice given in this chapter.
2 Read the manufacturer's handbook thoroughly and comply strictly with the advice on wiring, mounting and maintenance.
3 Get to know your lathe as quickly as possible and familiarize yourself with lathe terminology.
4 In the learning stages, buy as few accessories as possible, but buy the best you can afford.
5 Add to your basic accessories as your skill increases – you will never be short of ideas for birthday and Christmas presents!
6 A well-constructed, sturdy bench is essential for bench-mounted lathes to ensure smooth, vibration-free running.
7 While accepted as one of the safest woodworking machines, the bandsaw must be treated with respect. Always wear eye protection and use a push-stick to feed the wood past the blade.
8 When drilling other than very small holes on the pillar drill, make sure that the work is firmly clamped.

Chapter 3
Tools of the Trade

The greater part of my time-serving in the woodworking field was extremely enjoyable, despite the hard physical labour involved in the considerable amount of hand-dimensioning.

It is difficult to explain the feeling of satisfaction derived from the slow but sure acquisition of skill: the skills of planing straight and square; of being able to saw straight and true; of being able to fashion all kinds of profiles with hand moulding planes and of developing the 'feel' of the craft of woodturning.

One of the most important parts of the learning process is to acquire a comprehensive knowledge of all the tools available and to be able to use them to their full potential. The benefit of such knowledge is that unnecessary tool duplication is avoided, also any unnecessary expense.

My mentor always impressed upon me the importance of buying the best available tools for any branch of woodworking, stressing that quality work was easier and more pleasurable to achieve by using good-quality tools.

Quite clearly, making use of good-quality tools not only avoids the constant irritation and frustration you will inevitably experience when using inferior tools; it also instils a degree of confidence in the user. My advice, therefore, is the same as I had from my 'guvnor' 50 years ago – that is, buy the best available but buy only what you really need.

Broadly speaking, there are just two categories of woodturning. These are:

Turning between centres

This is often referred to as **spindle turning**. The workpiece is driven by an attachment fitted into, or screwed on to, the headstock mandrel, and is usually (but not always) supported by the tailstock.

In this category of turning the grain of the wood is usually parallel to the axis of the lathe bed, as shown in Fig 3.1.

The stock may be turned between centres without the support of the tailstock when accessories such as a screw chuck or a combination chuck are used; this applies in the making of hollowware such as goblets, vases or ornamental boxes.

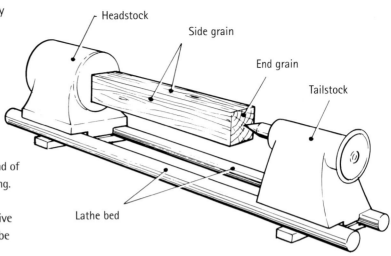

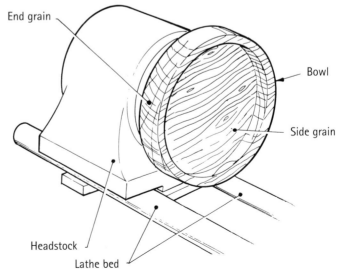

Faceplate turning

In this category, the wood is fixed to accessories such as a faceplate, screw chuck or spigot chuck, and almost always the wood is not supported by the tailstock.

Such work usually involves the turning of discs or bowl blanks where the grain runs along the *surface* of the wood and at right angles to the lathe bed. Thus, twice on every revolution of the stock, end grain will be encountered (Fig 3.2).

Fig 3.1 Turning between centres – grain parallel to the lathe bed

Fig 3.2 Faceplate turning – grain at right angles to the lathe bed

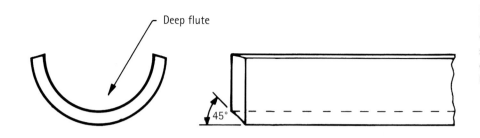

Fig 3.3 Profile of the roughing-out gouge. NB: In the interests of safety, this tool should not be used on bowl or platter blanks

Tools for between-centres turning

Gouges

These include roughing-out and spindle gouges. Roughing-out gouges are available in sizes between ¾in and 1½in (19–38mm). Sizes ranging from ⅛ to ¾in (3–19mm) are normally available in spindle gouges. Examples of both are shown in Figs 3.3. and 3.4.

Chisels

These include beading tools as well as skew and square-across chisels. They are available in widths from ½ to 1½in (13–38mm). The profile of the skew chisel is shown in Fig 3.5.

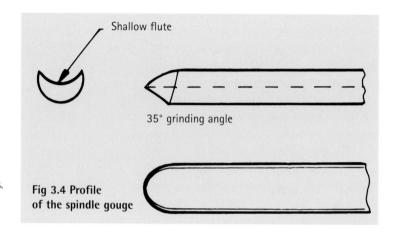

Fig 3.4 Profile of the spindle gouge

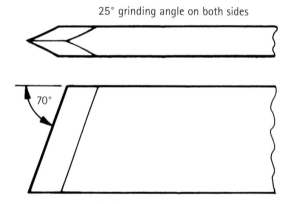

Fig 3.5 (left) Profile of the skew chisel

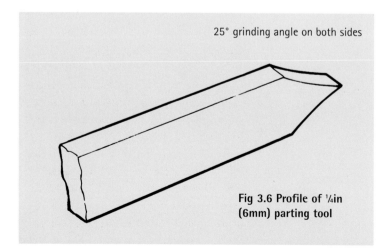

Fig 3.6 Profile of ¼in (6mm) parting tool

Parting tools

Strictly speaking these are chisels. They are available in a variety of widths and sections. I prefer and recommend the ¼in (6mm) parallel parting tool, as shown in Fig 3.6.

It is important to remember that gouges and chisels (including parting tools) are cutting tools and are generally used in the bevel-rubbing mode (see Chapter 5 on the Laws of Woodturning).

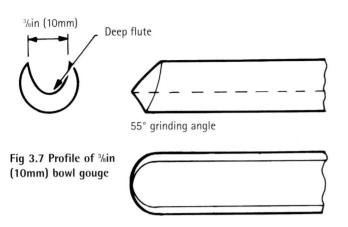

3/8in (10mm)

Deep flute

55° grinding angle

Fig 3.7 Profile of 3/8in (10mm) bowl gouge

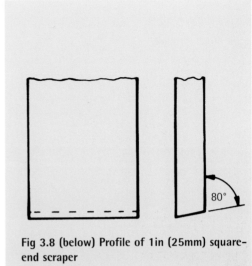

Fig 3.8 (below) Profile of 1in (25mm) square-end scraper

Tools for faceplate turning

Bowl gouges

These are available in sizes from 1/4 to 3/4in (6–19mm). The recommended 3/8in (10mm) size is shown in Fig 3.7.

Scrapers

These are available in sizes ranging from miniature to massive heavy-duty sections. All kinds of profiles are also available. The three recommended sizes and profiles are shown in Figs 3.8, 3.9 and 3.10.

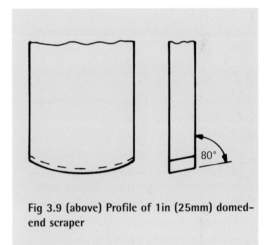

Fig 3.9 (above) Profile of 1in (25mm) domed-end scraper

Again, it is important to remember that bowl gouges, like any other gouge, are generally used in the bevel-rubbing mode, and that scrapers must be used in the trailing mode (see Chapter 5 on the Laws of Woodturning).

As a general rule, scrapers are not used on between-centres turning. Spindle gouges may be used on faceplate turning and bowl gouges between centres, but my advice to the novice is to wait until considerable skill and control has been attained before using such tools in these ways.

The catalogue description of certain tools is sometimes prefixed **L & S**, which is an abbreviation for **long and strong**. This simply means that the tool is normally heftier and longer than the standard tool (all bowl gouges are L & S), and consequently more expensive. The beginner will manage quite well with the standard-strength variety.

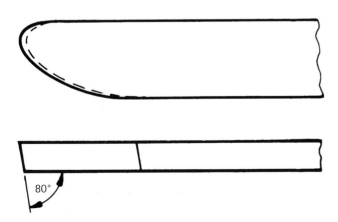

Fig 3.10 Profile of 3/8in (10mm) round-nose scraper

The preceding information is summarized in chart form in Fig 3.11, providing a quick and easy reference guide.

There are two categories of woodturning:

Turning between centres

(a) Grain runs parallel to lathe bed

(b) Work driven by 'pronged' centres and usually supported by tailstock

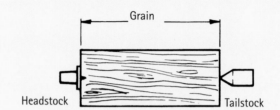

(c) Sometimes the tailstock is not used, e.g. in hollowware where 'open end' is necessary to shape the inside of goblets, egg cups, boxes, etc.

(d) In (c) the grain is usually in the same direction, but the work is driven and supported by accessories such as the screw chuck or combination chuck

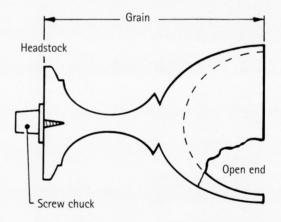

Tools for turning between centres

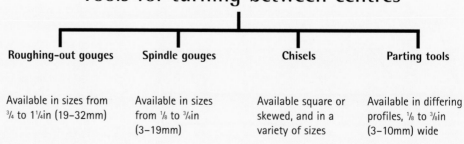

Roughing-out gouges	Spindle gouges	Chisels	Parting tools
Available in sizes from ¾ to 1¼in (19–32mm)	Available in sizes from ⅛ to ¾in (3–19mm)	Available square or skewed, and in a variety of sizes	Available in differing profiles, ⅛ to ⅜in (3–10mm) wide

Fig 3.11 Categories of woodturning and types of woodturning tools

Faceplate turning

(a) Usually entails the turning of discs and bowl blanks, where grain runs along the top surface. Therefore end grain is encountered twice on every revolution on the edge of the blank

(b) Initial fixing is by means of either a screw chuck, faceplate or spigot chuck

(c) Usually there is no support from the tailstock

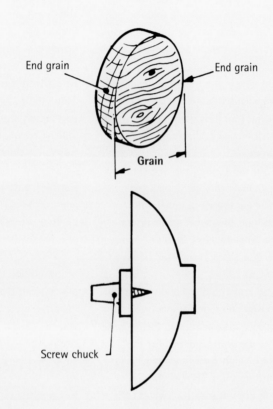

End grain

End grain

Grain

Screw chuck

Tools for faceplate turning

Bowl gouges

Available in sizes ¼ to ¾in (6–19mm)

Scrapers

Sizes range from 'miniature' section to massive heavy-duty 1½ x ⅜in (38 x 10mm) bar; numerous profiles available

Selection and purchase of tools

Woodturners in the UK are extremely fortunate in the choice and quality of turning tools available to them. Manufacturers such as Ashley Iles, Crown Tools, Record Power, Robert Sorby and Henry Taylor enjoy a worldwide reputation for producing quality woodturning tools. I am certain that anyone who purchases a set of tools bearing any of these brands would not be disappointed. In order to make your choice, spend time in the tool shops, comparing and handling each tool until you are satisfied that a particular tool feels right for *you*. To aid you, here are a few general comments regarding choice.

Some of the most attractive tools on the market are the handled Sorby brand. The handles, which are shaped as handles for woodturning tools should be, are made from beautiful hand-polished ash. Each one comes in its own individual sleeve, which can be used to hang up the tool.

I have used Robert Sorby woodturning and general woodworking tools for many years and I have never been disappointed in their quality.

Ashley Iles are world-famous for the manufacture of high-quality woodcarving and woodturning tools. The beechwood-handled tools are not so attractive as others, but the handles are adequate and well shaped. Their skew chisels have edges which are slightly radiused, a feature which greatly assists in smooth traversing when planing and rolling beads.

To my knowledge Iles is the only manufacturer producing a 1in (25mm) roughing-out gouge, which I consider to be the best and most useful size for the beginner (or for anyone who is purchasing only one size).

Record Power, a long-standing Sheffield company, supply a wide range of HSS (high-speed steel) tools distinguished by their highly polished, rosewood-stained handles.

Henry Taylor tools are also renowned for their superb quality. The design of some of their tools was influenced by the late Peter Child (an acclaimed and accomplished woodturner) and his designer/engineer son Roy, which is recommendation in itself.

Crown Tools, a relatively new Sheffield company, also supply an excellent range of quality tools and accessories.

The first set of tools

Finally, we come to my recommended first set of tools. Go for HSS (high-speed steel) tools. They are more expensive than the traditional carbon-steel tools, but they keep their edge much longer and the risk of accidentally drawing the temper during grinding is significantly reduced.

Roughing-out gouge Either the 1in or the 1¼in (25 or 32mm) for rapid removal of stock, particularly from square to round, fashioning long slow hollows and rounds, and for other functions which are described later.

Parallel parting tool ¼in size (6mm). In addition to parting-off and sizing cuts, it can be used extensively for rolling fine beads and also for feathering cuts.

Skew chisel 1in size (25mm). For general planing and tapering, the oval-section skew manufactured by Robert Sorby is unsurpassed, and the easiest for a novice to use. The same size manufactured by Iles, with its radiused edges, is almost as suitable.

Skew chisel ½in size (13mm). For fine V-cutting, rolling beads and general 'tidying up', this size is most useful. I prefer not to use the oval-section variety for this type of work, so it is a matter of choosing the brand that suits you best.

Spindle gouge ⅜in size (10mm). Spindle gouges are the 'master' tools in turnery, and this size, together with:

Spindle gouge ¼in size (6mm), will enable the experienced turner to fashion any shape or profile. Choose your spindle gouges by handling them and pick those which appeal to you personally. I have spindle gouges from all the manufacturers mentioned above, and I find that they all perform to my complete satisfaction.

Fig 3.12 The ¾in (19mm) round-nose scraper in use

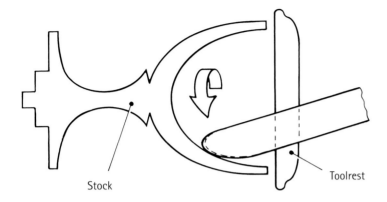

Stock

Toolrest

In addition to the six tools listed above, which are primarily intended for between-centres turning, I suggest that the initial set of tools should also include four tools to enable the beginner to undertake a certain amount of faceplate work:

Bowl gouge ⅜in size (10mm), this being quite suitable for bowls up to a diameter of approximately 10in (255mm).

Square-ended scraper 1in size (25mm), for flattening and smoothing convex surfaces.

Round-nose scraper ¾in size (19mm), for cleaning up the inside of hollowware such as goblets, vases, egg cups, and of course the inside of bowls or any concave surface. For such work, the tool will require profiling as shown in Fig 3.10. An example of this tool in use is shown in Fig 3.12.

Domed scraper 1in size (25mm), for cleaning up the inside of bowls, etc.

As you progress in your turning and your projects become more and more ambitious, you may wish to buy additional tools. Do remember, though, that managing with as few tools as possible teaches you to use them to their full potential. It may surprise you to know that in the course of a day's commercial repetition turning, I rarely use more than five tools.

Care of woodturning tools

Having invested in a good set of tools, it makes sense that everything possible should be done to keep them in good order. First of all, a tool rack (such as the one in Fig 2.24) is essential so that tools can be conveniently stacked, and to prevent the cutting edges becoming damaged.

An occasional rub with an oily rag will preserve the 'new look' and prevent rust forming. A trick used by some woodturners is to leave the tools under a pile of shavings overnight. Any moisture in the workshop is then absorbed by the shavings. Make sure the shavings are dry, and not the product of green turning.

The shavings trick does work, but I shall not admit to using it myself. My workshop insurance policy stipulates that I must clean the workshop of shavings at the end of each working day, which I do of course!

SUMMARY

1 Buy good-quality tools. They will make the learning process that much easier. You will also avoid the constant irritations and frustrations you will surely experience if you buy the cheaper varieties.
2 Buy high-speed-steel tools. The initial outlay will be nearly double, but the advantages are many.
3 Take care to store your tools properly so as to avoid damaging the cutting edges – a tool rack is essential.
4 An occasional wipe with an oily rag will prevent them rusting over.

Chapter 4
On Sharpening

f it were possible to assemble 100 novice woodturners under the same roof and pose the question, 'What is the greatest single problem you are encountering in your turning?', over 80 would reply 'Sharpening the tools correctly.'

This is the conclusion I have drawn from research I have carried out, and from talking to the hundreds of aspiring woodturners I have met while teaching and demonstrating. It is an irrefutable fact that to be capable of successful and therefore satisfying turning, a turner must use tools which have been ground accurately and to an acceptable degree of sharpness.

When individuals book courses with me, I always ask whether they possess any woodturning tools. If they do, I invite them to bring them along when they come on the course so that I can assess their tool-sharpening ability. Unfortunately, it is my experience that the general standard of tool sharpening is extremely low. The overwhelming majority of tools brought for me to assess 'would'na cut butter', as the old miners in my part of the world would say. When I demonstrate to the owners that I can only bludgeon the wood into some kind of shape, it convinces them of their inability to achieve worthwhile results using tools in such condition.

To borrow a phrase from Margaret Thatcher, tools such as those shown in Fig 4.1*a are not for turning*. Fig 4.1*b* shows what they should look like.

Immediately following the 'bludgeoning' demonstration, I give a quick demonstration using correctly prepared tools, to emphasize the difference in the *sound* that sharp tools make and the *results* they will produce.

1 Used as a roughing-out gouge. This tool is too flat in section for such use. The cutting edge is concaved, which would result in the protruding 'wings' engaging the wood before the centre of the tool, causing it to twist and dig in

2 File adapted for use as a scraper. The grinding angle is too acute (long) and it would rapidly overheat. It is too thin in section for so long a blade and could shatter in use

3 Spindle gouge. The edge has been ground to a point rather than to a flowing 'fingernail' profile, and with too obtuse (short) a bevel. The edge is multi-faceted and the tool is unhandled and dangerous to use

4 Parting tool. Bevel has been ground to a convex shape which will cause it to dig in

5 Another parting tool. Bevel is far too acute, making the edge extremely fragile and the tool unpredictable in use

6 Skew chisel adapted from a file. Too obtuse a bevel, and multi-faceted. Insufficient file tang driven into the handle

7 Hooked tool. Claimed by the owner to 'come in handy' for some turning jobs. I can't imagine what!

Fig 4.1a A set of totally unsuitable tools

1   2   3   4   5   6   7

Fig 4.1b A selection of good-quality British-brand tools. *Left to right:* **roughing gouge, oval skew chisel, bowl gouge, spindle gouge; square scraper, skew chisel; spindle gouge, two roughing gouges, parting tool; domed scraper, spindle gouge; french-curve scraper, bowl gouge**

The standard of the tools used in some schools, colleges and further education establishments also causes me concern. This really has to be regarded as an indictment of the teacher who, through ignorance or folly, allows turning tools in such poor condition to be used.

I recall going to an open day at such an establishment, and not unnaturally I was drawn to the woodwork section where a boy was demonstrating 'woodturning'. As usual there was a group of interested onlookers, including parents and the teacher.

What I beheld was nothing short of frightening. The pupil had a piece of 3in (75mm) square stock, about 18in (460mm) long, mounted between centres and was 'assailing' it with what was obviously a very blunt round-nose scraper. He was exerting so much force that the tool was overheating and smoking, but more alarmingly, on two occasions the wood flew off the lathe.

The teacher remained impassive and apparently unconcerned throughout the demonstration, so I could only assume that what I had just witnessed was the norm. Before beating a retreat to safer confines, I did manage a look at the results of the 'turning', and I can honestly say that better results are achieved by beavers on logs.

I mention this incident for no other reason than to convince the reader that using tools which are blunt, or using them for the wrong purpose, *can be dangerous.*

Equipment for sharpening

There are several types of grinders on the market, including dry grinders, wetstone grinders and combinations of the two. Personally, I prefer and use the double-ended 'dry' bench variety, as do most of the professional turners I know.

Buy the best grinder you can afford, made by a reputable manufacturer. My grinder is equipped with two 7in-diameter (180mm) wheels which are ¾in (19mm) wide, one being an 80-grit for general sharpening, the other a coarser 46-grit for heavier grinding and shaping. Both are 'ruby' cool grinding stones from C. & M. O'Donnell.

Avoid grinders with wheel diameters of less than 5in (125mm). They will impart too much of a hollow-ground effect to the tools, particularly the chisels and the 'parters' (see Fig 4.1a, no. 5). This can result in the tool becoming too fragile behind the cutting edge and lead to unpredictable tool behaviour and consequent loss of control.

Avoid also grinders with narrow-faced wheels. I consider that anything less than ¾in wide (19mm) is unsuitable, as they do make the grinding of wider tools more difficult.

Remember that a grindstone is a cutting tool and consequently needs to be kept in good order to retain an efficient cutting action.

Continued grinding results in the face of the stone becoming impregnated with metal particles or 'glaze'. If allowed to remain, it will impair the cutting action of the stone, and more force will have to be exerted to complete the grinding.

Extra force results in a greater degree of friction, which in turn generates more heat, leading to the tool edge being 'blued', which in the case of carbon steel tools renders them useless by 'drawing the temper'.

If you use the wheels for grinding softer metals such as copper or aluminium, they will rapidly clog up. It makes sense, therefore, to avoid these metals.

The faces of the wheels can be kept in good order by 'dressing' them with one of the proprietary products available on the market. The most expensive is the diamond dresser. The 'star wheel' type of dresser is a great deal cheaper. However, in my opinion this is one of the rare occasions where buying cheapest is the best, for you can buy a 'devil stone' for a small sum. These are perfectly adequate to maintain the quality of the cutting edge on the face of the wheels.

Siting and mounting the grinder

Everything possible must be done to encourage the turner to keep his tools sharp. The grinder must be sited adjacent to the lathe and not a 'route march' away. Similarly, the turner must be able to adopt a comfortable posture when grinding. Accordingly, the centre of the wheels needs to be approximately in line with the centre of your chest. This is particularly important if you are going to adopt the method of tool grinding that I advocate.

Safety considerations with the grindstone

Some form of eye protection is absolutely essential when using the grinder. While most manufacturers fix transparent visors over the wheels, these are not totally adequate and must be supplemented by wearing goggles to prevent particles of stone or metal getting into the eyes. There are several types on the market, so choose a pair which are comfortable to wear and store them in a box to keep them dust-free.

As part of my maintenance schedule, I remove the wheels from the grinder and do a test to ensure they are still sound and free from cracks. Simply hold the stone with a length of dowel passed through the centre hole and give the stone a positive flick with a finger on the other hand. If the stone is sound, a distinct high-pitched 'ping' should be heard (see Fig 4.2).

If there is any doubt in your mind about the stone being sound, discard it and buy another. Unsound stones can be *extremely dangerous* if they shatter in use. Workmen have been seriously injured and indeed killed by the shrapnel-like effect of an exploding stone.

Similarly, the mounting of an unenclosed stone on the outboard of the lathe is not only

Fig 4.2 Testing the grindstone. A wheel in good condition gives a distinctly clear ring when flicked with a finger

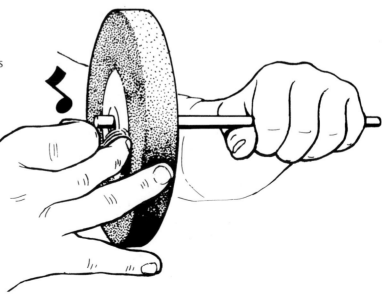

extremely dangerous, but also very stupid and irresponsible. Also, the practice of grinding on the sides of the stones should be avoided. This can have the effect of weakening the stone and could result in it disintegrating.

Grinding angles

If it were possible to examine and compare sets of turning tools belonging to half a dozen professional turners, it would be evident that hardly any two use the same grinding angles. Experience would have taught them to grind the angles *best suited to them*, taking into account the type of work they generally undertake and the hardness or softness of the wood they mainly work with.

The longer or more acute the bevel which is ground on a tool, the sharper the edge which can be achieved. There will obviously be less resistance to the tool being pushed into the wood, but the edge will be fragile and prone to overheating and crumbling.

Conversely, too short a bevel or too obtuse an angle on the cutting tools means there will be more resistance to their being pushed into the wood.

Accordingly, we are looking for a compromise so the tools will not only cut efficiently and without undue effort, but also stand up to their intended use and provide a reasonable 'tool-edge life'.

As will be explained in some detail in the next chapter, one of the laws of woodturning is that 'the bevel or grinding angle must rub the wood behind the cut'.

Now, if the grinding angle is too acute, the tool, in order to achieve the 'bevel-rubbing' mode, will need to be presented with the handle well down, not only in an uncomfortable position but also probably fouling the lathe bed or bench.

Conversely, if a short, obtuse angle is ground on the tool, it will need to be presented almost horizontally, and as the cut proceeds the tool will probably have to be raised to a most uncomfortable position (Fig 4.3).

As I undertake a great deal of commercial softwood turning, I keep a special set of gouges and chisels for this work, all ground with longer than average bevels. Paradoxically, turnings in softwood require sharper tools than hardwood turnings if an acceptable finish is to be

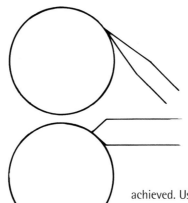

Fig 4.3 How acute and obtuse bevels affect tool presentation. If the bevel is too long the tool handle will be uncomfortably low. If the bevel is too short the tool handle will be uncomfortably high when turning small stock

achieved. Using other than very sharp tools on softwood will tear the fibres severely, but the effect of such tools used on hard, close-grained timbers would not be so pronounced.

The hobby turner will have no need to go to such expense. He will manage quite adequately with one set of tools ground to an average angle.

What then is the 'average angle'? Taking into account what I have said, I recommend the following approximate angles:

- Roughing-out gouges: 45°
- Spindle gouges: 35°
- Chisels and parting tools: 25°
- Bowl gouges: 55°
- Scrapers: 80°

By all means experiment with different angles. Having found the angles which suit you, it makes sense to keep a note of them. This can be done by drawing the optimum angles on a piece of stiff card or thin plywood and checking the tools from time to time by simply laying them on the 'datum line' and comparing (Fig 4.4).

Fig 4.4 A grinding-angle template for the angles that suit you

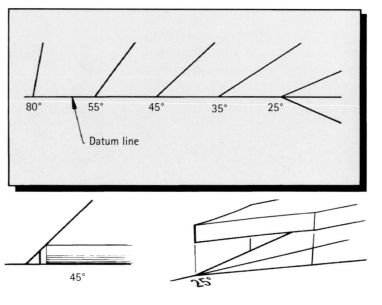

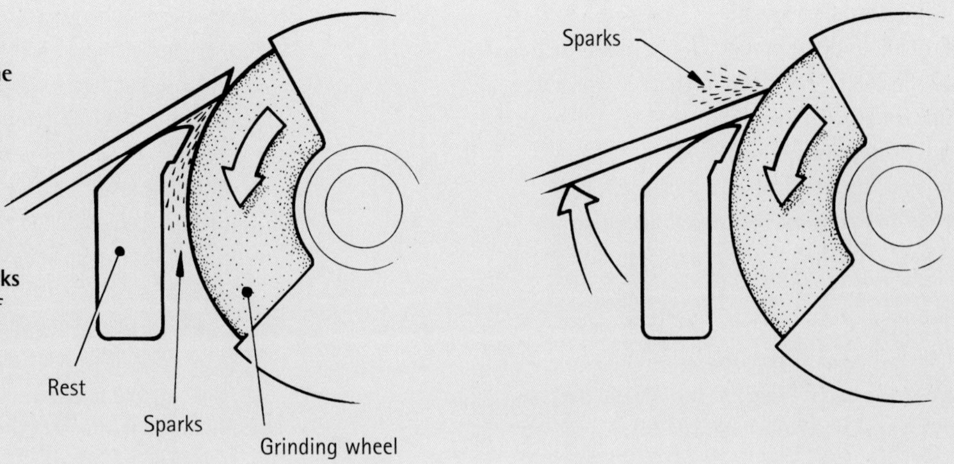

Fig 4.5 Freehand grinding. The tool is presented so that the heel engages the grinding wheel first. Sparks will flow beneath the bevel. The handle of the tool is gradually raised until the sparks flow over the top of the tool

Rest

Sparks

Grinding wheel

Sparks

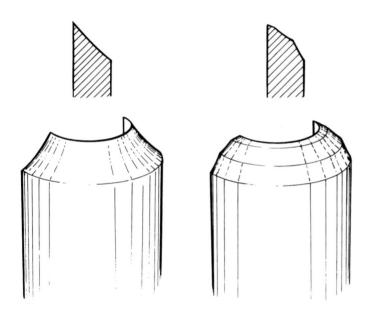

Fig 4.6 Correct and incorrect grinding. On the left is what we are trying to achieve: a single-facet concave bevel. On the right is what we are trying to avoid: a multi-facet convex bevel

stone on the heel of the bevel. The back end is then lifted until the grinding sparks just start to come over the top of the tool, indicating that the tool is being ground right up to the edge (Fig 4.5).

If anyone tries to persuade you that this method is easy, don't you believe them! To be able to freehand-grind to an acceptable standard takes considerable practice and no little time, particularly on the larger gouges and scrapers which require substantial rolling and swinging movements. It is not easy to avoid a multi-faceted or convex bevel, as opposed to the desired single-facet, concave bevel (Fig 4.6).

At the beginning of the chapter I drew attention to the fact that the greatest single problem the majority of novice woodturners encounter is tool sharpening. The reason is simple – they use the freehand method of grinding. I am convinced that more beginners to the craft give up woodturning because of sharpening problems than for any other reason.

When I began teaching the craft, and being aware of such problems, I decided to simplify the sharpening process for two very good reasons:

My final words on grinding angles are these. If you find the tool is not performing as well as it did when you first bought it, it generally means you have allowed the grinding angle to become too obtuse or too short. Try lengthening the bevel and I shall be surprised if it does not prove more satisfactory in use.

Methods of tool grinding

What is the best method of tool grinding? I was trained to use the 'freehand method', which most professional turners use and recommend. With this method the tool is offered up to the

1 It is absolutely necessary to have *one* continuous angle ground on the tools. The reason will be explained in Chapter 5 on the Laws of Woodturning.

2 It is of paramount importance for beginners to enjoy a certain amount of success, in order to motivate them and to maintain desirable degrees of interest and enthusiasm.

If they do not have success with their tool grinding, they most certainly will not have success with the subsequent turning. Interest and enthusiasm will dwindle, sharpening will be looked upon as a chore and the chances are that they will become disillusioned and give up. Even if they carry on, they will never make good woodturners using badly prepared tools.

Taking all this into consideration, I strongly recommend that not only beginners, but also any turner who is experiencing difficulty with sharpening, should adopt the 'jigged' method.

Most grinders are supplied with adjustable platforms, or 'jigs' if you like, but for the purposes of jigging for turning tools they are not suitable. Incidentally, if you do adopt the method recommended here, the existing slotted supports for the platforms will need to be sawn off with a hacksaw (Fig 4.7).

My particular method is to make use of a purpose-built wooden jig, which is easy to make, simple to use and will ensure accurate grinding after very little practice. The method is so simple, I rarely grind freehand these days. What is more, despite all the years of practice I have had freehand, I can grind the tools more accurately with the jig.

Basically the arrangement, as can be seen from Fig 4.7, consists of a baseboard on to

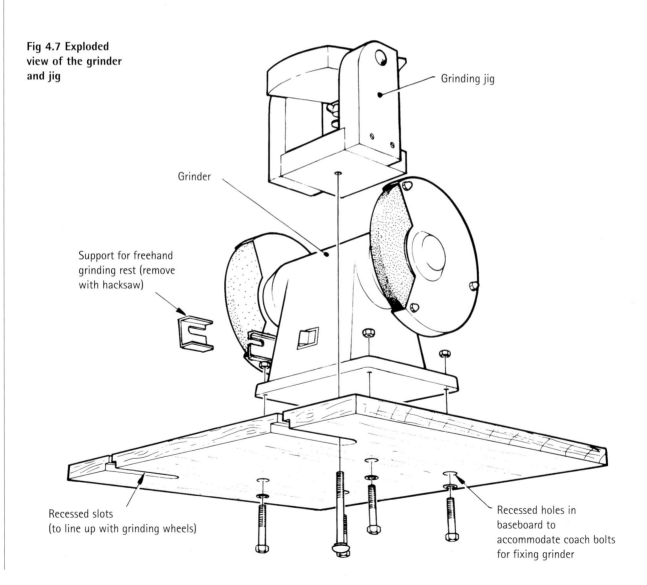

Fig 4.7 Exploded view of the grinder and jig

Grinding jig

Grinder

Support for freehand grinding rest (remove with hacksaw)

Recessed slots (to line up with grinding wheels)

Recessed holes in baseboard to accommodate coach bolts for fixing grinder

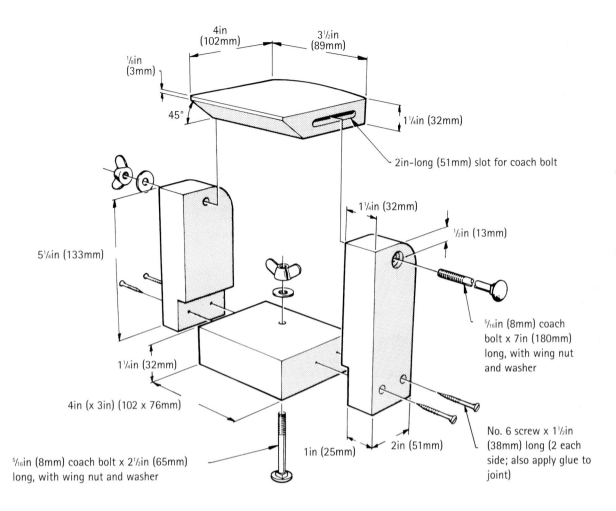

4in
(102mm)

3½in
(89mm)

⅛in
(3mm)

45°

1¼in (32mm)

2in-long (51mm) slot for coach bolt

1¼in (32mm)

½in (13mm)

5¼in (133mm)

5⁄₁₆in (8mm) coach
bolt x 7in (180mm)
long, with wing nut
and washer

1¼in (32mm)

4in (x 3in) (102 x 76mm)

No. 6 screw x 1½in
(38mm) long (2 each
side; also apply glue to
joint)

5⁄₁₆in (8mm) coach bolt x 2½in (65mm)
long, with wing nut and washer

1in (25mm)

2in (51mm)

which both the grinder and the jig are bolted. This makes it portable and capable of being G-clamped (C-clamped) to any flat surface.

The slots in the baseboard should be in line with the two grinding wheels, to facilitate use on both. The four bolts securing the grinder to the baseboard need to be countersunk flush with the underside to prevent rocking.

Similarly, the two slots in the baseboard should be routed out (alternatively, use tenon saw and joiner's chisel) to a depth and width sufficient to accommodate the bolt heads. This will enable the jig to be easily moved from stone to stone.

The actual jig platform on which the tools are placed needs to be no less than 3½in (90mm) wide. The need for this width will become apparent when you grind tools like the large-section round and domed scrapers which require substantial swinging movements (Fig 4.8).

The reason for this platform being slotted out – use brace and bit and square out with

Fig 4.8 The construction of the grinding jig, showing dimensions

chisels – will also become obvious in use. If it was not, you would have difficulty in adjusting to the various angles without the platform fouling the grinding stone.

Make sure you use wing nuts on the bolts securing the jig to the baseboard and the one passing through the platform. They are much more convenient to use than ordinary nuts, and more than adequate tension can be applied by finger pressure.

How to use the jig

At first, I suggest the correct angles are approximately determined with the grinding wheels stationary. (After very little practice, you will find you are able to adjust the jig with the grinder running, which of course speeds up the process.)

Take a roughing-out gouge and lay it on the jig. Slacken the wing nut on the platform and adjust to the approximate angle by 'sighting through' from one side (Fig 4.9a). Now it becomes obvious why the centre of the grinder needs to be high enough to line up with the centre of your chest – too low a position and you could finish up being wrynecked.

If anything, in the sighting-through process, err on the side of the heel of the bevel. If you 'dub' the cutting edge over, it means unnecessary time spent on restoring one continuous angle. Now lightly tighten the platform wing nut, start the grinder and offer the tool up to the stone *very gently*. Only a second's contact with the stone is necessary before examining the gouge to ascertain if it is being ground *all along* the existing bevel. If not, use the gouge to tap the platform in the appropriate direction. (You should tap on the

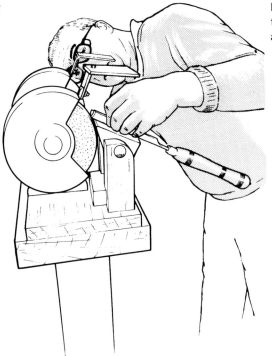

Fig 4.9a 'Sighting through' the grinding angle

Fig 4.9b The grinding jig in use

front edge if, when sighting through, you erred on the heel of the bevel.)

Repeat the process until the new, shiny grind can be seen all along the bevel. Nip the wing nut and complete the grinding (Fig 4.9b).

If this sounds difficult and complicated, I can assure you that it is not. After a few attempts, you will find you can set the platform to follow the existing bevel in a matter of seconds.

To make a *precision* grind, it merely remains for the tool to be kept flat on the platform

and rolled from side to side. I use the fingers of my right hand to both roll the tool and apply a gentle forward pressure to maintain tool contact with the stone. I use the fingers of the left hand to keep the tool perfectly flat on the platform and to assist in the rolling movements also.

Do not 'dwell' either at the beginning or the end of the roll, or you run the risk of 'blueing' the tool edge. Keep a pot of water adjacent to the grinder and dip the tool into it frequently during the learning stages. Constant practice develops the desired gentle touch and then you will have no need to dip the tools in the water.

Very little metal needs to be removed to restore an acceptable degree of sharpness to the tool edge, and you will find just a few rolls of the tool is sufficient. This, combined with the gentle touch, means that there is little chance of the tool edge overheating. A good test is to grasp the tool edge in the palm of the hand immediately after grinding. It should not feel uncomfortably hot. If it does, *drop it quickly*, taking care to miss your feet!

If you prefer not to make the wooden jig as suggested, a precision metal jig is available from C. & M. O'Donnell. Fig 4.10 shows it in use.

Fig 4.10 The O'Donnell grinding jig in use

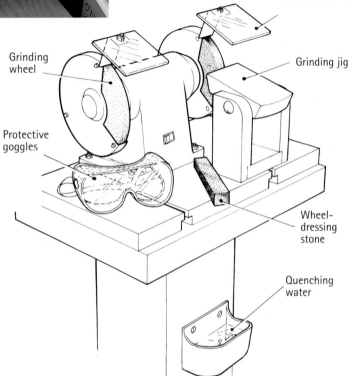

Fig 4.11 The requirements for tool grinding

Protective screen

Grinding wheel

Grinding jig

Protective goggles

Wheel-dressing stone

Quenching water

I will not go through the method of sharpening every type of tool in this chapter. Individual tools are dealt with in Chapter 6, Turning Between Centres, and Chapter 7, Faceplate Turning.

Acceptable degree of sharpness

This could be defined as: 'Preparing the tool edge to a degree of sharpness which will, in skilled hands, produce as good a finish as possible, taking into account the characteristics of the wood.'

As a general rule, this edge can be achieved direct from the grinder, without recourse to oilstones. This is the opinion of myself and a number of professional turners. However, a sharper edge can be achieved by honing the edge on an oilstone. The question is: 'Is it necessary?'

Other than for softwoods, I don't think it is. If you decide to hone, extreme care must be taken not to create a multi-faceted bevel, which can cause the tool to 'dig in'.

To avoid spending a disproportionate time on sharpening, I suggest you first of all try the tools straight off the grinder. I should be surprised if you were not satisfied with the results. By way of summary, Fig 4.11 illustrates a typical grinding set-up and the required ancillary equipment.

SUMMARY

1 Before successful and enjoyable woodturning can be achieved, there is an absolute requirement for the tools to be accurately ground with one continuous bevel and to an acceptable degree of sharpness.
2 Eye protection is essential when using the grinder.
3 The angles which are used to grind the tools are not critical, but having found the angles that suit you, make a note of these on a template.
4 Making use of a grinding jig ensures accurate grinding, the wooden jig being easy to make and simple to use.

Chapter 5
Laws of Woodturning

When it comes to actually using your tools to shape the wood in woodturning, there are certain rules, or as I prefer to call them, 'laws', which need to be complied with in the interests of safety, tool control and quality of finish. Just as you may expect punishment if you offend the criminal law, you will certainly receive punishment in the form of pain if you offend these 'Laws of Woodturning'!

Drawing on my own and other turners' experience, I have always been reluctant to make definitions relating to woodturning 'laws' and procedures, because you can be assured that someone, somewhere, is doing exactly opposite to what you are preaching.

For instance, I was demonstrating at a local woodworking show when I was approached by a man who had brought along some of his work for me to assess. There were items of both spindle and faceplate work and the standard, taking into account the short time he had been turning, was quite good.

He went on to say that he had not read any books on the subject, neither had he ever seen anyone else demonstrate the craft. Then in all sincerity, and to my utter amazement, he enquired if it was usual for turners to stand at the side of the lathe on which I was standing, because he always stood at the back of the lathe!

Nevertheless, being well aware that there are loopholes in every law, and that in stating or defining laws I am likely to be in conflict with other turners, I put forward and define what I consider to be the Laws of Woodturning.

Law 1 The speed of the lathe must be compatible with the size, weight and length of wood to be turned.

Law 2 The tool must be on the rest *before* the whirling timber is engaged, and must remain so whenever the tool is in contact with the wood.

Law 3 The bevel (grinding angle) of the cutting tools must rub the wood behind the cut.

Law 4 The only part of the tool that should be in contact with the wood is that part of the tool that is receiving *direct support* from the toolrest.

Law 5 Always cut 'downhill' or with the grain.

Law 6 Scrapers must be kept perfectly flat (in section) on the toolrest and presented in the 'trailing mode', i.e. with the tool handle higher than the tool edge.

Law 1

The speed of the lathe must be compatible with the size, weight and length of wood to be turned.

Considerable downward forces can be encountered in woodturning, such forces increasing in proportion to increased speeds and the size, weight or imbalance of the timber being turned.

The inherent *dangers* in mounting large pieces of out-of-balance stock in the lathe cannot be overstressed. Perhaps relating two separate incidents will serve to illustrate and highlight such dangers.

The first incident involved an acquaintance who, at the time of the mishap, had not acquired much turning experience. Thinking that large-bowl turning was the thing for him, he decided to tackle an 18 x 4in (460 x 100mm) disc of unbalanced elm.

He neglected to adjust the lathe to its slowest speed, but started the machine up while it was set to run at its fastest speed – about 2000 rpm.

The inevitable happened: the wood came loose on its mounting and flew from the lathe with considerable force, smashing into his face. He sustained serious facial injuries and his nose was shattered. He still bears the scars.

The second incident happened to me personally and was really caused by carelessness. Again it highlights the absolute requirement to comply with Law 1 *before* the lathe is switched on.

I had been engaged in turning some newel posts in 5in square (125mm) stock and exceeding 5ft (1.5m) in length. Shortly before lunchtime and just as I was removing a completed newel from the lathe, one of the farm labourers came into the workshop and asked me to turn a bung for a device on a farming implement. I adjusted the lathe from the slow, safe speed that I had been using for turning the newels to the top speed of 2000 rpm for the small-diameter bung. I completed this 'free' job and went to lunch.

You can no doubt guess what happened when I returned to continue with the newel posts. I neglected to adjust the lathe back down to the slower, safe speed. Fortunately for me, however, I was standing to one side and out of the 'firing line' when I pressed the start button.

There followed a terrifying and nerve-shattering noise, the whole of the substantial lathe mounting started to vibrate severely, and before I could press the stop button, the wood flew out of the lathe, sending the bottles of polish and sealer stacked on an adjacent bench to all corners of the workshop.

Obviously, I could have been seriously injured. It is now a habit of mine to stand out of the 'firing line' when I press the start button. I strongly recommend you do so also.

What, then, can be considered to be safe turning speeds?

The general rule is that the larger, heavier or longer the stock, the slower the lathe speed that should be set.

If in doubt, always err on the side of safety – that is, on a slower speed than you think it should be, particularly when using unbalanced stock. It is no trouble to stop the lathe and increase the speed once you have reduced the timber to a cylinder and thus to balance. This is common practice anyway, because too slow a speed makes it extremely difficult to get an acceptable finish and invariably results in a 'thread' effect, particularly if the tool is traversed other than very slowly.

So far as the length of timber is concerned, it will become evident that fast lathe speeds and long pieces of timber do not go together. Longer lengths usually mean increased weights in any case, but even if the stock is not particularly heavy, as in long, slender work, the tendency for it to 'whip' increases as the lathe speed is increased.

Taking all these things into consideration, I put forward the following guide to safe lathe speeds. But remember that such speeds can only be approximate, because of the differing range of speeds available from lathe to lathe.

Between-centres turning

Stock size	Up to 24in (600mm) long	Over 24in long
Up to 2½in (65mm) square	2000 rpm	1500 rpm
2½–4in (65–100mm)	1500 rpm	1000 rpm
Over 4in	1000 rpm	750 rpm

Faceplate turning

Stock size	Up to 2in (50mm) thick	Over 2in thick
Up to 8in (200mm) dia.	1000 rpm	750 rpm
8–12in (200–300mm)	750 rpm	750 rpm
Over 12in	Slowest available	Slowest available

Remember that your personal safety is the most important consideration, so the general rule of slow speeds for larger and heavier stock must always be in the forefront of your mind.

Law 2

The tool must be on the rest before the whirling timber is engaged, and must remain so whenever the tool is in contact with the wood.

I make no apologies for stating this law, although some observers might claim that it should not be classed as a law or rule, but merely a matter of common sense. I have never yet taught anyone who has not offended this law, even though I had stressed its importance.

In teaching, I rarely allow students to work on stock exceeding 2in (50mm) square during the first morning of the course. Thus, if this or any of the other laws are disobeyed, the consequences are less of a shock to the nervous system than if large-section stock was being turned. One of my objectives is to instil confidence in the student, and offending the laws on large-section timber does not go far in achieving this aim.

I have already mentioned the considerable downward forces which can be encountered in woodturning, and these forces are increased as mass (or weight) and velocity are increased.

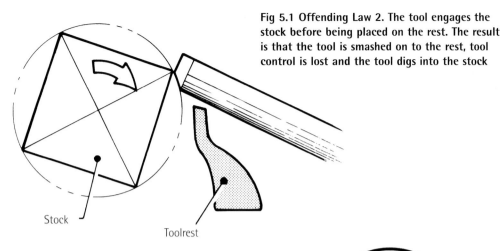

Fig 5.1 Offending Law 2. The tool engages the stock before being placed on the rest. The result is that the tool is smashed on to the rest, tool control is lost and the tool digs into the stock

Stock

Toolrest

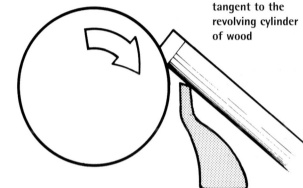

Fig 5.2a The cutting tool is presented at a tangent to the revolving cylinder of wood

If the tool comes into contact with the wood *before* it is in contact with the rest, it will be smacked downwards on to the rest with some force and you may well finish up with bruised fingers and black fingernails. Additionally, the tool may be snatched from your grasp, there will be tearing of wood fibres, and your nerve and courage will be dented (Fig 5.1).

In my experience, beginners are more likely to offend this law in the roughing down of square-section stock than during any other operation. The reasons for this are discussed in Chapter 6 on Turning Between Centres.

I have mentioned that there are loopholes in most laws. So far as this particular law is concerned, one is in the use of scrapers on the outside of bowls and discs. Some turners will use 'scraper bars' without bearing them on the toolrest. I have never found any particular advantage in the practice, and I certainly do not recommend that newcomers to the craft try it.

Law 3

The bevel (grinding angle) of the cutting tools must rub the wood behind the cut.

Before discussing how to present the cutting tools to the whirling wood in order to achieve the 'bevel-rubbing' mode, we should first of all distinguish between cutting tools and scraping tools. This may be helped by stating that there are two distinct methods of shaping or turning the wood to the desired profile.

The first is by use of the cutting tools, these being the gouges, chisels and parting tools,

which are presented at a tangent or 'bevel-rubbing' angle to the spinning wood (Fig 5.2a).

The tools in this category, as described in Chapter 4, On Sharpening, are ground at angles ranging from 25 to 55°, depending on the type of tool. Such tools will remove stock from most species of timber at a desired rate, and in skilled hands will give an acceptable finish and retain their cutting edge for a surprisingly long time.

As a general rule, the cutting tools, with the exception of the bowl gouge, are used only on between-centres turning, where the grain runs parallel to the bed of the lathe.

The second method of shaping wood is by the scraping method. You may have read theoretical arguments claiming that a scraping tool cuts, and indeed I agree that a sharp scraper will produce cleanly cut shavings on some varieties of timber, even when being used in between-centres turning. However, for the purposes of this book and in the interests of clarity, 'cutting' means using the cutting tools and 'scraping' means using the scraping tools.

By referring back to Chapter 4 it will be seen that the scraping tools are ground with a much more obtuse angle (shorter bevel) than the cutting tools. In the same chapter it was also explained that the shorter the bevel, the

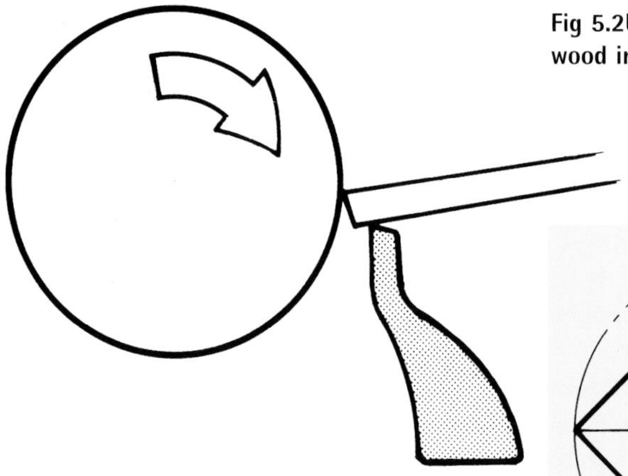

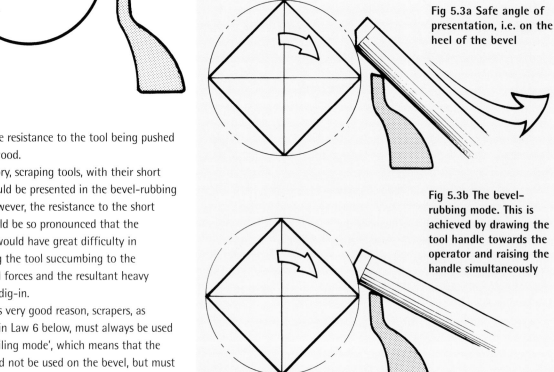

Fig 5.2b The scraper tool is presented to the wood in trailing mode

Fig 5.3a Safe angle of presentation, i.e. on the heel of the bevel

Fig 5.3b The bevel-rubbing mode. This is achieved by drawing the tool handle towards the operator and raising the handle simultaneously

greater the resistance to the tool being pushed into the wood.

In theory, scraping tools, with their short bevels, could be presented in the bevel-rubbing mode. However, the resistance to the short bevel would be so pronounced that the operator would have great difficulty in preventing the tool succumbing to the downward forces and the resultant heavy 'catch' or dig-in.

For this very good reason, scrapers, as indicated in Law 6 below, must always be used in the 'trailing mode', which means that the tool should not be used on the bevel, but must point slightly down (Fig 5.2b).

Now a scraping action with any tool generates considerably more friction and heat to the tool edge, which of course means the tool may rapidly overheat. This is why scrapers are ground with an obtuse angle so the heat can be absorbed and give acceptable 'tool-edge life'.

Applying the same logic, if cutting tools, with their longer bevels, are used scraper fashion, the edge will rapidly overheat, having the effect of both softening and dulling the tool edge extremely quickly.

This is why accomplished turners, using the cutting tools as they should be used, spend less time at the grindstone than the less skilled turner, whose part-scraping, part-cutting technique necessitates more frequent visits to the grinder.

Hopefully, by now I have convinced you that the gouges and chisels (parting tools are really chisels) should be used in the bevel-rubbing mode, and the scrapers should be used in the trailing mode.

I dismiss those who say that there is no craftsmanship in using scrapers, and I will discuss this further in Chapter 7, Faceplate Turning.

How to achieve the bevel-rubbing mode

I like to compare this technique with 'clutch control' when driving a motor car.

In driving, the clutch must be raised slowly and smoothly to avoid 'biting' or engaging too quickly. The consequence of too quick a bite is the embarrassing and sometimes nerve-racking 'kangarooing' known to us all.

To achieve a smooth 'takeaway' with the cutting tools, they must first of all be presented to the whirling wood so that they will not cut at all, or at what I like to call *the safe angle of presentation*.

This is done by placing the tool on the rest with the tool handle well down so only the heel of the bevel is making contact with the wood.

The engaging, biting or cutting is brought about by the smooth drawing down of the tool towards the turner, while at the same time the back end is lifted. (Fig 5.3a and b).

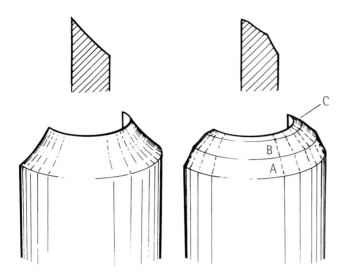

Fig 5.4 Correct and incorrect grinding. On the left is the single-facet concave bevel which would provide adequate bevel-rubbing potential. In the example on the right it would be impossible for the bevels marked A and B to give support to the cutting edge. The only part of the bevel that could possibly rub behind the cut is C, which is inadequate. A rounded or convex bevel would be similarly inadequate

This will ensure that you *find the bevel*, a term I shall be using frequently throughout the book. In clutch control, the more you lift your foot, the greater the degree of bite. In tool control, the more you lift your back hand (after having 'found the bevel') the greater the bite, or in other words, the thicker the shaving you will fetch off.

When learning clutch control in a car, the learner driver practises on an up-slope until able, by lifting or depressing the foot, to move slowly forward or remain stationary.

A direct comparison can be made between 'holding the car on the clutch' and bevel-rubbing: when the whole of the bevel is rubbing, it is like holding the car on the clutch, because *nothing is happening*. The car isn't moving; no wood is being removed.

In both cases, all that is needed to make something happen is to lift. Lift the foot on the clutch or lift the back end of the cutting tool: the car moves or, similarly, cutting commences.

Does this appear to be a paradox? First I say the bevel must rub, then I say that if the whole of the bevel is rubbing, nothing is happening.

The truth of the matter is that *behind the cut* the bevel must be rubbing, and a frequent comment I make to students who are struggling to make balanced shapes is, 'put the bevel where you have just cut'.

Also, remember with scrapers that the shaving thickness is dictated by the amount of forward pressure applied to the tool. With the cutting tools, the amount of forward pressure does not affect the shaving thickness in the slightest if the correct technique is used. Try it,

by first of all 'finding the bevel' with a roughing-out gouge, lifting the back end of the tool along the rest, applying as much forward pressure as you like. The shaving thickness remains constant because of the bevel rubbing on the wood behind the cut, supporting the cutting edge.

The only thing which can affect the thickness of shaving is the *lifting of the back hand*, but despite the thickness of the shaving, the bevel of the tool must rub the wood behind the cut.

If the tool edge is not receiving such support, it is free to bury itself into the wood. This is likely to happen if you present a cutting tool in a scraping mode because it will be impossible for the bevel to support the cut.

In the chapter On Sharpening, the importance of grinding the tools with one continuous bevel was emphasized. The reasons should by now be obvious, because if you use a multi-faceted tool, it will not take a shaving until it is lifted off the bevel nearest to the cutting edge. This means the other 'bevels' cannot possibly support the cut (Fig 5.4). A tool ground to a rounded or convex profile will likewise give no support to the cutting edge.

Other advantages of bevel-rubbing

The ability to make the bevel rub behind the cut also helps to provide flowing, balanced shapes in your turning.

Additionally, bevel-rubbing imparts a burnishing effect on the wood, making it smooth and shiny. This manifestation is one of the hallmarks of the skilled turner.

If you doubt this, take a roughing-out gouge and reduce a piece of 2in-square (50 x 50mm) pine to a cylinder, leaving as good a finish as your level of skill allows.

Now drop the back end of the tool until it just stops cutting (remember holding the car on the clutch?) and apply a moderate or, if you like, a positive forward pressure as you traverse the tool along the rest. Now see the wood take on a burnished, shiny look!

This is what you should be aiming for in the use of all your cutting tools, and when you can consistently achieve it, you have progressed a long way down the path to being an accomplished woodturner.

Law 4

The only part of the tool that should be in contact with the wood is that part of the tool that is receiving direct support from the toolrest.

Failure to obey this law will nearly always result in a catch or dig-in.

Let me then explain this and make it as simple as possible to understand. I have already mentioned the downward forces encountered in woodturning, such forces increasing as the mass (weight of timber) and velocity (speed of lathe) are increased.

To counteract these forces, it has been stressed that the tool must be on the rest during the cutting process (Law 2).

Notwithstanding your obedience to Law 2, a dig-in will almost certainly occur if the downward forces are applied to a part of the tool edge which is not receiving *direct support* from the toolrest.

The principle of a child's seesaw provides an adequate analogy. If the seesaw was perfectly balanced on its centre pivot or support, it would remain perfectly parallel to the ground. If downward force is applied where the seesaw is balanced – that is, over the centre support – the seesaw will remain in the same position. Applying downward force either side of the centre support will tip the seesaw in the same direction. The further away from the centre support the downward force is applied, the faster the 'unsupported' end smacks down on the ground (Fig 5.5).

Apply the same principle to using a roughing-out gouge. If the tool is being used on its back, the *only* part of the tool edge receiving *direct support* is the corresponding centre of the gouge.

Just like the seesaw, if the downward forces are allowed to contact either side of the centre of the tool, it will be smacked downwards on to the rest. Tool control will immediately be lost and the tool will almost certainly bury itself into the wood (Fig 5.6).

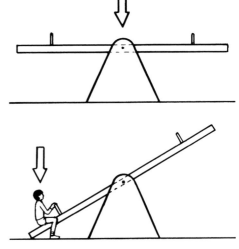

Fig 5.5 The seesaw principle. A load applied to the centre of the seesaw (top) would not affect equilibrium. A load applied off centre (below) without support would affect equilibrium

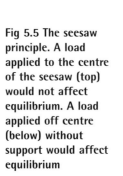

(a)

Toolrest

Area of support

(b)

(c)

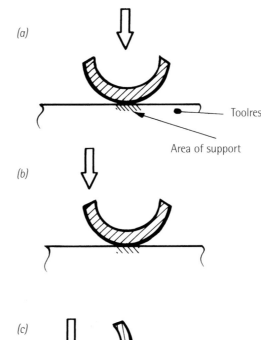

Fig 5.6 Supporting the tool edge. The cut should be made with the portion of the tool that is supported on the rest (a). When the cut is made with a portion of the tool not supported on the rest (b), the stock will force the tool to rotate until that portion of the tool finds support (c). Damage may occur to both the operator and the stock!

Fig 5.7 Using the supported part of the tool edge

Fig 5.8 Using the supported part of the tool edge

Fig 5.9 (below) Using part of the tool edge unsupported by the toolrest

A practical example of how this law can be offended is shown very clearly in Figs 5.7–5.10.

The example shows a length of wood being turned to a cylinder, but with a pummel or square end being left on, typical of table and chair legs, etc., allowing them to be mortised to receive the cross rails.

Fig 5.7 shows the gouge being used on its back with the shaving coming from the corresponding part of the tool receiving direct support from the toolrest.

Fig 5.8 shows the gouge position altered in that it has been rolled right over on its edge to allow it to cut right up to the square section without fouling it. Law 4 is not being offended because the shaving is still coming from the part of the tool receiving direct support from the toolrest.

If you study Figs 5.9 and 5.10 you will see the consequences of failing to roll the gouge over on to its edge. The tool is receiving support only in its centre, but the leading 'wing' of the gouge (*unsupported*) has been allowed to engage the square section. Just like the child's seesaw, the downward forces on an unsupported section will smash the tool down on the rest, resulting in the heavy 'catch' shown in Fig 5.10.

Fig 5.10 The consequence of using an unsupported part of the edge: the dig-in

This particular law will be enlarged upon when I come to describe the functions of the various cutting tools in Chapter 6, Turning Between Centres.

Law 5

Always cut 'downhill', or with the grain.

In all branches of woodworking, from carpentry to carving, from joinery to cabinetmaking, smoother and easier cuts are achieved by 'working with the grain'. Woodturning is no exception.

On spindle turning or working between centres, cutting with the grain invariably means cutting from larger to smaller diameters, hence the saying 'cutting downhill' (Fig 5.11).

On faceplate turnings, cutting from larger to smaller diameters does not necessarily mean you are cutting with the grain. This will be explained later in the book when I deal with bowl turning.

Perhaps the easiest way of appreciating this law is to try this exercise. Take any piece of timber in which the grain is clearly not parallel to the surface of the wood. By making use of a hand plane we can see the effects of planing with the grain and against the grain. The former will produce a clean, smooth surface, but the latter results in a rough, torn surface (Fig 5.12a and b).

Another less appreciated consequence of cutting uphill is that you are in danger of offending Law 4, particularly when cutting hollows or coves with the spindle gouges. I will expand on this when describing the use and functions of the gouges in Chapter 6, Turning

Between Centres. Suffice at this stage to repeat that disobedience to Law 4 nearly always results in a dig-in.

Law 6

Scrapers must be kept perfectly flat (in section) on the toolrest and presented in the 'trailing mode', i.e. with the tool handle higher than the tool edge.

Appreciating and understanding the foregoing laws really makes this easy to understand.

I have discussed at some length under Law 3 the reason why scrapers, because of their obtuse or short grinding angle, must not be presented in the bevel-rubbing mode, as the resistance to the tool would be so great that a dig-in would most certainly ensue.

Accordingly, these tools must point slightly down (bevel underneath) so that only the extreme edge of the tool is in contact with the wood (Fig 5.2b).

It is equally important for the scrapers to be kept perfectly flat on the toolrest. If you do not do this, and allow the part of the tool corresponding to that *not in contact* with the toolrest to touch the wood, you will be offending Law 6 and Law 4 as well (Fig 5.13). The result will be a dig-in which will probably live in the memory.

I strongly recommend that you regularly review this chapter until you fully understand the six laws.

Bad and unsafe habits can creep up on you, so in the interests of safety, particularly in the learning stages, take your time, have regard to these laws, and *relax*.

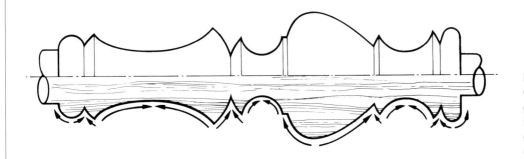

Fig 5.11 Law 5: Cutting with the grain. The arrows indicate the direction of cutting 'downhill' or 'with the grain' in between-centres turning

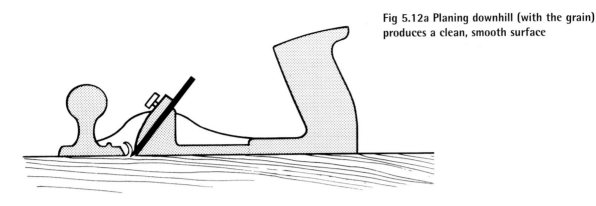

Fig 5.12a Planing downhill (with the grain) produces a clean, smooth surface

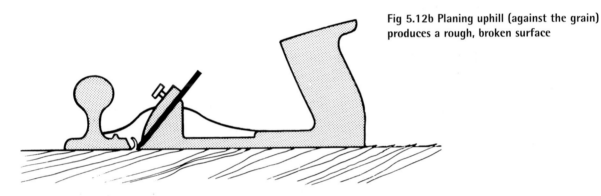

Fig 5.12b Planing uphill (against the grain) produces a rough, broken surface

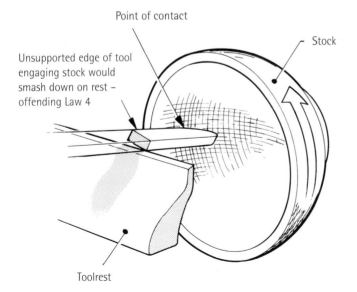

Point of contact

Stock

Unsupported edge of tool engaging stock would smash down on rest – offending Law 4

Toolrest

Fig 5.13 Offending Laws 6 and 4

SUMMARY

1 A thorough understanding of the laws will ensure that when things go wrong, you will be able to identify the reason and thus avoid a repetition.
2 Such an understanding will also help you to grasp not only *how* a tool is used, but also *why* it is used in a certain manner.
3 Compliance with the laws makes it most unlikely that you will sustain any serious injury.
4 Control of the cutting tools is determined to a great extent by bevel-rubbing. Remember therefore to practise 'clutch control' and to master it, not only on straight cylinders, but also in hollows and around convex shapes.

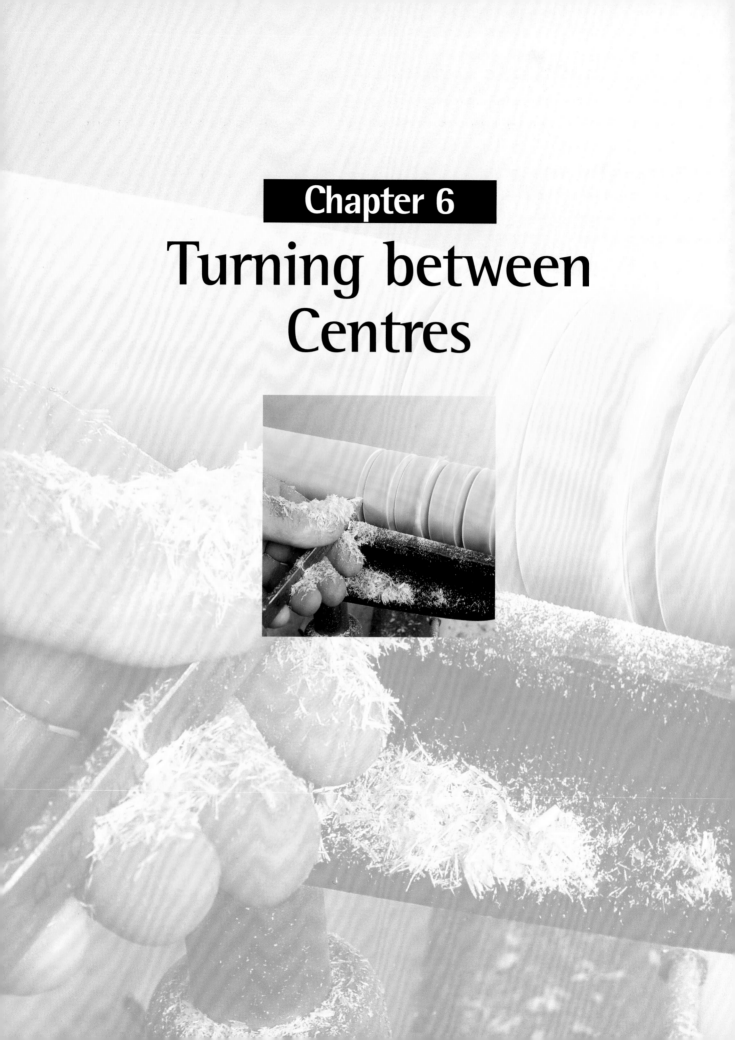

Chapter 6
Turning between Centres

t is now time to decide which category of woodturning we ought to begin with. Would it be better to start with faceplate work, or turning between centres?

The majority of people to whom I give instruction are under the impression that a turner's merit is judged by his ability to produce quality faceplate work, such as bowls, platters and vases.

While I agree that a great deal of skill may be required to produce such work, I certainly do not believe *more* skill is called for in faceplate work than in turning between centres.

A good faceplate turner will almost certainly be an accomplished turner between centres, but conversely, a turner who is accomplished in spindle work will also be quite capable of producing quality faceplate work.

Taking this a stage further, it is quite possible for the *mediocre* faceplate turner to produce attractive artefacts, but cloak the fact that they may have been made using methods that are *crude, uncraftsmanlike, dangerous, dusty and slow*.

For example, a turner may make bowls which are of an acceptable standard and which sell. However, his knowledge of the correct function and use of the bowl gouge may be minimal as he relies to a great extent on power sanding to arrive at an acceptable finish. Ask the same person to turn a leg for a Windsor chair, where crisp, cleanly cut, traditional profiles are required, and his lack of craftsmanship would quickly become evident.

In other words, it is my view that the mediocre turner can get away with crude, uncraftsmanlike methods on some types of faceplate work, but he will most certainly be exposed for what he is when using other than correct cutting techniques on between-centres work.

Another good reason for starting your education on spindle turning is that, generally speaking, larger pieces of wood are used in faceplate work, which means increased downward forces will be encountered (see page 45).

Gouges and scrapers presented incorrectly to large chunks of wood whirling round on the faceplate can be dangerous, and the severity of the resultant dig-ins or catches can be alarming. Such experiences will make the operator nervous and tense, almost certainly denting his confidence for some considerable time.

It is vital that the learning process should be as calm, unhurried and tension-free as possible, and therefore I am firmly of the opinion that 'early learning' should be restricted to between-centres turning with pieces of wood that are neither too long nor too large in section.

Accordingly, for our initial exercise we will make use of a piece of Scots pine about 10in long and 2½in square (255 x 65 x 65mm). I have chosen this length for demonstration as one of my toolrests is 12in (305mm) long, and consequently the need to keep moving the toolrest is avoided.

In this chapter we will go through my usual order of working, examining each step in detail:

1 Rough down to a cylinder.
2 Mark out the wood with template and pencil to indicate the positions of the various design features and key diameters.
3 'Size in' in these marked places with the parting tool, making use of callipers, verniers, etc. to establish the correct diameters (more of this later).
4 Cut in the required shapes with the spindle gouges and chisels, blending in the profiles to the predetermined depths.

Preparation of the timber

You may have read elsewhere that stock to be mounted between centres should be reduced to an octagonal shape, in the interests of safety. Not only is this procedure time-consuming, it is totally unnecessary. If this work is done with a hand plane, it will take some considerable time. If the turner makes use of a power planer or saw, it will be more dangerous than turning it to a cylinder on the lathe.

Centring the workpiece

After a little experience you will be able to guess the centre of a piece of square stock well enough for practice purposes, but initially it is best to draw diagonals on the ends of the stock. In many instances, it is important to be as accurate as possible in determining centres, for example when squares or 'pummels' are being left on the workpiece, as with table or chair legs.

Take a pointed awl and make small locating holes at both ends. Place your drive centre in one of these holes and give it a sharp rap with a mallet or lump of wood, preferably with the workpiece over the bench leg or something solid. Avoid the use of hammers or you may 'burr' over the end of the drive, thus preventing it homing in properly in the mandrel's Morse taper (Fig 6.1).

Mounting the stock

Insert the drive centre into the headstock mandrel and offer the wood up to it, ensuring the indentations you have just made receive the driving spurs. Your other hand serves to keep the wood pulled up to the drive while you position the tailstock to within about ½in (13mm) of the other end.

Next, lock the tailstock in position and advance the tailstock barrel with the handwheel until the revolving centre engages the hole made in the centre of the end of the wood.

Determining correct tailstock pressure

The tailstock should apply only sufficient pressure to drive the wood efficiently. Do not overtighten the workpiece, as this can have the effect of damaging the headstock bearings if done repeatedly. I recommend the following simple method. **The power to the lathe should be isolated during this procedure.**

Place your left hand on either the drive belt or pulleys and with your right hand try to revolve the wood. If you can feel movement on the drive spurs, tighten a little more until all the play is taken up (I call this the *test of tightness;* see Fig 6.2).

Fig 6.1 Use a mallet or a block of wood for this job

Fig 6.2 Applying the 'test of tightness'

Fig 6.3 Positioning the toolrest

Positioning the toolrest

The general rule is that the height of the toolrest is not critical in between-centres turning. Fix it at approximately 'centre height', i.e. with the top edge of the rest in line with the centre of the wood. This will be fine. (There are occasions when the rest height *is* critical, and these are dealt with in Chapter 7.)

My method of determining both the height of the rest and the safe distance from the workpiece is to revolve the wood by hand until the diagonals are parallel to the bench top. I then position the rest in line with the nearest corner, leaving no less than a ¼in (6mm) gap for the roughing-down process (Fig 6.3).

If the toolrest is not long enough to span the length of the workpiece, it is important to position it so that no less than ¾in (19mm) is

protruding by the end of the wood where you are working. Why? Assume your toolrest is positioned just short of, or in line with, the end of the workpiece. In attempting to cut to the end of the wood, you would probably drop the tool off the end of the rest and the downward forces would almost certainly twist the tool in your hand and trap one or more fingers. I have seen more than one black fingernail as a result of people disregarding this advice.

Holding the tools

Some teachers and books use the word 'grip' when describing the application of the hands to the tools. I prefer to use the word 'hold', as 'grip' implies a high degree of tightness and strength. A secure 'hold' is needed, but not the vice-like grip which most novices tend to use.

While at first a certain amount of tension and apprehension is understandable, flowing, fluid tool manipulation can only be achieved by a relaxed approach and the absence of tension, not only in the hands and wrist but in the whole body.

There are basically only two methods of holding the tools:

1 The underhand hold

This is the hold I use for the majority of my between-centres turning.

As shown in Fig 6.4, the thumb of the hand nearest the toolrest (be it right or left hand) is

Fig 6.4 The underhand hold

Fig 6.5 Principle of gauging or cutting parallel lines

placed on top of the tool while the fingers cradle it from underneath.

The thumb serves to keep the tool pressed down on the rest (which avoids offending Law 2) and the index finger *lightly* presses against the toolrest. This assists balance and facilitates the cutting of straight lines in the roughing-down process, in much the same way as the carpenter draws parallel lines on a board with a pencil (Fig 6.5).

This same hand, particularly the thumb and index finger, provides fine control and flexibility on spindle turning, where intricate shapes and positive entry are often called for.

The 'back' hand cups the tool handle in a position that is comfortable and where the tool is balanced when placed on the rest. Positioning this hand too far back results in exaggerated and tiring movements.

The 'back' hand is also the 'dominant' hand, determining the thickness of the shaving by virtue of lifting or lowering the handle. It also dominates the swinging and rolling movements called for in many techniques.

2 The overhand hold

This is the hold I use for the greater part of my faceplate turning.

The back hand holds the tool in exactly the same way as before, but the front hand is positioned with the fingers overlapping the tool from the top and with the outside of the palm resting on the toolrest, which assists balance and control (Fig 6.6).

Because this hold is used primarily on faceplate work, it will be dealt with in greater detail in the next chapter.

Stance, balance and movement

Positioning of the feet, balance, weight transference and movement are of vital importance in woodturning.

Your stance should feel comfortable, with your feet sufficiently parted to afford optimum balance and therefore movement. In long traversing cuts (e.g. when roughing down) or when substantial swinging movements are called for (e.g. when shaping a bowl), widen your stance to enable you to sway from side to side without losing balance.

Both elbows should be tucked in to your body, enabling your hips, legs and shoulders to

Fig 6.6 The overhand hold

play their part in assisting the hands, wrists and forearms. This provides for greater control and is certainly less tiring.

Balance and movement can be assisted in some operations by leaning on part of the lathe structure or the lathe bench. It is amazing what assistance to balance is afforded by the index finger of the front hand being pressed up to the toolrest.

Most beginners are far too stiff and restricted in their movements around the lathe, probably because they are apprehensive at the sight of a piece of wood whirling round at 2000rpm; but it is essential to learn to relax and be fluid in your movement.

The time has come

Before you press the button, let me remind you of the *very important* safety considerations. Impress upon your mind the word **SAFER**, from which we can develop the most useful mnemonic:

S for **Speed** – is it compatible with the size of wood to be turned?
A for **Aside** – stand out of the 'firing line'.
F for **Fastened** – are all locking handles secure?
E for **Eye protection**.
R for **Revolve** the wood 'freehand' to ensure it spins freely.

Fig 6.7 Cut commencing behind the high spot

Why not write down the above mnemonic on a piece of card or plywood and put it close to the lathe to act as an *aide-mémoire*? *Remember*: safety must be number one priority.

The tool that you will invariably pick up first for between-centres turning, and certainly for reducing a piece of square stock to a cylinder, is the:

Roughing-out gouge

Start the lathe and take hold of the tool as described above. The first cut will start about 2in (50mm) in from one end of the piece of wood; in this exercise, start at the right end as you view it. (There are two very good reasons for starting the cut this distance from the end; see page 62.)

Technique

The tool must be on the rest *before* the wood is engaged (Law 2, page 46). Present the tool with the handle well down so that the tool will *not* cut (Safe Angle of Presentation, Fig 5.3a), with the heel of the bevel rubbing the wood.

Remember how 'clutch control' was achieved to provide a nice smooth takeaway by finding the bevel? (Law 3, page 47) To refresh your memory, this is brought about by drawing down the tool towards your body and simultaneously lifting the back end. The tool will now start to cut, the thickness of the shaving (and we do not want too much removed at one pass) being determined by how much the back hand is raised. (Refer back to Figs 5.2a, 5.3a, 5.3b in Chapter 5 on the Laws of Woodturning.)

Now incline the tool approximately 15° in the intended direction of traverse (to the right, in this case) and roll it slightly in the same direction. This angling induces a slicing, paring action and it is important to maintain this same angle to ensure a parallel cut. This is best achieved by body movement and not movement by the hands and arms.

Commence subsequent cuts behind the high spot you have created and with the shaving coming from below the centre of the tool — that is, where it is receiving direct support. Make sure you traverse past the end of the workpiece or you will create an 'uphill' situation (Fig 6.7).

Fig 6.8 Feeling for roundness at the back of the workpiece

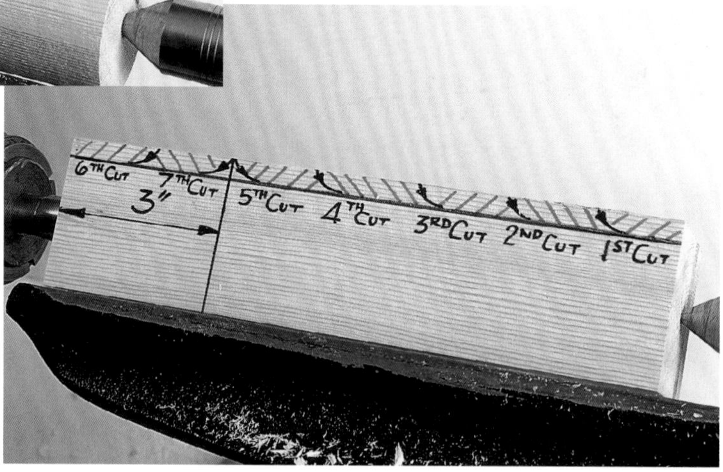

FEEL FOR ROUND HERE

NEVER HERE

Fig 6.9 The order of cutting on square stock

6TH CUT 7TH CUT 5TH CUT 4TH CUT 3RD CUT 2ND CUT 1ST CUT

3"

When the end of the wood is reached, *do not* lift the tool off the rest to return it to where you intend starting your next cut. If you do, you will run the risk of engaging the wood *before* engaging the toolrest (offending Law 2). The consequence of this is a dig-in.

Draw the gouge back slightly towards your body and slide it back on the rest to the required entry point. This is the reason why the toolrest should not be positioned less than ¼in (6mm) away from the square stock in the roughing-down operation.

With experience, you will be able to detect by sound when you have turned the wood to a cylinder. It is also quite safe to cup the *back* of the whirling wood with your fingers, to feel for roundness (Fig 6.8). *Do not ever*, in any operation, touch the *front* of the whirling workpiece, or you may get your fingers wedged between the wood and the toolrest, resulting in a nasty accident.

When you reach a position about 4in (100mm) from the left end of the workpiece, reverse the process and cut towards the headstock until the cylinder is parallel along its full length. Fig 6.9 shows the order of cutting.

Do not allow a large gap to appear between the wood and the toolrest. As soon as the stock has been reduced to a cylinder, stop the lathe and move the rest inwards to leave approximately a ¼in (6mm) gap as before.

To ensure that you are bevel-rubbing correctly, I suggest that you occasionally lower your back hand and 'hold it on the clutch', and then by gently raising the back hand, bring the cut back on.

Most beginners do not exert enough forward pressure on the tool, probably because they mistakenly think this will cause the tool to dig in. When it is realized that the bevel of the tool prevents this from happening, then the desired moderate forward pressure is applied.

Normally, within a few minutes of acquiring the basic technique, the beginner visibly becomes more relaxed. As a means of further increasing confidence, I recommend that this first exercise be repeated on three or four more pieces of wood, reducing each one to a straight cylinder of approximately 1in (25mm) diameter.

Supporting technique

You will find that if the diameter of the wood is reduced to much below 1in it begins to 'whip', accompanied by a tell-tale sound. This is a problem encountered often in spindle work, and the 'whip' increases as diameter is reduced.

It is therefore necessary to 'steady' the work, and on pieces of up to 18in (460mm) long, the beginner will have little difficulty in steadying the workpiece with his front hand. The fingers on this hand 'cup' the whirling wood, and the thumb, placed on top of the tool, serves to keep it in contact with

Fig 6.10 Preventing 'whip' with the supporting technique

the rest. Note that the fingers of the front hand are kept well to one side of the cutting edge (Fig 6.10).

The back hand should be positioned so as to hold the gouge where it is balanced, that is, well forward on the handle, adjacent to the ferrule.

Exert only an equal and opposite steadying pressure, which in the case of small-diameter work should be light.

Excessive steadying pressure may result in the flesh overheating and, in extreme cases, smoking. If it does, let go and start again, making use of something to absorb the heat, such as a pad of leather or a handful of shavings.

Please note that this technique must only be used *after* the stock has been reduced to a cylinder, *never* on square-section stock.

Mechanical steadies

There are several types of mechanical steady, both manufactured and home-made, which can be employed for long, slender turnings, and these are described on pages 119–20.

Other uses

The roughing-out gouge is really inappropriately named. Although its basic function is to rough down, it can be used for many other operations. In skilled hands, and with a sharp edge taking fine cuts, it is possible to obtain a finish on the wood almost equal to that obtained by the skew chisel. The novice

will improve his skill with this tool if he regularly attempts:

Hollows It is important to understand that no gouge can cut a hollow or concave shape 'quicker' than the radius of the tool. It follows, therefore, that the roughing-out gouge will only cut fairly 'slow' shapes, be it hollows or rounds.

Rounding over Because this tool is ground square across, it is not possible to fashion other than a 'slow' rounding-over profile, as the wings of the gouge prevent it.

Exercise

Reduce your piece of wood to a parallel cylinder. Set it out, lathe running, with the aid of a ruler and pencil into approximately 2in (50mm) spaces. Make sure the toolrest is close in to the work while marking.

The object of this exercise is to form hollows in alternate spaces, and practise cutting rounds on the others. Start with the hollows by presenting the gouge approximately in the centre and pushing it into the wood with a slight scooping action, at right angles to the workpiece. Gradually widen the hollow out to your pencil lines by taking cuts from either side, taking care to stop the cut at the bottom of the hollow. Don't cut uphill and thus offend Law 5 (page 52). Complete all the hollowing (Fig 6.11).

Fig 6.11 Forming hollows with the roughing-out gouge

Now for the rounding over. As a profile is being fashioned exactly opposite to a hollow, the tool must be used in an exactly opposite manner, that is with a slight rolling action. Commence the cut close to the corner of a flat and roll the tool gently towards the hollow. To blend the rounding over into the hollow, final cuts will necessitate a rolling action followed by a slight scooping action (Fig 6.12).

Finally, before passing on to the next tool, I think that a technique to deflect the shavings (perhaps more accurately described as 'chippings' until the wood is cylindrical) away from the turner's face is well worth mentioning. Fig 6.13 shows this technique, which entails the fingers of the front hand being positioned to divert the shavings, and the thumb again serving to keep the gouge in contact with the toolrest. **Whatever technique is used, it is still essential to wear eye protection.**

I have advised starting the cut approximately 2in (50mm) from the end in the roughing down of square-section stock. This is basically in the interests of safety. If there are any shakes or 'pith' close to any of the square corners, you may well get long flying splinters of wood. If, however, you start the cut 2in from the end and work towards this open end, the length of the splinter is limited to the same length. Additionally, you will encounter less resistance to the tool because subsequent cuts will be slightly 'downhill'.

Sharpening

The roughing-out gouge should be ground square across with a bevel of approximately 45°. The method of sharpening by means of the grinding jig has been explained in Chapter 4, On Sharpening.

Parting tool

Having attained a certain amount of skill and familiarity with the roughing-out gouge, it is time to turn attention to the parting tool, which is the tool I would be most likely to use next during the course of my everyday turning between centres. From my order of working (page 55), it will be appreciated that the

Fig 6.12 Forming rounds with the roughing-out gouge

Fig 6.13 Deflecting shavings away from the face with the fingers

parting tool is used more in the role described in step 3 below than in actually 'parting off'.

Additionally it can be used for several other purposes, and its versatility is often not recognized by a good many turners. After all, the ¼in (6mm) parallel parting tool which I recommend as part of your first set of tools is really a chisel, and a chisel can perform many different functions.

Technique: normal two-hand hold

As with all cutting tools, the parting tool should be used wherever possible in the bevel-rubbing mode, (Law 3, page 47).

Fig 6.14 The 'fraying' effect when the cut with the parting tool is begun in the bevel-rubbing mode

Do not continue in this scraping mode. The abrasive action will quickly dull the sharpest of tools and undue force will be required to push it forward. Instead, lower the handle and 'find the bevel'. The cut is then brought on and continued by lifting the back hand until the desired diameter has been reached.

Technique: one-hand hold

When making use of callipers or any device to **size in** (that is, to reduce the wood to a predetermined diameter) obviously the parting tool must be held in one hand.

I take hold of the tool well up the handle, finger and thumb in line with the ferrule. The tool handle rests on my wrist and forearm for greater stability and control. Sizing cuts should be *started* with both hands holding the tool, the front hand being released to pick up the callipers when approaching the desired diameter.

Complete the cut as before by merely lifting the back hand (Fig 6.16).

Fig 6.15 Fraying prevented by horizontal presentation

It will be found, however, that when this tool is presented to the stock in this mode, it will more than likely fray the sides of the intended groove as it enters the wood. This fraying, or slight spelching, is more pronounced on softwoods and coarse-grained hardwoods (Fig 6.14).

This problem is exacerbated if the tool has been sharpened so that the cutting edge is not dead square across, but slightly domed. Some turners intentionally grind a slightly concaved edge on the tool so that the extreme tips 'scribe' the wood first to avoid the fraying.

I prefer to keep my parting tools ground square across, because I think they lose their versatility if ground otherwise.

The problem can be overcome (if it matters, and on many projects it does not) by *initially* presenting the tool horizontally (scraping mode), entering the wood to a depth just sufficient to get through the first fibres (Fig 6.15).

Fig 6.16 Sizing in with the vernier, using the one-handed tool hold

Cautionary notes

1 The parallel parting tool must be kept at right angles to the work or the tool will quickly bind.
2 Even when the tool is kept at right angles, it is advisable not to go below a depth of ½in (13mm) without withdrawing the tool and widening out the groove on the 'waste wood' side.
3 When using verniers to size in, do not hold them on the points. If they 'jump' or bind, they could stick in your flesh.
4 When you reach the required depth, place the vernier on the bench and withdraw the tool with two hands in the same plane as you finished the cut. Do not lift the tool out of the groove you have just cut, or you will leave the toolrest and most likely foul the side of the groove, causing a dig-in.
5 Ensure that the tool is kept perfectly flat on its edge when parting or sizing. The full width of the tool is being used and therefore the full width must be supported by the toolrest (Law 4).

Parting off

A typical example of when this is done is shown in Fig 6.17. Here, a clock finial has been turned on a screw chuck, and the dowel at the headstock end is about to be parted off. The left hand is shown 'catching' the finial as it is cut off. As the parting cut nears completion, only gentle pressure should be applied to the cut.

Fig 6.17 'Cradling' a clock finial just before parting off

Other uses

The parting tool's versatility includes the following operations:

Feathering cuts

A parting tool entered at right angles to the work will cut directly across the grain, and the completed shoulder, fillet or trench is consequently rough. This can be remedied by a 'feathering cut'. The tool is tipped very slightly in the direction of traverse, allowing the leading tip to gently 'feather' under the fibres as it moves along the grain in either direction. The roughness will be transformed to a nice smooth finish (Fig 6.18).

Fig 6.18 Feathering cut with the parting tool

Fig 6.19 Rolling a bead with a parting tool

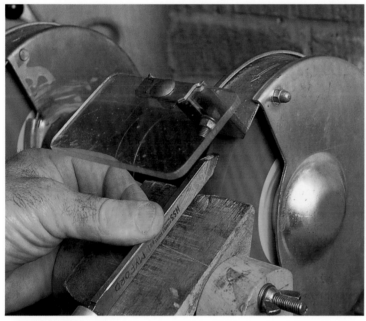

Fig 6.20 A method of grinding the parting tool using the grinding jig

Beading (rounding over)

The parallel parting tool is particularly useful for the forming of small beads, although I use it extensively for rolling beads of all sizes. Here's how it is done, and the exercise will provide practice for using the tool in the ways described above.

Prepare a piece of Scots pine as before, roughing it down to a true cylinder. Mark it out with ruler and pencil, lathe running, with alternate ¾in and ½in (19 and 13mm) spaces. The ¾in spaces are for the trenches and the ½in spaces will form our beads. Size in on either side of all the beads to a depth of about ¼in (6mm), making use of the vernier. Remove the waste wood between these sizing cuts, using *both* hands on the tool. You will see that the

bottom of the trench is quite rough, so practise the feathering cut to smooth it off (Fig 6.18).

To cut the beads, the tool is presented to the work at right angles and in the bevel-rubbing mode. Now feather the right-hand tip of the tool under the wood about ⅛in (3mm) in from the right-hand side of the bead. The tool handle is then lifted *and* rolled in a nice smooth action, ensuring that only the leading tip of the tool is in contact with the wood. Repeat the process until the centre of the bead is reached. The left-hand side is then cut in the same manner, reversing the whole process (Fig 6.19).

For successful, balanced bead cutting with the parting tool, movements must be smooth, unhurried and tension-free. It is courting disaster to try to take too much wood in one pass, this being the reason why the cut is started near to the corner of the bead. The most common reason for getting a 'catch' is that the trailing edge of the tool is allowed to touch the wood (using the unsupported part of the tool edge – Law 4). This should not happen if you remember to keep the tool *rolling* as you lift it.

Sharpening

As outlined in Chapter 4, On Sharpening, the tool is ground square across with a bevel of approximately 25° either side. Sharpening this tool by making use of the jig is very simple. Fix the adjustable jig platform as explained, lay the tool on its edge and apply the 'gentle touch' to grind right up to the tool edge. Now turn the tool over and repeat the process. You should finish up with a precision-ground tool (Fig 6.20).

The 'real' shapers

In simplistic terms there are only *three shapes* (and combinations of such) in any design in woodturning, these being straight lines, hollows and rounds (but see below).

Again in simplistic terms, only *four tools* are required in spindle turning to cut such shapes. Two have already been dealt with, that is, the roughing-out gouge and the parting tool. The two remaining tools are what I refer to as the 'real' shapers, namely the skew chisels and the spindle gouges.

Before dealing with these two tools, it is advisable to expand on the more common shapes and profiles that go to make up traditional turned designs.

Terminology: shapes and profiles

Many of these terms are derived from classical Greek and Roman architecture and refer to flowing curves (serpentine lines), concave shapes (hollows or coves), and convex shapes (rounds or beads). These are very often interspersed with fillets or V-cuts. Fig 6.21 depicts a typical piece of spindle turning which includes some of these traditional profiles.

Spindle gouge

The tool most likely to be used following the roughing-down process and sizing in is the spindle gouge. The reason these tools are made in sizes ranging from ⅛ to ¾in (3–19mm) is that no gouge will cut a cove 'quicker' than the radius of the tool. It follows that a large, wide cove can be shaped with a very narrow gouge, taking repeated cuts, but it is not possible to fashion very narrow coves with a large gouge.

The principles of using any size do not vary, however, and proficiency in the use of, say, the ⅜in (10mm) spindle gouge will ensure proficiency in the use of the others.

In skilled hands spindle gouges will fashion almost any profile and also leave a first-class finish on the wood. It is possible to complete virtually the whole of the piece of turning shown in Fig 6.21, for example, using spindle gouges only. (Of course, it would be more convenient and quicker to rough down with the roughing-out gouge, size in with the parting tool and 'clean up' the fillets and intersections with a chisel, but the fact remains that almost all the operations *could* be carried out with the spindle gouges.)

Fig 6.21 Traditional turning profiles

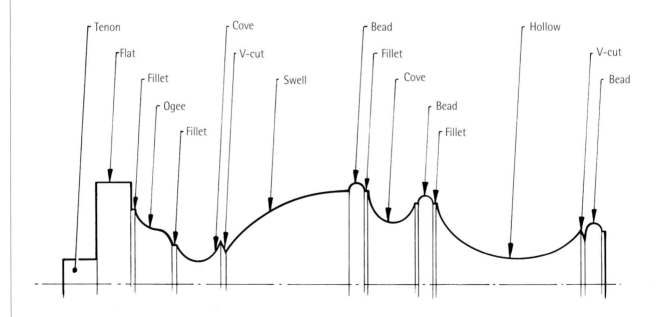

Fingernail profile
– and why?

Advice from all the authorities is to grind the end of the spindle gouge to a nose or 'fingernail' profile. But why must we grind it so?

It is definitely *not* so ground to form coves by presenting it horizontally to the workpiece and *scraping* hollows, as some people imagine. Not only would this tear out the grain, particularly on the extremes of the cove, but you also run the risk of a dig-in. *Why?* The underneath of the gouge is round in section, but you would be using the whole width of the edge as the scrape proceeds. Result: the downward forces on the unsupported sides could twist the tool over, thus causing it to dig in. The wider the gouge, the more likely this becomes.

It may be simpler to understand why the fingernail profile is ground if it is explained what would happen if it were *not* ground this way. Assume the tool was ground square across or only with a very slight nose. Cutting tools must be used in the bevel-rubbing mode (Law 3) and because of the reasons described above, you cannot offer the tool up on its back. The tool must be offered up to the work right over on its edge, flute facing the centre of the intended cove.

The action called for to form a cove is a twisting, scooping movement combined with a forwards push. *If* you were able to get the cut started and then used sufficient force to twist the tool, you would almost immediately be cutting wood with an unsupported part of the tool edge (Law 4). The tool would eventually succumb to the downward forces and you would have a dig-in.

It is also important that the fingernail profile is one flowing curve. If a pronounced point is ground on it or there are 'high spots', it will prove difficult to use without the cut becoming 'blocked'.

Method of grinding

This therefore seems an appropriate point at which to describe how to grind the tool to the desired profile. I will not pretend this tool is easy to grind correctly, even with the aid of the grinding jig, but continued practice with the method I recommend will quickly overcome initial shortcomings.

Determine the correct angle on the platform of the grinding jig as described in Chapter 4 (this should be about 35°). To form or maintain a flowing, rounded profile, the handle must be swung from side to side. Place the tool on the jig platform on its side and at an angle of about 25°. (The more you increase this angle, the more likely you are to finish up with an undesirable pointed profile.)

Now, as you slowly begin to roll the tool on to its back, swing the handle in a smooth arc so that when the centre of the tool is in contact with the grindstone, the handle is dead in line with the face of the stone. Continue both the roll and the swing until you have gone the equivalent 25° the other way, by which time the tool should also have been rolled right over on to its other side. Repeat the process until the desired degree of sharpness has been attained. The value of the wide platform on the grinding jig now becomes obvious.

The action sounds much more complicated than it really is, and Fig 6.22 shows the required movements in detail.

Technique: cutting coves

Choose a spindle gouge of a size compatible with the width of cove to be cut. Very narrow coves can be completed with a couple of 'scooping' cuts from either side, but the starting cuts on wider coves will need to be begun just either side of centre and widened with successive cuts.

Use a piece of softwood about 11in long by 2½in square (280 x 65 x 65mm). Rough it down to a cylinder and set it out (lathe running and toolrest close in) with a pencil and ruler to give alternate spaces of 1¼ and ¾in (32 and 19mm). The ¾in spaces will form the coves and the larger spaces will provide for bead and V-cutting practice.

Offer the gouge up to the workpiece so it is well over on its side, flute facing the intended centre of the cove. To observe the 'law of cutting', the handle should be well down in the bevel-rubbing mode and for the initial cuts the gouge should be at right angles to the work.

It is at this stage of entry into the wood that things can go wrong. Unless a *positive* entry is made, the gouge has a tendency to

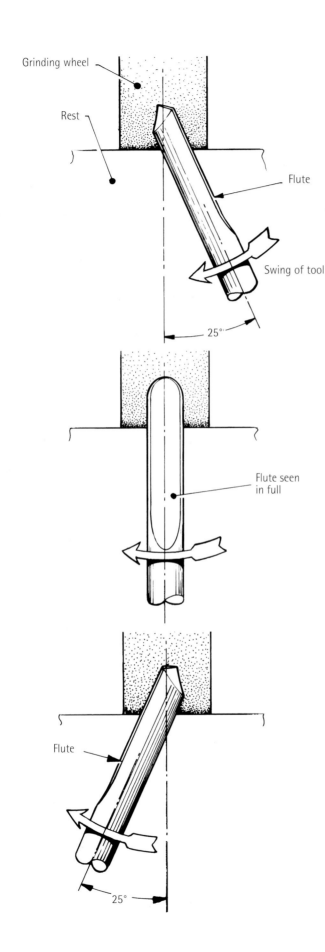

Grinding wheel

Rest

Flute

Swing of tool

25°

Flute seen in full

Flute

25°

Fig 6.22 Method of grinding the spindle gouge

Position 1: The gouge on its right-hand side
Position 2: The gouge on its back
Position 3: The gouge on its left-hand side

'skid' sideways, and always in the direction of the bevel, scarring the work. This irritating lateral skid is caused because the bevel has nothing to bear against until it has started the cut. The problem can be overcome by several methods.

1 By making slight V-cuts with the skew chisel or parting tool on the marked-out coves (several cuts will be necessary on wide coves). The small 'nicks' will give the bevel immediate support and prevent the skid (Fig 6.23). The coves can now be cut by employing the 'normal hold' – that is, with the thumb on the top of the gouge and the fingers cradling it underneath as shown in Fig 6.24.

2 By making a slight adjustment on the front-hand hold, so the thumb is pressed down on to the toolrest to act as a stop. This will prevent the skid towards the headstock (Fig 6.25). To prevent the skid towards the tailstock, swing the same thumb right over the gouge and secure it to the toolrest on the other side (Fig 6.26).

3 Remember how the parting tool was used so it was presented horizontally, scraper-fashion, to ensure a clean entry to the wood and prevent fraying (see page 63). A similar technique can be used with the spindle gouges to effect 'precise point of entry'. Line the bevel of the tool up with the *intended* shape of cut (for the final cuts on a well-shaped cove, this means the handle must be inverted towards the centre of the cove). Ensure the gouge is almost horizontal and on its side. Now push forward into the workpiece with the *tip* of the gouge (Fig 6.27). This is one of the few occasions when I suggest the tip of the gouge should be used.

As soon as entry is effected, drop the handle from this scraping mode and continue the cut with the bevel-rubbing mode, the tool being rolled and swung down to the bottom of the cove. Do not go past halfway, or not only will

Fig 6.23 Making V-cuts with the skew to prevent skids

Fig 6.24 Normal hold on spindle gouge

Fig 6.25 Hold adjustment no. 1 to prevent skid to left

Fig 6.26 Hold adjustment no. 2 to prevent skid to right

Fig 6.27 Horizontal entry with gouge will also prevent skid

you be cutting uphill, you will also be using an unsupported part of the tool edge, which could result in a 'catch'.

My method

I use none of the above aids. I present the tool on its side, with handle well down in the bevel-rubbing mode, and then I lever upwards, forwards and *positively* into the workpiece. It takes a good deal of practice and confidence, but it is certainly the quickest and best method for me. Fig 6.24 shows the cut about to commence.

Fig 6.28a shows the commencement of the cove cutting process and 6.28b and c show the necessary rolling and swinging movements from both sides of the cove. Used in this manner the shaving is coming from where it should do, that is, below the tip of the tool, inducing a nice slicing action.

I suggest you try all the above methods and settle for the one that suits *you*. For the purpose of this exercise, I suggest you use a ⅜in (10mm) spindle gouge and complete the whole of the shaping with it. After cutting all the coves, the next step is:

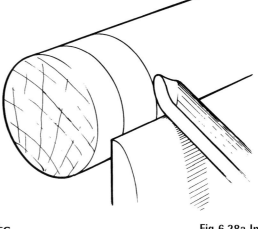

V-cuts

Present the tool in the bevel-rubbing mode and inclined on its side at an angle of about 25°. The gouge is at right angles to the workpiece and you want to start the cut on the edge of the cove. The handle is then lifted to about the horizontal in a 'guillotine' action, which will shape one side of the V. Now repeat the process (flute of the tool facing the opposite direction) from the other side until the V is formed. To ensure a nice, crisp bottom to the V, *draw the*

Fig 6.28a Initial position of gouge for turning a cove

Fig 6.28b Movement of the gouge – right-hand side

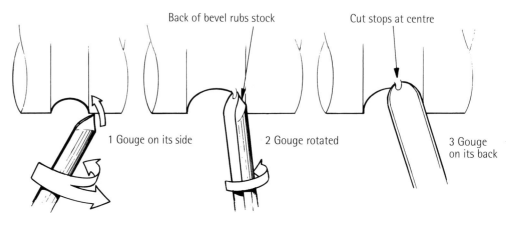

Back of bevel rubs stock — Cut stops at centre

1 Gouge on its side   2 Gouge rotated   3 Gouge on its back

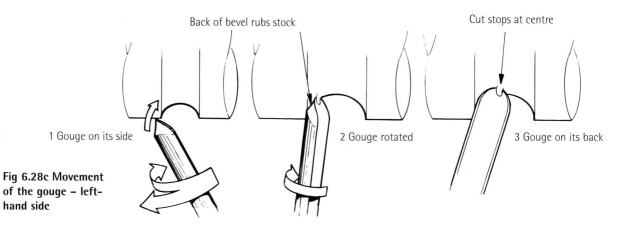

Back of bevel rubs stock — Cut stops at centre

1 Gouge on its side   2 Gouge rotated   3 Gouge on its back

Fig 6.28c Movement of the gouge – left-hand side

gouge back towards your body and again use the tip of the gouge — otherwise the side of the gouge will 'scar' the other side of the V.

Proceed now to cut the V-shapes along the full length of the wood. Fig 6.29 shows the position of the gouge to start the cut on the last V.

Bead cutting

A bead is the exact opposite profile to a cove, and it follows that to produce one an exactly opposite action is required. Again, present the gouge to the wood in the bevel-rubbing mode, but this time on its back. Before proceeding with the cut, it is important that the following facts are firmly ingrained in the mind:

1 To cut the right side of a bead, the gouge must be rolled, lifted and swung to the right, ensuring that the shaving is coming from below the tip of the tool. Unfortunately, the natural action is to swing the handle to the left, and a conscious effort must be made to avoid this.
2 To cut the left side of the bead, the only difference is that the tool is both rolled and swung in the opposite direction. If the tool handle is swung in the wrong direction, a pointed bead will result.

Fig 6.30 shows these movements.

On wider beads or convex shapes, in addition to the three movements described, the tool must also be *traversed*. I suggest you form the right-hand side on all the beads to get into a 'rhythm' and then repeat the process on all the left-hand sides. Do not try to take too

Fig 6.29 Forming a V-cut with the spindle gouge

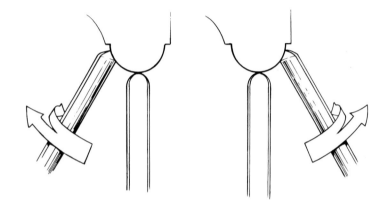

Fig 6.30 Turning a bead with a spindle gouge

much wood in one pass, and make the movements slow, smooth and deliberate.

The forming of balanced beads is not easy, because you are trying to synchronize three, sometimes four movements. If any one is 'out of time' with the others, the desired smooth, flowing shape will not materialize. Perseverance and patience will bring their rewards, however, so keep trying. Fig 6.31 shows the completed exercise.

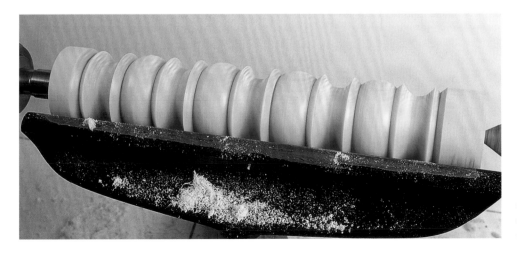

Fig 6.31 The completed exercise straight off the gouge

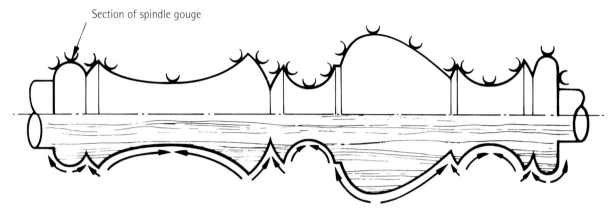

Section of spindle gouge

Fig 6.32 Examples of rolling movements made with the spindle gouge in cutting different profiles. Cutting is safest when shaving appears just below tip of gouge

Fig 6.32 shows the position of the gouge (in section) relative to the shape to be cut and also to the grain direction. Remember that the shaving should leave the *supported* part of the tool edge (Law 4). A true cutting action can only be achieved if the gouge is presented in the bevel-rubbing mode (Law 3). By referring back to Fig 6.28 it will be seen that the shaving should not come from the tip of the tool (this would be a scraping action), but from either side of the tip, depending on which side of the cove the cut is started. Fig 6.33 shows how the bevel of the tool is 'lined up' with the intended

profile, and also indicates the necessary swinging movements.

There are other functions which the spindle gouge will perform, and these are described on pages 79–81.

The limitations of the spindle gouges will be obvious when trying to create nice crisp intersections where the beads and V-cuts merge, and when feathering fillets. Access to these 'tight' profiles is best achieved with our fourth and last tool, and the one that seems to cause more consternation than any other, namely the skew chisel.

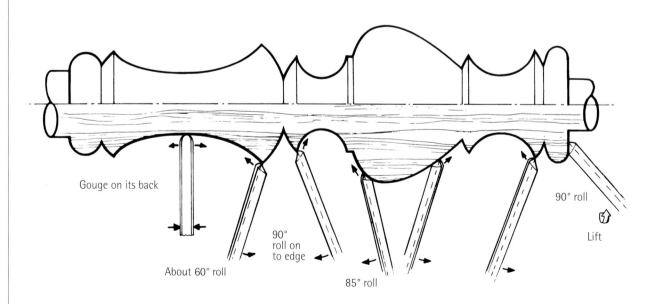

Gouge on its back

About 60° roll

90° roll on to edge

85° roll

90° roll

Lift

Fig 6.33 The bevel should be lined up with the intended profile and the handle should be swung in the directions indicated

The skew chisel

It is true the skew is peerless in *some* operations (more of this later), but because it is probably the most 'unforgiving' of tools, a lack of knowledge and incorrect technique can result in severe and unwanted 'impressions' being left on both wood and memory. Naturally, subsequent attempts with the tool will be accompanied by even more anxiety, apprehension and tension, and the tool will most likely be held in a powerful grip. This is a vicious circle, the operator now doing everything he should not be doing, and another dig-in of gigantic proportions results. The skew will probably now be banished to a distant corner of the workshop to gather dust and cobwebs.

I have taught a good few people, and I can say, hand on heart, that with the exception of two or three, I have had no one who has not learned to use the skew safely and satisfactorily. The few that have failed did so because, having experienced so many heavy 'catches', they found it impossible to relax.

Another word of encouragement: the skew chisel is not as important as some people would have you believe. Sure, it is versatile, but not so versatile as the spindle gouges. Sure, it will leave a super finish, but so will the gouges. Perhaps of greater importance to the beginner is the fact that many operations are a great deal safer when using the gouges.

Where the skew is supreme is in the planing of cylinders and 'slow' contours, but even more so (in the case of the ½in (13mm) skew) for the finishing cuts on fillets, 'tight' detail and intersections.

The skew can be used basically in two modes:

1 by making use of part of the long cutting edge for smoothing or planing cuts;
2 by making use of both the long point (toe) and short point (heel) for such operations as rolling beads, V-cuts, and pummel cutting, and in the case of the ½in skew, cutting those tight details and intersections referred to above.

Planing or smoothing cuts

It is necessary to understand not only *how* the skew is presented, but also *why*. When using any woodworking chisel, be it carpenter's, carver's or turner's, removing a shaving from a piece of round-section wood is best achieved by using that part of the tool close to the centre. It would not be possible to remove a shaving by using only the points or tips of the tool, this only serving to 'scour' the work.

Let us now apply this principle to a piece of wood mounted in the lathe, the wood having been turned to a cylinder.

Stop the lathe and remove the toolrest. Lay the chisel on the workpiece and you will discover that the only way to get the centre of the chisel to remove a shaving is by presenting it at an angle of approximately 25° in the intended direction of traverse (unless it is positioned on the very top of the workpiece and the tool parallel to the lathe bed — this of course would prevent the use of a toolrest, which is not to be recommended!). By altering this angle of presentation you can dictate at which point the shaving will leave the cutting edge.

Replace the toolrest and, with the lathe still stationary, offer the tool up to the wood at about the same angle and with the tool *flat* down (in section) on the rest. You will soon realize that with the chisel in this position, it is not possible to get the desired centre portion of the chisel in contact with the wood. No matter how much you alter the angle of presentation (with the tool still flat on the rest), the only way to get the centre of the chisel to engage the wood is when the *whole width of the cutting edge* contacts the workpiece. The only cut it would be possible to achieve with the tool so presented would be a wide 'parting' or 'peeling' cut, which of course we do not want.

To make the shaving leave the tool from the desired centre portion, it is necessary to tip it so that the long point or toe is clear of the wood. This means, of course, that the area of tool close to the toe is unsupported. If this is allowed to touch whirling wood, you will get a nasty dig-in!

I recommend all the above experiments and presentation variations be carried out with the lathe *stationary*, and it does help to get the 'feel' if you can get someone to revolve the work slowly by hand, as I do in teaching.

In addition to understanding this bit of theory, another prerequisite to attaining proficiency with the skew is to make sure you use the type most suited to the task. Without doubt, the most user-friendly skew chisel on the market, for smoothing or planing cuts, is the oval-section variety first introduced by Sorby.

Fig 6.34 'Planing' on tramlines

Fig 6.35 Shaving coming from the desired centre/heel area

Fig 6.36 The extreme leading tip of the skew is used to feather up to a square shoulder

Some other manufacturers leave the corners of their chisels square. Tool steel is harder than the mild steel rest, and you can find yourself removing shavings from the rest and coming to a halt in the slightest nick in the toolrest.

The oval skew is a joy to use, and it is much easier to acquire that elusive 'feel' by making use of it. The section of the tool is such that when it is tipped sideways, it comes to rest at just about the optimum angle of tip. With some of the other skews, it is possible to tip the tool too far, resulting in bevel contact and control being lost.

For your first 'practical' with the skew, reduce your cylinder of wood to about 1½in (38mm) diameter. It does help in the early stages to raise the height of the rest above centre. Now present the tool as described, at about 25° and tipped towards its leading edge. Make sure the handle is well down, feel for the wood and commence slowly traversing and lifting (in that order) until a shaving appears. As with all the cutting tools, the shaving thickness is dictated by the back hand lifting or lowering. Maintain the same angle to the workpiece by imagining you are cutting down a set of tramlines (Fig 6.34).

Repeat the process, keeping your 'north eye' on the dangerous trailing edge to ensure it is clear of the work. Practise to your heart's content. The pile of ribbon-like shavings appearing on the bench should be testimony to your skill (Fig 6.35).

As confidence increases, vary the angle of presentation, but beware of allowing the 'danger' portion of the tool to contact the workpiece. Practise also forming a taper, cutting from large to small diameter, and up to a square shoulder formed with a parting tool.

As the cut approaches the shoulder, you will need to alter the angle of presentation, so the extreme leading tip of the chisel is feathered under the wood to facilitate access to the almost 90° intersection (Fig 6.36). Failure to do this would result in the leading tip fouling the side of the shoulder.

Those people who are particularly nervous about using the skew chisel for planing cuts can be assured that if you induce the leading tip under the work in the feathering action, it is *virtually impossible* to get a dig-in because you *must* be using the *supported* part of the tool edge. The only disadvantage of this method is that unless you take other than a fine shaving, you will have difficulty in traversing the tool (this is called 'blocking the cut') — but you will not dig in.

Traversing in the opposite direction can be achieved by employing the same hands (your stance obviously being to one side), or by swapping hands and working left-handed. I prefer the latter because you are in a position to see the developing profile much more easily than in the former method. Have a go at both — being ambidextrous is a great asset.

Supporting technique

As outlined in the section dealing with the roughing-out gouge, long slender work needs to be steadied, and the method of achieving this when using the chisels is identical to the method employed when using the gouge.

Cautionary notes

1 Do not attempt to start the planing cut from a position *outside* the length of the workpiece. It is difficult to find the bevel in fresh air. (Experienced turners do this all the time, but it demands considerable practice of the safer method described to attain the necessary 'feel'.)
2 In finding the bevel, make sure you are traversing the tool *before* lifting the tool to engage the cut. Control is much easier and safer.

Shaping

The chisels, particularly the ½in (13mm) size, can be used extensively for rolling beads, V-cutting, feathering cuts, and smoothing fuller convex and concave surfaces. (I prefer the flat-section ½in skew for finer detail cuts, but I radius the edges very lightly on the grinder to facilitate easy movement.) As mentioned earlier, some of these can be achieved just as well with the spindle gouges, but mastery of the skew is not complete until you can produce the same profiles with it.

Fig 6.37 The skew is rolled to the right to form a radiused pummel

V-cuts

These can be used as an integral part of a design, or as preliminary cuts when fashioning beads or forming pummels. A pummel is the square section left on a good deal of spindle turning, such as table and chair legs, newel posts and balusters.

Accurately centre a piece of 2in-square (50 x 50mm) stock and mount it between centres. With the aid of a try square, pencil in pairs of parallel lines about ¼in (6mm) apart, leaving about 2in (50mm) space between each pair.

Cutting pummels

The wood has been marked out, so make use of the toe (long point) of the chisel to first of all form a V, and then develop it into a radiused pummel. Present the chisel on its edge with the tool handle only slightly down from the horizontal and at right angles to the workpiece. Aim the toe of the chisel at the right-hand mark, pushing forward and slightly lifting the handle.

Do not try to force the chisel too deep or you will only succeed in overheating the tool edge. Withdraw the chisel and widen the V by taking cuts from alternate sides, progressively inclining the tool so that the tip is 'aimed' at the centre of the V. The radius is formed from the left-hand mark by slightly rolling the tool as you lift in the direction of the intended cylindrical section to your right (Fig 6.37).

The wood to the right of the pummel can now be reduced to a cylinder. Remember to roll the roughing-out gouge right over on to its left edge to facilitate cutting right up to the square section, and to avoid causing a dig-in by fouling the square with an unsupported part of the tool edge (Fig 6.38).

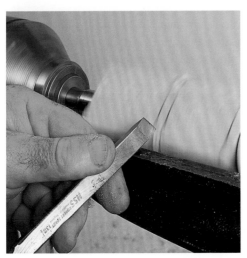

Fig 6.38 The roughing-out gouge is used right over on its side to cut up to a pummel

Cautionary notes

1 Do not attempt to use any part of the cutting edge *other* than the extreme tip (supported tool). If you do, you are *sure* to have a dig-in. When forming a deep V or radiused pummel, it is advisable to tilt the cutting edge of the chisel away from the shoulder *very slightly* to avoid this happening.

2 If the tool starts bumping about, it is a sure sign that the heel of the bevel is pushing the cutting *tip* off line. Do not try to force the cut deeper, but withdraw the tool and re-present at a slightly shallower angle by lifting the handle.

Square shoulder cutting

Many pummels are designed to finish with a square-faced shoulder, and these are a little more difficult to cut than a radius. As with all cutting tools, the bevel or grinding angle must be lined up with the intended shape or cut. Applying this principle to the forming of a square shoulder, it becomes obvious that for the finishing cuts, the grinding angle, and *not* the tool, must be at right angles to the workpiece. I usually start by making a V-cut to reduce the resistance to the tool before applying the finishing cuts.

When cutting or cleaning square shoulders, particularly deep ones, remember again to tilt the tool very slightly away from the face you are cutting, or you will experience a heavy 'catch'. Do not take other than very light cuts. Attempting to take too much wood will result in the tool overheating and the cut becoming 'blocked' (Fig 6.39).

Bead cutting

As an exercise, mark out your cylinder with varying widths from, say, ½in to about 1¼in (13–32mm), and then make a series of V-cuts, all cut with the toe of the skew, to a depth which is in proportion to the width of the intended bead (Fig 6.40).

Use either the toe or the heel of the chisel to shape the beads. Using the long point is safer, but in my opinion not so good as using the heel, there being very little bevel contact to assist in producing a balanced shape. Additional advantages of using the heel are that the finish

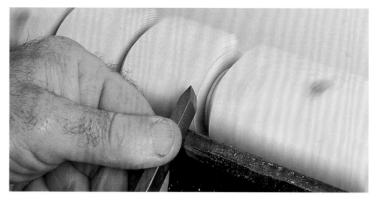

Fig 6.39 Cutting a square-shouldered pummel – grinding angle (and not the tool) at right angles to the wood

Fig 6.40 Forming a V-cut with the toe of the skew

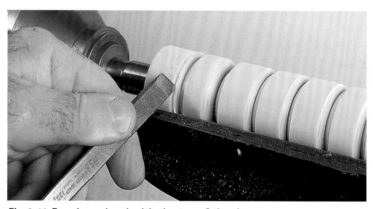

Fig 6.41 Forming a bead with the toe of the skew

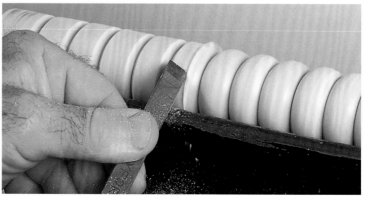

Fig 6.42 Forming a bead with the heel of the skew

Fig 6.43 The method of grinding the skew, making use of the O'Donnell jig

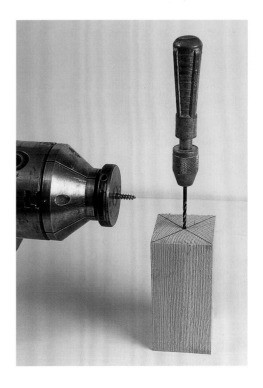

is superior, since the bevel is imparting a burnishing effect, and for me it feels less awkward. Try both methods and adopt the one that feels right for you.

Whatever method is chosen, you must obey the Laws. First of all, present the tool at the bevel-rubbing angle, or 'on the clutch'. The cut is brought on by tilting the blade slightly in the direction of cut while simultaneously lifting. With either toe or heel, the lower hand should control the tempo of the rolling and lifting movements, and the thumb and fingers of the front hand serve to keep the bevel pulled on to the wood. The leading tip of the tool is feathering under the wood and it is *only* this tip that should cut. Fig 6.41 shows a bead being formed with the toe of the skew, while Fig 6.42 shows the heel being used.

As with the spindle gouges, narrow beads can be completed with just a couple of rolls. On wider beads, the first cuts must be made nearer to the V-cuts or the cut will be 'blocked'.

Sharpening

Again by using the grinding jig, standard-type chisels are very easy to grind accurately. After determining the correct angle, the tool is offered up to the grinder with the cutting edge parallel to the face of the stone and flat down on the jig platform. Lateral movements are then necessary to ensure the full width of the stone is used (Fig 6.43). The oval skew is a little more difficult because it has a tendency to roll, but a little practice keeping it centrally balanced will also ensure accurate grinding.

Fig 6.44 Stock prepared for mounting on the screw chuck

Woodscrew chuck technique

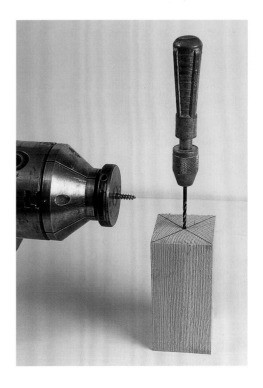

In some types of spindle turning, as pointed out in Chapter 3, the workpiece is not always supported by the tailstock. Examples of this are when hollowware such as egg cups, goblets, ornamental boxes, etc. are turned (the grain of the wood still being longitudinal to the lathe bed), where the tailstock would obviously prevent the hollowing-out process.

The woodscrew does not afford the same grip in end grain as it does in side grain. This applies even more so when using softwoods. Therefore everything possible must be done to prevent the workpiece becoming loose on the woodscrew. If it does, you may as well discard it and start again.

Here are two methods I adopt, which enable me to turn ornamental goblets in pine up to 10in (255mm) long, using a screw chuck only.

Method 1

Centre the workpiece and drill a pilot hole suitable for the screw. I use the appropriate size drill fixed into an old screwdriver handle which is fitted with an adjustable collet (Fig 6.44), but it can also be done on the pillar drill or with a

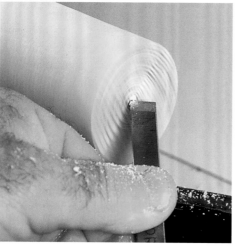

Fig 6.45
Undercutting the
open end with the
parting tool

Fig 6.46 Centre-
finding with the
skew chisel

Fig 6.47 (below)
Drilling the pilot hole
before reversing ends

wood is screwed right up, it is bearing on the outer edge, which prevents rocking, thus providing the best possible fixing. (Rarely will you get this secure hold on a surface straight from any type of saw.) *Do not* overtighten or you may strip the threads.

Method 2

Where it is necessary to avoid leaving a screw hole at the now 'open' end, the initial turning can be done between centres, with A (Fig 6.48) at the headstock end and B at the tailstock end. The parting tool, in forming the undercut at end B, will obviously need to be stopped just short of fouling the tailstock revolving centre. The resultant little nib of wood assists in finding dead centre, and it can then be pared away. After drilling a pilot hole, end B can then be remounted on the screw chuck. (Refer also to Fig 6.62 on page 83, where the same method is employed.)

It is normal to lose a little centricity in the reversing process, so the first job is to make *light* cuts with a roughing-out gouge to restore the wood to a true cylinder.

hand brace. I still prefer the standard woodscrew to the modern parallel-thread type. Mount the stock on the screw, bring up the tailstock for support, and turn to a cylinder with the roughing-out gouge.

Take a parting tool and cut in about ⅛in (3mm) from the tailstock end. Angle the tool inwards a little to create a slightly concaved end. The tailstock will obviously have to be taken away to complete the cut (Fig 6.45).

With the toe of a skew chisel, make a shallow cut in the dead centre of the stock to allow for a pilot hole to be started easily and accurately (Fig 6.46). Make the pilot hole, lathe running, by pushing the drill forward to the required depth (Fig 6.47). It is perfectly safe to do this without the support of the toolrest. Alternative methods would be to grip the drill bit in a pair of pliers, or in the Jacobs chuck fitted in the tailstock.

Stop the lathe and reverse ends. The concaved face now ensures that when the

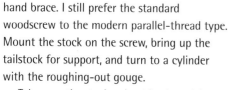

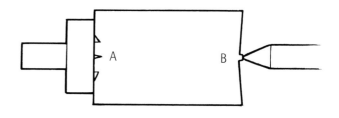

Fig 6.48 Preparation of the stock for Method 2

Please note that to succeed with this type of fixing, you will need patience, good technique, and to take only *light cuts* with *sharp tools*. Any tool presented at right angles to the workpiece, particularly at the unsupported end, will exert considerable leverage on the fixing. Matters are made worse if the tools are used in other than the bevel-rubbing mode, there being much more resistance to a scraping action.

Hollowing and end-grain techniques

Mount a piece of softwood about 5in long and 2½in square (125 x 65 x 65mm) on the woodscrew chuck, using either of the 'reversing' methods described above. After reducing the stock to a cylinder, position the toolrest across the open end at a slight angle. Making use of a ⅜in (10mm) spindle gouge presented well over on its side, and with its bevel lined up with the square end, take a couple of fine arcing cuts from outside to centre. The shaving should leave from *below* the tip of the tool, and an exceedingly good finish on the end grain should ensue (Fig 6.49).

Before deciding on what method of hollowing to employ, and there are several, I think it is advisable to reflect on Law 5, which concerns cutting downhill, or with the grain. Study Fig 6.50 and note that the grain direction changes twice on both the inside and outside of the cup. It should be noted that the grain direction on the outside is *exactly opposite* to that on the inside.

The rule to remember on this type of work is that on the *inside* of the cup, cutting with the grain is always *from small to large diameter*. On the *outside* of the cup, cutting with the grain is always opposite, that is *from large to small diameter*. Wherever possible, it is advisable to comply with this Law, particularly on the finishing cuts, or the resulting finish may well be less than satisfactory.

Hollowing by scraping

The whole of the hollowing process can be achieved with scrapers alone, and I certainly do not frown on their use in this situation as they perform very well in end grain, if they are sharp. Although not so rapid in removing the stock as in the method described below, the technique is easy to acquire, so long as the Law applying to scrapers is complied with.

To refresh your memory, Law 6 states that 'Scrapers should be kept perfectly flat on the rest and presented in the trailing mode.' The consequence of offending this law can be a heavy dig-in, and in woodscrew chuck work, the wood could come loose from its fixing.

To get the tool edge to cut at centre height, as it must, the height of the toolrest is important, if Law 6 is to be complied with. Making use of your ¾in (19mm) round-nosed scraper, ground to the profile suggested in Chapter 3, start the hollowing in the centre of the wood and gradually widen it out until the desired depth and internal profile are arrived at (in this example a simple egg-cup profile). Remember, the final cuts

Fig 6.49 Facing up in fine arcing cuts with the spindle gouge

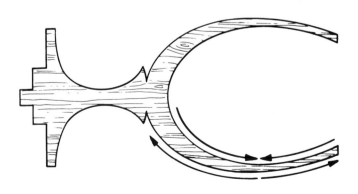

Fig 6.50 A bellied goblet. The arrows indicate the direction of cut with the grain

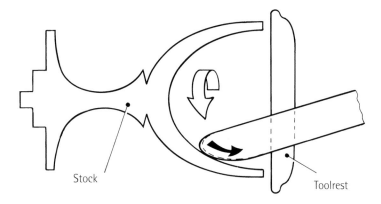

Stock

Toolrest

Fig 6.51 Hollowing out with the ¾in (19mm) scraper

Fig 6.52 The hollowing-out operation with the ¾in (19mm) round-nose scraper shown in more detail

should be from centre to rim so as to cut *with* the grain (Figs 6.51 and 6.52).

Hollowing by gouging

Proficiency in the use of a small spindle gouge for hollowing out is something that all woodturners should strive for. Not only is it by far the quickest method, but it will only need a couple of passes with a scraper to achieve the best possible finish.

Use the gouge (in this case a ⅜in (10mm) spindle gouge) to good advantage to determine the depth of the cup. I stick a small piece of masking tape on the inside of the flute at the required depth. The toolrest should again be across the face of the workpiece, and the height adjusted so the tip of the gouge lines up with the dead centre of the wood. The gouge can be made to function just like an auger if it

is presented almost on its side (about 10 past 7 on the clock) with the flute facing towards you. The gouge is pushed firmly into the spinning wood and 'wriggled' from side to side to achieve easy passage down to the required depth (Fig 6.53).

Having established the depth, the inside can now be gouged out. There are three methods for doing this, but I shall only describe the one I consider to be the easiest and safest.

Drop the height of the toolrest about ¼in (6mm) below centre and present the gouge as described above for determining the depth. Now induce the leading edge of the gouge under the wood to the left of the hole and swing the tool outwards and towards you. In close-grained hardwoods, nice shavings will be brought out; don't be disappointed if you get only chippings from the end grain of softwoods (Fig 6.54).

Fig 6.53 (bottom left) Boring to depth with the taped spindle gouge

Fig 6.54 (below) The spindle gouge being swung from centre to rim to complete the hollowing

To ensure a nice flowing internal profile, it is important that the tool handle is swung in a flowing arc. A series of fluid, swinging cuts should therefore leave you with a smooth, continuous curve. Just a couple of passes with the round-nosed scraper will remove any remaining undulations.

It does help in the hollowing-out process if a gouge with a much shorter bevel, say about 60°, is used, as opposed to the normal angle of 35°. This shorter bevel enables the profiling of a 'tighter' curve while maintaining bevel contact.

PROJECT

Making a goblet

Having practised the hollowing technique, and hopefully attained a fair level of competence, why not make yourself a goblet?

Fig 6.55 Profile and dimensions of the goblet

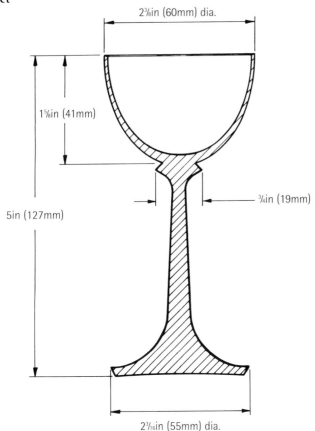

2⅜in (60mm) dia.

1⅝in (41mm)

5in (127mm)

¾in (19mm)

2³⁄₁₆in (55mm) dia.

Design

For the first attempt it is advisable not to make the goblet too long or too slender, or unnecessary problems may be encountered. Fig 6.55 provides a fairly simple profile with dimensional details.

Choice of wood

Any close-grained hardwood may be used, such as sycamore, hornbeam, beech, walnut, etc. For photographic convenience, Scots pine has been used for the sequence photographs.

Method

Mount the stock on the screw chuck using Reversing Method 2 described earlier, and 'face off' as shown in Fig 6.49.

Determine the depth of the inside of the goblet with the ⅜in (10mm) spindle gouge, using masking tape positioned on the blade at the required depth. Remove the interior with the same tool, as described earlier. If required, an inside template can be made in thick card or thin plywood to assist in attaining the desired profile. (It is important, in the interests of safety, to stop the lathe when testing with the template.) Any ripples left by the gouge can be cleaned off by making use of the round-nosed scraper. Sand and polish the inside as described in Chapter 9.

Measure and mark the depth of the cup on the outside of the goblet, allowing ⅛in (3mm) more than the internal depth. Size in with a parting tool, aided by callipers, to the required depth of ¾in (19mm) (refer to Fig 6.16). Make two further cuts in the waste wood to the left of the first cut; this will enable the spindle gouge to be swung in a nice arc down the base of the cup. The overall length of the goblet can now be defined by making a shallow parting cut near to the bottom of the workpiece. Fig 6.56 shows the goblet completed to this stage.

Profile the outside of the cup. The ⅜in spindle gouge will complete the whole of this profiling. In essence we are cutting an elongated half-bead profile, so the gouge is initially presented on its back in the bevel-rubbing mode. As the cut proceeds the handle is swung gradually to the left, with the tool being rolled well over on to its side when it

Fig 6.56 Goblet completed to the hollowing and sizing-in stage

Fig 6.57 Outside profile of the cup completed

Fig 6.58 Refining the stem, using finger support to prevent 'whip'

Fig 6.59 Parting off. Note the fingers cradling the goblet

Fig 6.60 A completed goblet in walnut

reaches the bottom of the cup. Aim for an even wall thickness; it may be necessary to stop the lathe frequently and test with a pair of callipers. The V-section where the stem merges with the bottom of the cup is easily achieved with the long point of the skew.

When you are satisfied with the profile so far, it is advisable to sand and polish this area before cutting the stem. Fig 6.57 shows the goblet completed thus far.

To provide added stability and to boost confidence, the inside of the cup can be packed with soft tissue paper and the tailstock can be used to advantage to apply gentle pressure. A revolving tail centre is essential for this operation.

The profiling of the base and stem can now be done, always remembering to cut 'downhill' with the spindle gouge. The required technique is to present the gouge very much on its back, and roll it on to its side as the cut merges with the one from the opposite direction. As the stem nears the finished diameter, it may be necessary, if the tailstock is not being used, to make use of the supporting technique (refer to Fig 6.10) to prevent 'whip'. When satisfied with the profile, sand and polish. Fig 6.58 shows the supporting technique being used to refine the goblet stem.

With a newly sharpened parting tool, carefully part off, keeping the base as flat as possible (Fig 6.59). By making use of a sanding disc held in a Jacobs chuck, the underside of the base can now be cleaned up and a dab of polish applied to finish the project. A completed goblet made in walnut is shown in Fig 6.60.

Goblets are very satisfying projects to make, and as your level of competence increases, more difficult and pleasing designs can be attempted.

Making wooden fruit

The woodscrew chuck is a most useful piece of equipment and can be used to good effect to make wooden fruit. Apples and pears are particularly good sellers, and allow some of the many short ends of wood which we all accumulate to be put to profitable use.

Apple

I prefer the stalks of both apple and pear to leave the fruit at an angle, and this factor influences the chucking techniques. My method means that slightly longer stock than normal is required, but I am quite happy to waste a little wood to make the fruit more natural-looking. Accordingly, the stock required is of 3in-square section and 4in long (76 x 76 x 102mm).

Choice of wood

Exotic hardwoods can produce stunning grain patterns, but for some people the cost of such species can be prohibitive − particularly in the early learning stage, when mistakes are not unusual. Native hedgerow and garden trees or shrubs can also produce dramatic grain. Yew-wood, laburnum, cherry and plum are eminently suitable, as are spalted woods, particularly beech. I have used North American tulipwood for both the sequence photographs and the finished examples.

Method

Mount the wood between centres and prepare it for the woodscrew chuck using Method 2 above. Taking light cuts with the roughing-out gouge, reduce the stock to the suggested 2¾in (70mm) diameter. The profiling can now commence at the open end (the stalk end), using a ⅜in (10mm) spindle gouge. A rolling action is required to form the rounded-over section, merging into a swinging, scooping action to form the undercut profile. At a distance of 2¾in (70mm) from the open end, size in with a parting tool to a diameter of approximately ¾in (19mm). The remainder of the profiling down to the depth of the sizing cut can now be completed with the same tool.

Before reverse-chucking it is necessary to sand and polish the completed section, and also to drill the ⅛in (3mm) hole to accommodate the stalk. Stop the lathe and drill the hole to a depth of about ½in (13mm) and at an angle of about 15°. Fig 6.61 shows the drilling operation, and Fig 6.62 shows the profiling thus far.

The underside or blossom end now needs to be profiled, and in order to do this it is first

Fig 6.61 Drilling the angled hole for the apple stalk

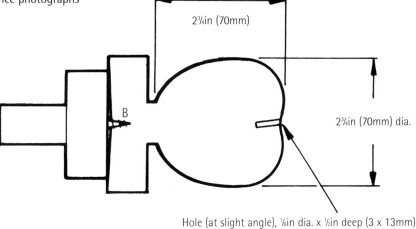

Fig 6.62 Profile and dimensions of the apple

2¾in (70mm)

2¾in (70mm) dia.

B

Hole (at slight angle), ⅛in dia. x ½in deep (3 x 13mm)

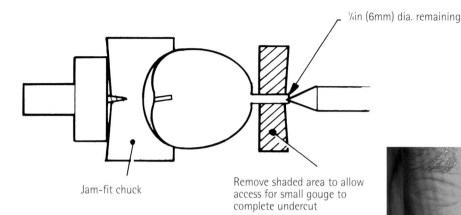

¼in (6mm) dia. remaining

Jam-fit chuck

Remove shaded area to allow
access for small gouge to
complete undercut

Fig 6.63 The apple reverse-chucked to allow work on the blossom end

necessary to mount a short length of 3in-square
(76 x 76mm) softwood on the screw chuck and
gouge out a shallow hemisphere to take the stalk
end of the apple on a gentle push fit. By locating
the tailstock revolving centre in the exposed
screw hole, gentle pressure can be applied to
ensure stability and true running. If necessary,
line the wooden jam-fit chuck with soft tissue
paper to prevent damage to the polished area.

Now reduce the waste wood down to about
¼in (6mm) diameter to allow access for a ¼in
spindle gouge to refine the base (Fig 6.63). The
final little raised nib which represents the
blossom end can be refined with the tailstock
removed, taking very light, delicate cuts (Fig
6.64). It is important that the blossom end does
not protrude beyond the main profile, or the
apple will not stand up. The sanding and
polishing process can then be completed.

My final touches to the blossom end are to
'rough it up' a little with a skew chisel, and
finally burn and blacken it with a pyrography
unit. A hot poker or soldering iron will serve the
same purpose.

Fig 6.64 Refining the blossom end, with the tailstock removed

45°

⅜in (10mm) dia.

⅛in (3mm) dia.

1½in (38mm)

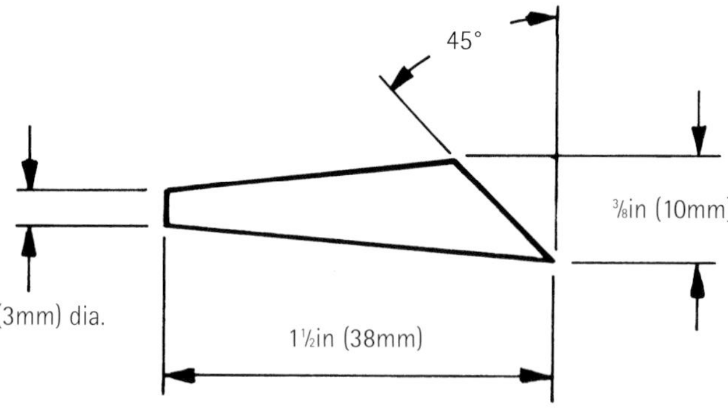

Fig 6.65 Profile and dimensions of a typical stalk

Stalk

My method is to prepare ⅜in-square stock about
5in long (10 x 10 x 127mm) and turn it to a
cylinder between centres. This is then transferred
to the Jacobs chuck and fixed in the headstock
mandrel. The tailstock can provide gentle
pressure while the stalk is profiled (starting at
the tailstock end), sanded, polished and parted
off. This procedure allows me to make three
stalks on one fixing. The top end of the stalk can
now be sanded to the angle required. Fig 6.65
gives dimensions of a typical stalk, which is
subsequently glued into the top of the apple.

Pear

The shape of natural pears (and apples) varies
considerably, but I prefer to maintain some kind
of uniformity in both designs. By referring back
to Fig 6.62 it will be seen that the largest
diameter of the apple is equal to the length,
and to me this looks in proportion. Similarly, I
consider that the length of a pear should
exceed the largest diameter by about 1in
(25mm). Accordingly, a minimum 4¾in length
of 3in-square section (120 x 76 x 76mm) is
required to fulfil the desired proportions.

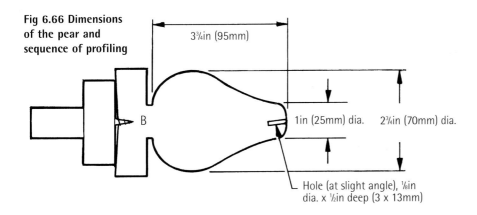

Fig 6.66 Dimensions of the pear and sequence of profiling

3¾in (95mm)

B

1in (25mm) dia. 2¾in (70mm) dia.

Hole (at slight angle), ⅛in dia. x ½in deep (3 x 13mm)

Choice of wood

As described above for the apple.

Method

The methods and techniques used for producing the pear are identical to those used in turning the apple. The only things that are different are the profile and the overall length (Fig 6.66). It will also be necessary to produce another jam-fit chuck in softwood. This can be hollowed out to approximately 1in (25mm) diameter to receive the stalk end of the pear in the reverse-chucking process (Fig 6.67). The stalk can be identical to the apple stalk.

Fig 6.68 shows some examples of completed and polished fruit.

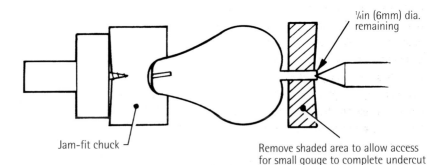

¼in (6mm) dia. remaining

Jam-fit chuck

Remove shaded area to allow access for small gouge to complete undercut

Fig 6.67 Refining the profile with the pear reverse-chucked

Fig 6.68 Some completed and polished fruit

SUMMARY

1 Regular practice, using the four basic tools on the three basic profiles, will inevitably lead to rapid improvement.

2 For the novice woodturner, the 1in (25mm) oval-section skew chisel is a 'must' for planing straight cylinders and slow contours. Used as described, it will quickly instil confidence.

3 In bead cutting, the spindle gouge is presented on its back and rolled on to its side.

4 In cove cutting, the spindle gouge is presented on its side and rolled on to its back.

5 The ½in (13mm) skew chisel is indispensable for cutting crisp intersections, fillets and general tidying up.

6 It is a fundamental principle of woodturning that the bevel or grinding angle is *lined up* with the intended shape to be cut.

7 Much pleasure can be derived from the making of small-section hollowware on the screw chuck, so ensure you practise your hollowing-out techniques frequently.

8 Making simple objects like apples and pears builds confidence and offers practice in producing balanced, flowing profiles.

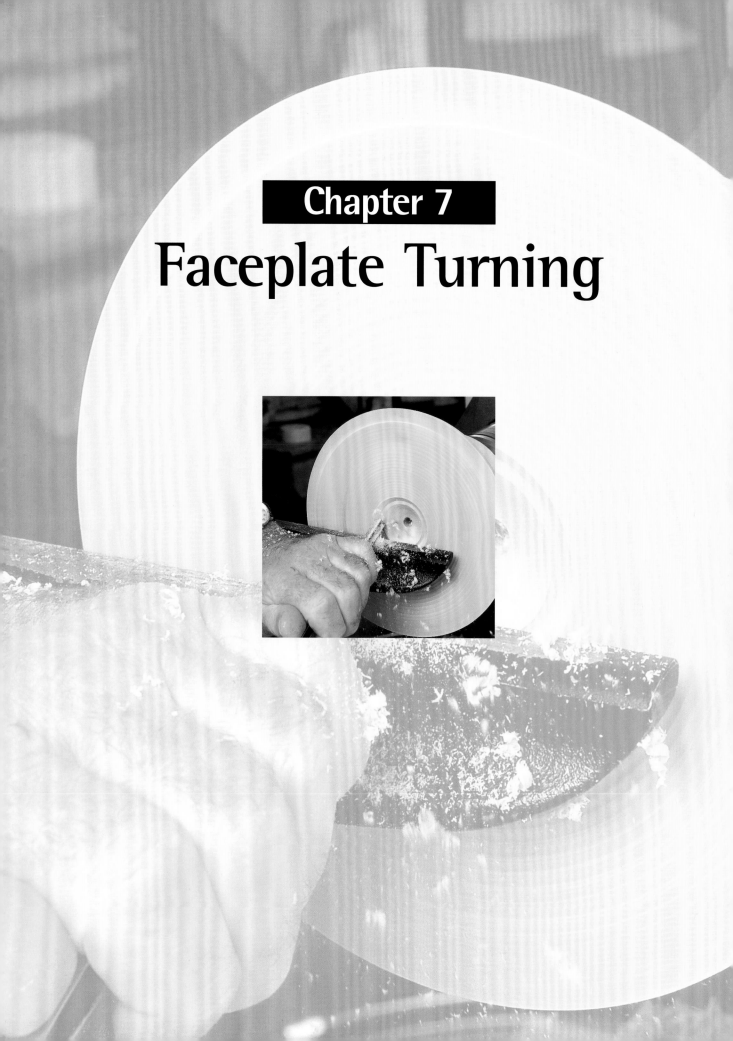

Chapter 7
Faceplate Turning

As the reader will have gathered from previous chapters, my message is that turning large-diameter pieces of wood *can* be dangerous, unless the turner has acquired the fundamentals and fully understands the Laws of Woodturning.

Such understanding and development of technique and confidence can be best and most safely acquired on small-section spindle work. Several weeks' concentrated practice in this category of turning should be undertaken *before* tackling bowls, etc.

The alternative is to go on a course with a professional turner. You will probably tackle a medium-size bowl on the second day of the course (the first day on some courses), the essential difference being that the teacher is beside you to supervise, prompt and, if necessary, guide the tool movements to avert any potentially dangerous situation. Advice regarding the choice of courses is given later in the book, on page 170.

Woodturners and bowl turning go together like eggs and bacon; in my early days of turning I was always extremely eager to turn bowls of all shapes and sizes, and examples of these are still dotted about the country in relatives' homes. There is something uniquely satisfying about making a nicely designed bowl, and the thrill of sending long, rope-like shavings flying across the workshop adds to the satisfaction and fascination.

Certainly, the turning of bowls, vessels and platters must have constituted a substantial amount of ancient turning, arising from the need to utilize one of the planet's most abundant raw materials as a substitute for animal skins, hollow stones, leaves and shells, etc. The first bowls were purely functional, but gradually as tools, equipment and skill improved, so did the form and appeal of turned vessels and platters. Despite this, for well over two thousand years turnings of this type were designed to be practical, rather than aesthetically decorative or appealing.

However, the last forty years have seen a resurgence of interest in the craft, and gradually there has been a growing tendency to produce artefacts that are first and foremost aesthetically appealing, even at the expense of utility. I welcome this change in direction, although I have certain reservations about some of these 'modern art' turnings.

Grain formation and timber preparation

In spindle turning, the grain of the wood invariably runs parallel with the lathe bed. In faceplate work, the grain normally runs along the surface of the disc or bowl blank, which means end-grain is encountered twice on every revolution.

The problems of using a hand plane on the end of a piece of wood are familiar. If the edge is planed all along, the wood will split away because the grain at the far end is unsupported. The heavier the shaving, the more the wood is split away (Fig 7.1). To avoid this, either a slight chamfer is made at the far end and fine cuts taken (Fig 7.2), or you can plane inwards from

Fig 7.1 Cutting up to the unsupported edge causes the wood to split

End grain

Unsupported edge

Side grain

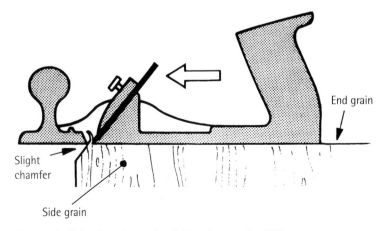

End grain

Slight chamfer

Side grain

Fig 7.2 A slight chamfer and a light cut prevent splitting

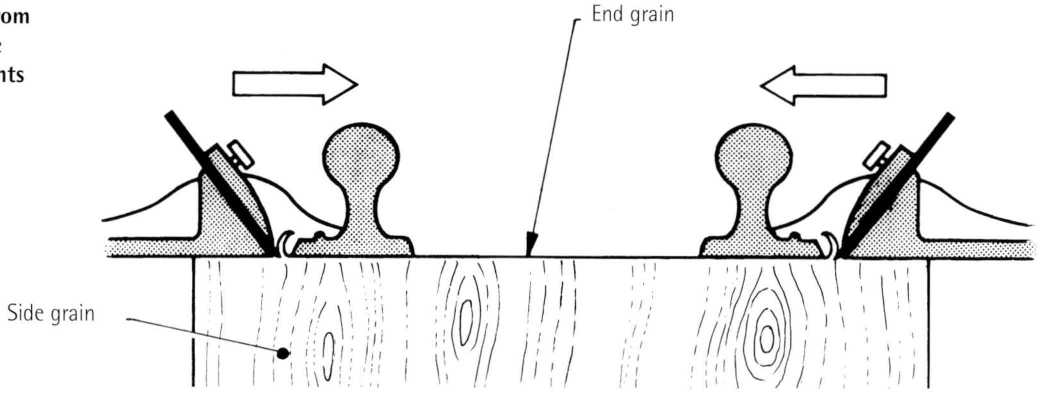

Fig 7.3 Cutting from both edges to the centre also prevents splitting

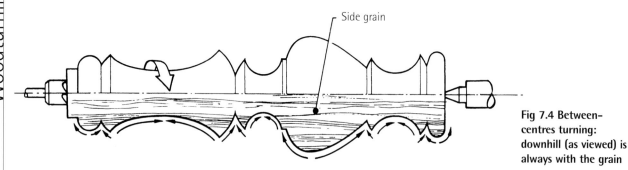

End grain

Side grain

Side grain

Fig 7.4 Between-centres turning: downhill (as viewed) is always with the grain

both ends to the centre (Fig 7.3). Similar techniques must be used on the edges of discs and blanks to prevent the same problem.

One of the Laws of Woodturning is to cut downhill, or with the grain, wherever possible. In spindle turning this is always 'downhill' as viewed with the wood in the lathe (Fig 7.4). However, in faceplate turning, downhill as viewed with the wood mounted on the lathe is not necessarily cutting with the grain.

Fig 7.5 shows a blank that has been mounted on the lathe by means of a screw chuck. Viewed from the front, 'downhill' is obviously from the chuck side towards the open

end. Remove the wood from the lathe and lay it flat on the bench as shown in Fig 7.6, and 'downhill' has changed. It is now from the small diameter to the larger. The question is, 'What constitutes cutting with the grain on bowl blanks and discs?' The answer is as follows:

- Cutting with the grain on the *outside* of a bowl or convex shape is achieved by working from *small* to *large* diameter.
- Cutting with the grain on the *inside* of a bowl or concave shape is exactly *opposite* and is achieved by working from *large* to *small* diameter.

Fig 7.5 Turning a disc: cutting with the arrow is downhill (as viewed) with the blank mounted on the lathe, but this is *against* the grain

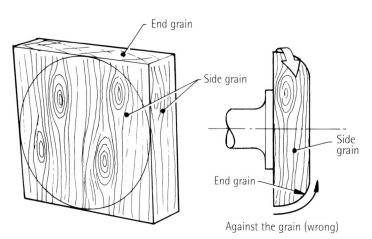

End grain

Side grain

Side grain

End grain

Against the grain (wrong)

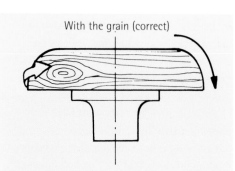

With the grain (correct)

Fig 7.6 The blank is removed from the lathe and placed on the bench. Downhill is now opposite to the direction shown in Fig 7.5. Cutting with the arrow is *with* the grain.

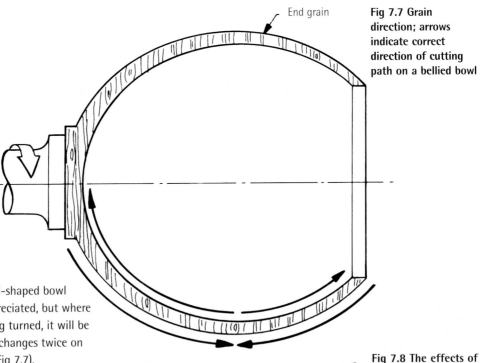

Fig 7.7 Grain
direction; arrows
indicate correct
direction of cutting
path on a bellied bowl

End grain

On a simple, conventional-shaped bowl
these facts are easily appreciated, but where
a full-bellied bowl is being turned, it will be
seen that grain direction changes twice on
both inside and outside (Fig 7.7).

Next to be considered is whether the
timber should be used heart-side up or heart-
side down. In the process of seasoning, timber
always shrinks away from the heart, resulting
in this side becoming rounded. Thus, if there is
any movement and the heart side is at the
bottom of the bowl, the bottom will become
rounded and consequently the bowl will not
sit flat and may well spin or rock on any level
surface (Fig 7.8). Traditionally, bowls were
always designed so that the heart side was
uppermost to avoid this problem (Fig 7.9).

This principle is disregarded by many
modern bowl turners because of the popularity
of 'natural-edge' bowls, or where there is a
marked colour contrast between the
heartwood and sapwood. Such features can
obviously only be incorporated in the design
when the principle is waived. The problem of a
rounded bottom is then avoided by making the
base slightly concaved (Fig 7.10).

Green or wet turning

This is not something new, for after all, the
bodgers made virtually all their chair
components from green wood. As the wood
moved, the joints became tighter, the round
mortises shrinking to an oval shape. There has
been a revival of this form of turning,
particularly in bowl work. Here are some of the
advantages of green or wet turning:

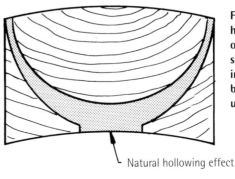

Fig 7.8 The effects of
shrinkage, with the
heart side at the
bottom of the bowl,
can make it rounded
and unstable

Natural rounding effect

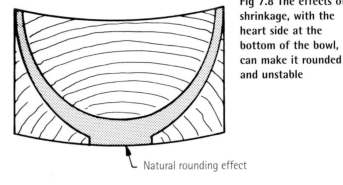

Fig 7.9 With the
heart side at the top
of the bowl, any
shrinkage will result
in *hollowing* of the
base, with stability
unaffected

Natural hollowing effect

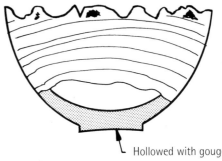

Fig 7.10 The above
rule is waived for
natural-edged bowls,
but for stability the
base must then be
slightly hollowed

Hollowed with gouge to counter
effect of shrinkage

- Green timber is considerably cheaper than seasoned timber.
- It cuts much more easily than dry timber.
- The tools stay sharper longer.
- Seasoning time is reduced considerably if the wet wood is rough-turned to a wall thickness of about ¾in (19mm). Subsequent air-drying should not take more than about six months, and this can be halved if the blanks are stored in airing-cupboard conditions. (It is normal and advisable to coat the rough-turned blanks with wax to prevent uneven drying, the cause of splitting.)

Turning wet is also very good for the ego. On spindle turning you can expect to see streamers of ribbon-like shavings leaving the tools, and in bowl work the rope-like shavings will quickly cover both bench and floor.

Methods of fixing

Faceplate only

Traditionally, as the name implies, faceplates were screwed on to a prepared blank and mounted on the lathe. The turning was completed all in one operation without using any re-chucking device. The main disadvantages of this system are:

- The screw holes in the bottom will be seen, although they can be plugged or covered with baize.
- The bottom of the bowl is required to be a minimum of ½in (13mm) thick to accommodate the screws. Invariably, this is too thick and makes the bowl inelegant and bulky.

Combination or multi-purpose chucks

Mention was made of these in Chapter 2. I made the point that these sophisticated chucking devices are not essential in developing basic skills, but they are extremely useful in speeding up and simplifying many projects. In essence, these chucks will grip internally and externally and also, by using the various accessories, can be converted to a woodscrew chuck or pin chuck.

Faceplate (or screw chuck) combined with home-made friction chuck

This was the method I was brought up with, and making use of it entails the use of either the faceplate or the screw chuck for the initial mounting. After the external shaping has been completed, the bowl is reversed and driven by a friction-fit chuck (again secured to either faceplate or screw chuck), made from a waste piece of wood. Not only does this system avoid unsightly screw holes in the base, but it is very satisfying to be able to complete such a project by making use of a device that itself needs careful preparation to make it function efficiently.

Tools for bowl work

Bowl gouge

Your recommended beginner's set includes a ⅜in (10mm) bowl gouge, a tool that will be quite adequate to complete virtually all the shaping on bowls up to about 10in diameter and 3in deep (255 x 75mm). For bowls larger than this (and beginners are advised not to tackle such), the heftier ½in (13mm) size is recommended. It is as well to know that bowl gouges are measured across the *inside* of the flute; thus the ⅜in bowl gouge is made from ½in (13mm) round bar, and the ½in gouge is made from ⅝in (16mm) bar.

Some turners, including myself, use spindle gouges on faceplate work of all kinds, particularly for finishing cuts and the forming of decorative detail. The novice would be best advised to stick with the bowl gouge (its deep U-section making it much easier to control on this type of work) and scrapers. Roughing-out gouges must *not* be used on faceplate work. They should be restricted to use on between-centres turning. Some bowl turners do use them, but the practice is *dangerous* for a novice.

Grinding profile of the bowl gouge
Traditionally these were ground 'square across', and some manufacturers still supply them so. Specialist bowl turners usually possess several bowl gouges, all ground to different profiles including square across,

fingernail, and some ground back as much as 1in (25mm) from the tip. This is done in the interests of speed and efficiency, but the beginner, with only one such gouge, will have to settle for a good, general profile.

My opinion is that a slight rounding of the cutting edge will prove to be the most useful and versatile grinding profile, easy to control and efficient in use. To sharpen the tool, determine the correct angle on the grinding-jig platform (about 55°; see pages 38–42). Now offer the tool up well over on its side and roll it right over to its other

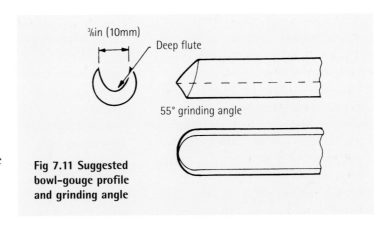

Fig 7.11 Suggested bowl-gouge profile and grinding angle

³⁄₈in (10mm)

Deep flute

55° grinding angle

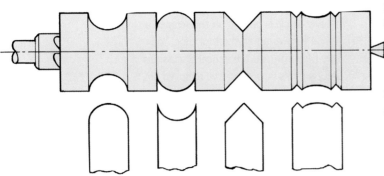

Fig 7.12 Selection of forming tools (scrapers) that can be used on both spindle and faceplate work

side. The rolling should be accompanied by a slight swinging action to produce the slightly rounded profile. Continue (remembering to apply only gentle forward pressure on the stone) until the 'acceptable degree of sharpness' has been achieved. Fig 7.11 shows the suggested profile.

Scrapers

These come in all shapes and sections, and I possess probably twice as many scrapers as cutting tools, a strange admission from someone who has stressed the use of cutting tools wherever possible. However, I undertake a good deal of faceplate work in the form of plinths, which are required with many different edge profiles, and my scrapers are ground to match the desired profiles. They are used to form the desired shape *after* I have removed as much waste as possible with gouges. The saving on marking out and execution is considerable.

It is obvious that scrapers can be used for two entirely different functions:

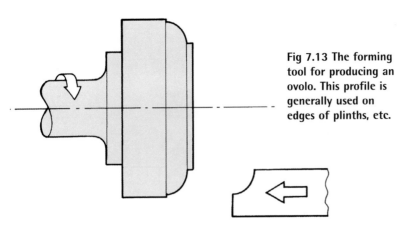

Fig 7.13 The forming tool for producing an ovolo. This profile is generally used on edges of plinths, etc.

As forming tools

The tool is ground to a profile exactly opposite to that required on the finished plinth, disc, or whatever, and is pushed straight into the work. Pattern-makers use this method of shaping to a great extent, not only on faceplate work, but also on between-centres turning, where accuracy rather than quality of finish is of more importance. Figs 7.12, 7.13 and 7.14 show examples of such tool profiles.

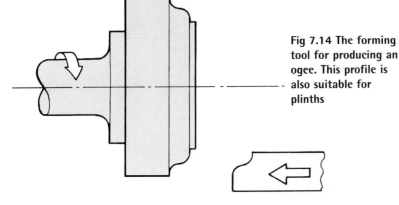

Fig 7.14 The forming tool for producing an ogee. This profile is also suitable for plinths

As improvers

The attainment of a satisfactory finish straight from the gouge is in many cases extremely unlikely. The areas of end grain, particularly on the 'unsupported' fibres, tend to lift up under the action of the gouge. This will happen to some extent even when the sharpest of gouges is being used in extremely skilled hands. This 'lifting' of the end grain is more pronounced in the coarse, open-grained timbers like elm and oak. Unskilled hands, employing a dull gouge, will probably lift these fibres up to a depth of ¼in (6mm), and thus nowhere is the keenness of the tool edge more urgently needed.

Very sharp scrapers will very often improve the finish on the end grain. It has been said that there is *no* skill in using scrapers. I disagree! While I do accept that considerably more skill is required to use the cutting tools correctly, to say no skill is required in scraping is bunkum. In the case of 'forming' scrapers, the demand on skill starts with the shaping of the tool on the grindstone. A 'feel' must be developed to get the best results, as with any other tool, and this indefinable asset is even more difficult to attain when making use of scrapers as 'improvers'.

The amount of timber removed is directly proportional to how much forward pressure you exert. For 'improving' this must be very light and the scraper must be kept on the move. Shavings and not dust should leave the edge on all but the odd species of timber. If this is not happening, the scraper edge is dull. Scrapers which are not extremely sharp will have a worse effect on the end grain than a dull gouge, and no amount of sanding will remedy this.

Your recommended first set of tools contains three scrapers, and these should prove adequate for some considerable time. If, however, you want a special profile of some kind, you can make use of a defunct carpenter's firmer chisel and grind it to the required shape.

Sharpening

For the reason discussed in great detail in Chapter 4, a grinding angle of about 80° is required on all scrapers. Adjust the platform on the grinding jig accordingly and offer the tool up very lightly on to the stone. Grinding the square-ended scraper entails nothing more than traversing the tool parallel across the face of the stone. As with the smoothing-plane blade, it is

as well to radius the ends of the square-across scraper slightly to prevent the tips scouring the work. Obviously the round-nose scrapers must also be swung in an arc to maintain or form the desired profile. Again, the value of the large platform on the jig will be obvious.

As your skill and confidence increase, the suggested grinding angle of 80° on scrapers can be lengthened. Some bowl turners grind them as long as 45° to facilitate a technique called **shear scraping**. This is not for beginners, however, and is best left well alone until a fair degree of proficiency has been attained in the traditional scraping techniques which are described fully in Chapter 5 (pages 52–3).

Whatever angle is ground on the scraper, a **burr** will be thrown up on the tool edge. You may have heard or read theoretical discussions as to whether this burr should be removed or left on. My advice, based on my personal experience, is to leave it on *except* when the scraper is being used on end-grain projects such as goblets, boxes, etc., and when dense exotic hardwoods are being used. On such species the burr can make the cut too aggressive and tool control so much more difficult.

Removing the burr from a newly ground tool can be done with an oil slipstone or by drawing the tool along a piece of fine-grade wet-or-dry abrasive paper.

PROJECT

Turning your first bowl

Before going into the mechanics of chucking and tool technique, it seems appropriate to spend a little time discussing bowl design.

As mentioned earlier in this chapter, for hundreds of years wooden bowls were produced largely for functional, utilitarian purposes and designed to be practical rather than aesthetically appealing. For the past 20 years or so, the inclination has been to produce bowls along more artistic lines. Wafer-thin bowls, natural-edged bowls, enclosed forms, hollow forms, wet-turned bowls, etc., have all had their share of exposure at galleries and seminars.

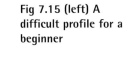

Fig 7.15 (left) A difficult profile for a beginner

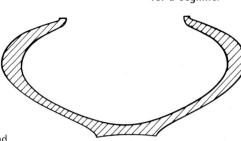

Fig 7.16 An even more difficult profile for a beginner

Some turners have even built international reputations for their innovative techniques and ideas, and for the development of specialist tools and equipment to undertake such work.

Whole books have been dedicated to this type of turning, but I would suggest that until a thorough understanding of the basic techniques has been acquired it is *dangerous* to attempt much of the work that specialist headstock turners produce. It is an irrefutable fact that the thinner the bowl wall, the larger the bowl, the *more unbalanced* the stock on natural-edge pieces, or the deeper the hollowing on enclosed forms, the more dangerous the turning can be.

This book is aimed at the relative newcomer to woodturning, and my advice is to concentrate on open, flowing profiles which will serve to develop good and safe technique and, perhaps more importantly, confidence. The nearer the outside profile gets to a U-shape (Fig 7.15), the more difficult the hollowing becomes. It becomes even more difficult on enclosed-form profiles such as that shown in Fig 7.16, and these should be avoided until you have much more experience.

With a little bit of forethought, it is possible to produce bowls and platters that are both functional and good to look at, even though the designs are based on simple, flowing profiles. Fig 7.17 shows a bowl designed along these lines, while Fig 7.52 on page 105 shows a platter of similar character; I shall describe the making of both.

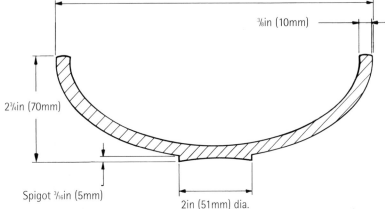

8¾in (222mm) dia.

⅜in (10mm)

2¾in (70mm)

Spigot ³⁄₁₆in (5mm)

2in (51mm) dia.

Fig 7.17 A simple, open bowl profile suitable for the beginner

Your first bowl

Not to be too ambitious, begin with a medium-sized bowl blank, 9in diameter by 3in thick (230 x 76mm). The design is also influenced by the fact that I shall be using and describing the friction-fit method of reverse-chucking, as discussed briefly on page 90. This necessitates the forming of a 2in (51mm) plinth on the base of the bowl, and allows turners who only possess a faceplate or a screw chuck to complete the bowl without any visible initial chucking (screw holes) being evident.

The wall thickness is generous, and it will be seen by studying Fig 7.17 that the rim has been slightly radiused, and also undercut on the inside to make for a nice crisp start to the inside curve.

Choice of wood

Any of the home-grown hardwoods, such as elm, ash, beech or cherry, are suitable. If available, sycamore is probably the kindest species on which to develop your skills. It is a nice clean wood, stable, and cuts easily. It is also comparatively inexpensive. I have used North American tulipwood again for the sequence photos, and also for the completed bowl shown on page 104.

Method

The method of fixing and reverse-chucking is described in Fig 7.18. Ensure that the screw chuck is accurately centred on the blank – or unnecessary vibration will be set up – and mount the wood on the lathe. It is as well to ensure that the surface receiving the screw chuck is planed flat to prevent any rocking.

Adjust the speed of the lathe to approximately 750–1000rpm and position the toolrest across the edge of the stock, the first task being to reduce it to a true cylinder.

As it is absolutely *vital* in the interests of personal safety not to allow the tool to lift off the rest while in contact with large-diameter turnings, I recommend (and use to a great extent) the 'overhand' hold. This method of holding, as explained and illustrated in the preceding chapter (page 58), provides for the weight of the palm and fingers of the front

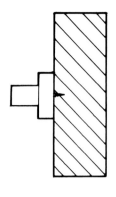

Fig 7.18a Mount the bowl blank on the woodscrew chuck or faceplate and true up both the face and the edge with the ⅜in (10mm) bowl gouge

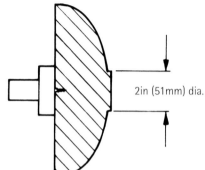

Fig 7.18b Set out and form the plinth with the parting tool. Shape the outside of the bowl, sand and oil. It is vital that the edge of the plinth is cut dead square. Now remove the blank from chuck or faceplate

2in (51mm) dia.

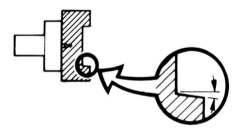

Fig 7.18c Mount a piece of waste wood about 5 x 1½in (125 x 38mm) on the chuck and true up both the edge and the face. With the dividers, scribe the diameter of the plinth on to the face and form the recess with a parting tool and skew chisel. Ensure that you form a slight taper as shown

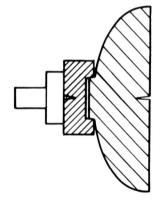

Fig 7.18d A good tight fit is required. When this is achieved, true up the face and hollow it out with the bowl gouge. Start the cuts near the centre and gradually open out towards the rim

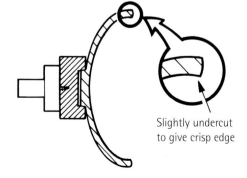

Slightly undercut to give crisp edge

Fig 7.18e Improve the internal finish with the domed scraper, then sand and oil. The bowl is removed from the chuck by tapping with the heel of your hand.

method could be used; see Figs 7.2 and 7.3 on pages 87–8.)

Correct presentation and angling of the gouge should result in the shavings leaving the edge *below centre*, that is, where it is receiving optimum support. The angling of the tool and the slightly radiused edge assist in inducing a slicing action to minimize the lifting of the end-grain fibres (Fig 7.19).

Next, stop the lathe and position the toolrest across the face of the bowl blank, adjusting the height so that the gouge can cut on the centre of the disc when pointing slightly upwards. Two methods can be used to true this face:

1 With the handle held slightly down and the gouge rolled well over on its side (flute facing you), pull the tool from the centre to the outside edge in a smooth traversing cut. Very flat and true surfaces can be cut in this manner, particularly when the 'underhand' hold is employed and the index finger bears on the toolrest, which has been set parallel to the face of the wood. Unless the bevel is very short, stock removal will be part scraping, part cutting, but don't let this bother you — the finish should be fine! (Fig 7.20).

2 Again with the handle down, commence the cut on the outside of the blank and traverse towards the centre. The bevel must be lined up with the intended square face and the cut takes the form of a shallow arc, with bevel in contact throughout. The shallow arc is

Fig 7.19 Truing up the edge of the blank with the bowl gouge

hand to keep the tool pressed down on the rest. Again, nothing more than a normal, relaxed hold is called for.

Gouge presentation

Remember that the gouge is a cutting tool and all the relevant Laws must be complied with. Remember also to revolve the work freehand before starting the lathe. Vibration of some kind will be experienced when the lathe is started, however careful you were in centring. Offer the gouge up to the whirling wood, handle well down (safe angle of presentation), and pass it across the edge of the blank *without cutting*, just to get the feel. You will experience a certain amount of bumping until the blank is reduced to a true cylinder, but do not be alarmed. Gradually bring the cut on by lifting the handle until a fine shaving appears. Best results are obtained when the gouge is rolled well over on its side, flute facing the intended direction of traverse, and also angled in the same direction.

Having 'found the bevel' in your mind's eye, it is quite safe to start off the end of the wood, then pick the cut up and traverse the gouge across the whole edge. Practise going from left to right and vice versa, taking only light shavings to avoid splitting the unsupported grain at the extremes. (In the case of plinths or discs requiring perfectly square edges, traversing the tool would need to be done from outside to centre from both ends, to avoid splitting, or alternatively the chamfering

Fig 7.20 Truing up the face from centre to rim, Method 1

Fig 7.21 Truing up
the face from rim to
centre, Method 2

effected by pushing the tool edge towards the
centre, while at the same time the handle is
levered upwards (Fig 7.21). This method is
perhaps a little more difficult than the first, but
in both cases it is usual to remove any slight
nipples or undulations with a square-ended
scraper.

This facing off is not absolutely vital on a bowl,
as most of the wood is later cut away, but it is
good practice for when a flat surface is
required, such as when turning wine-table tops.

The bottom and plinth can now be set out.
For this size of bowl, a base about 2in (51mm)
across will ensure the development of a nice
flowing curve on the bowl wall. With the lathe
running, pencil in this measurement and with
the parting tool, handle slightly down, go in to a
depth of about ³/₁₆in (5mm). Make a couple more
identical cuts in the waste side and then remove
the remainder with the bowl gouge (Fig 7.22).

To fashion a flowing curve on the outside of
the bowl, commence the cutting on the square
edge you have just formed and remember to
cut (where possible) from small to large
diameter, with the gouge well over on its side,
flute facing the direction of cut. The tool will
need to be swung round the developing curve,
and if you stand in close you should be able to
see the bevel rubbing behind the cut,
supporting the tool edge. If you swing the
handle too quickly, bevel support will be lost
and the tool will dig in and kick back to you.
The remedy is obvious (Fig 7.23).

It is not possible to get the gouge on that area
of the bowl wall adjacent to the plinth whilst
observing the rule of cutting from small to large
diameter. Consequently, light cuts in the other
direction will have to be made, but with enough
care no great damage will be done (Fig 7.24).

Fig 7.22 Forming the
plinth with the
parting tool

Fig 7.23 Developing
the outside curve
with the bowl gouge

Fig 7.24 Gouging in
the opposite direction
up to the plinth. Note
how the toolrest has
been positioned close
to the bowl to
minimize leverage on
the tool edge

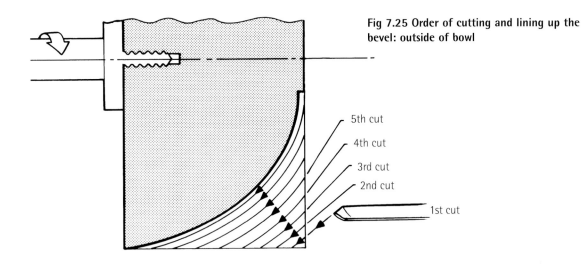

Fig 7.25 Order of cutting and lining up the bevel: outside of bowl

5th cut
4th cut
3rd cut
2nd cut
1st cut

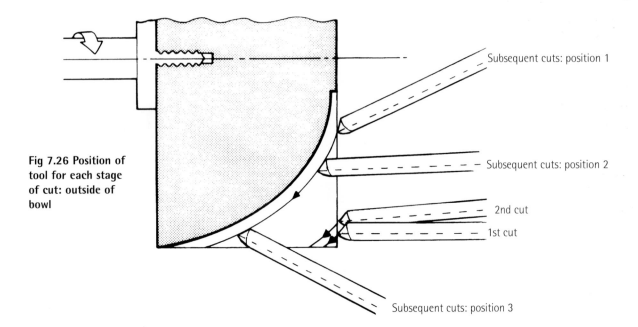

Fig 7.26 Position of tool for each stage of cut: outside of bowl

Subsequent cuts: position 1

Subsequent cuts: position 2

2nd cut
1st cut

Subsequent cuts: position 3

Fig 7.25 shows the order of cutting and the 'lining up' of the bevel on the outside of a bowl, while Fig 7.26 shows how the tool handle is swung as the cut progresses from near the plinth to the rim of the bowl.

Your first efforts with the bowl gouge will probably not leave a nice flowing curve, and you will need to practise a good deal to develop the technique. Do not despair. The square-across scraper in your set will help put things right. Position the height of the toolrest so the scraper is cutting dead on centre or slightly below. Should you have a dig-in, the tool will be knocked into fresh air and not deeper into the wood, which would increase the severity of the dig-in (Fig 7.27).

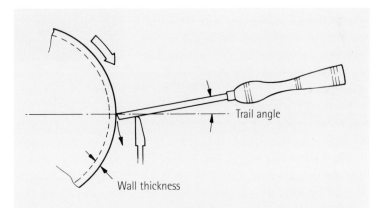

Trail angle

Wall thickness

Fig 7.27 Scraping: outside of bowl. (1) The scraper must trail and be kept dead flat on the rest (Law 6). (2) Adjust the rest height so that the scraper cuts on or just below centre. (3) If the tool digs in, the cutting edge will be forced downwards into fresh air

Fig 7.28 Improving the finish with the 1in (25mm) square scraper

Fig 7.29 Forming decorative V-cuts in the base with the skew

Keep the scraper perfectly flat on the rest and point it slightly downwards (trailing). For sweeping cuts, as on the outside of a bowl, I place my fingers on top of the scraper, lock the handle to my side and let body movement pull the tool edge round in a flowing sweep. A few passes from centre to rim should give you a surface free from undulations (Fig 7.28).

The plinth now needs to be completed by slightly concaving the base. This, again, can be done with the square-across scraper, and in doing so you will understand why the extreme tips of the tool should be slightly radiused to prevent them scouring the wood. If you think this base is in need of a little decoration, a couple of shallow V-cuts with the toe of the ½in (13mm) skew chisel, used on edge, will add to the effect as shown in Fig 7.29.

The sides of the plinth should be dead square, or trouble will be experienced in obtaining a good friction fit. My final cuts to achieve this are usually done with the toe of the small skew chisel, laid flat on the rest and used virtually scraper-fashion — cutting tools are occasionally used as scrapers to good effect (Fig 7.30).

Now stop the lathe and examine the work. You will be extremely fortunate if there are no rough areas of end grain. There are ways to improve this. One method is to power-sand, which many bowl turners do. Another method is to soak the end grain with oil, sealer or wax (depending on your chosen finish), which has the effect of softening up the stubborn fibres.

Assuming you choose a Danish oil finish, which is suitable for most bowls, you can use

Fig 7.30 Accurate forming of the plinth edge with the skew

the same product to soften the fibres. Apply a liberal coat of oil with a rag and allow a couple of minutes for penetration. Now take a freshly sharpened scraper and make a few light cuts around the bowl wall, traversing from the centre to the rim of the bowl. I would be very surprised if this treatment did not dramatically improve the finish. Bear in mind, however, that the product used for the initial softening in this method must be chemically compatible with the product to be used as a finish.

Fig 7.31 The outside of the bowl completed, ready for sanding

Fig 7.32 The home-made depth gauge in use

Fig 7.33 Tape stuck to gouge at same depth

Fig 7.34 Determining plinth diameter with dividers

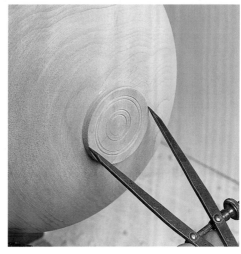

The outside of the bowl can now be sanded and the chosen finish applied. Details of power-sanding, hand-sanding, polishing and finishing are given in Chapter 9, Sanding and Finishing. The completed outside of the bowl is shown in Fig 7.31.

Before reversing the bowl to gouge out the inside, it is best to plan ahead and determine the required internal depth, thus avoiding the mishap of gouging through the bottom. This is easily done if you get carried away with the sheer pleasure of 'sending the shavings flying'.

A simple but effective method is to prepare a piece of wood slightly longer than the diameter of the bowl and about 2 x 1in (50 x 25mm) in section. Drill the appropriate-sized hole in the centre to take a tight-fitting length of dowel, and determine the depth by tapping the dowel with a hammer until it is positioned as shown in Fig 7.32. This measurement can then be transferred to the bowl gouge and indicated by means of a piece of tape stuck to the blade (Fig 7.33).

The next step is to remove the partly finished bowl from the screw chuck and replace it with a disc of wood intended for our friction-drive chuck. A piece of softwood about 5 x 2in (125 x 50mm) will do fine, so first of all true up both the edge and the face with bowl gouge and scraper. Measure the base of the bowl with dividers (Fig 7.34) and transfer this measurement to the wood now in the lathe. Be careful when doing this, and allow *only one leg* of the dividers (the one at 9 o'clock) to touch the whirling wood.

This operation is difficult for beginners, and an aid to 'marrying up' the points of the

Fig 7.35 Scribing plinth diameter on piece intended for chuck

Fig 7.36 Forming the chuck recess with the parting tool

Fig 7.37 Forming a slight inward taper on the chuck with the skew

dividers is to pencil in concentric rings on the intended friction chuck while the lathe is running. This obviously almost pinpoints where the dividers need to scribe the wood (Fig 7.35).

Another method used by many turners is to measure the *radius* of the base and set the dividers to this measurement. A pointed awl is used to make a small hole in the centre of the wood, allowing each leg of the dividers to be in contact with both wood and toolrest.

Whatever method you use, make sure the dividers point slightly down and both legs are firmly on the rest, otherwise you are inviting a dig-in.

Now, making use of the parting tool, go forward with a series of cuts just over ¼in (6mm) deep (Fig 7.36).

For the final cuts adjacent to the scribed line, I prefer to use the toe of a skew chisel, scraper-fashion again, to form a *gentle* decreasing bevel so the plinth tightens as it is inserted (Figs 7.37 and 7.18c).

Stop the lathe and try the fit (Fig 7.38). Further light cuts may be needed to arrive at a good friction fit. I do not mean by this that the bowl has to be hammered into the recess; a good push fit will prove more than secure. For those in doubt of the effectiveness of this method — and most people are until it has been demonstrated — wetting the recess in the chuck will allow the wood to expand and grip even better. Where the fit is a little sloppier than desired, it can be remedied by packing the recess with damp newspaper. It does look a trifle 'greenhorn', but it does work! With a little experience, however, the need to resort to such tactics will decrease.

Fig 7.38 Testing the fit

Now start the lathe, and the bowl should be running dead true. If it is not, stop the lathe, and a moderate blow with a light hammer, directed at the centre of the bowl face, will quickly remedy the situation. Turning can now commence, and the first thing to do is to dress the face of the bowl as we did with the bottom.

Bore a hole in the centre of the workpiece in the same way as in the hollowing-out process on page 80. Lay the gouge horizontally on the toolrest and positioned so the tip is in line with the centre of the wood. The tool is slightly rolled over on to its side (with the flute positioned at about 10 past 7 on the clock), and a positive pushing action combined with a 'wiggle' from side to side will comfortably bore the hole up to the tape mark (Fig 7.39).

Before beginning the hollowing process, just refresh your memory on grain direction. Remember that on the inside of a bowl, cutting with the grain is achieved by working from large to small diameter. With this in mind, start gouging just left of centre as you look at it and gradually widen the bowl out with a series of arcing cuts, each one starting a little further from the centre than the last. Use the 'overhand' hold and present the gouge well over on its side, flute facing away from you; for the initial cuts the gouge is almost at right angles to the wood (Fig 7.40).

To achieve the bevel-rubbing mode, the handle needs to be well down, but remember how in spindle turning the gouge had a tendency to skid sideways until entry had been made? The same problem will be encountered here, and the nearer we get to the rim, the greater the tendency to skid and inflict serious damage to the bowl rim. This can be avoided by making a series of V-cuts with the tip of the square-across scraper or skew chisel near to the rim. These will afford immediate support to the bevel of the gouge, thus preventing the skid (Fig 7.41)

The professional way to do it, or rather my way, is to present the gouge just below the horizontal and boldly lever upwards and forwards, in much the same way as described for the spindle gouge. As soon as entry is effected, the handle should be dropped and the path of the cut should be a shallow arc, finishing at the centre of the bowl. The shaving, as always, should be coming from below the centre of the tool (i.e. the part receiving direct support), and in this manner a dig-in is averted (Fig 7.42).

Fig 7.39 Boring with the bowl gouge up to the tape mark

Fig 7.40 Beginning the hollowing

Fig 7.41 Forming V-cuts with the skew to prevent skids

Fig 7.42 (left) Arcing cut with the gouge from rim to centre

Fig 7.43 (left) Lining up the bevel near the rim

Fig 7.44 The gouge in mid-cut, the handle being swung towards the body. Note how the toolrest has been positioned inside the bowl to minimize leverage on the tool edge

Fig 7.45 Testing for even wall thickness with callipers. NB: The lathe must be stopped for this operation

As the bowl widens and deepens, substantial swinging movements will be necessary to make the shape 'flow'. Fig 7.43 shows the start of a cut near to the rim; the tool handle is well over towards the right-hand side of the bowl, as it must be in order to line the bevel up. As the cut proceeds the handle will need to be swung towards the operator's body (Fig 7.44).

To maintain these substantial swinging movements, body sway, balance and weight transference are very important if a flowing internal profile is to be achieved. After the rim thickness at the top of the bowl has been determined, it is good practice to radius the top edge and perform the slight undercut *before* removing too much wood from lower down the bowl. This way, stability is maintained whilst performing these refining cuts.

Continue by aiming for an even wall thickness; this should be tested with a pair of double-ended callipers. The lathe *must be stopped* while you are using the callipers in this mode (Fig 7.45). Do not forget occasionally to

Fig 7.46 Order of cutting: inside of bowl

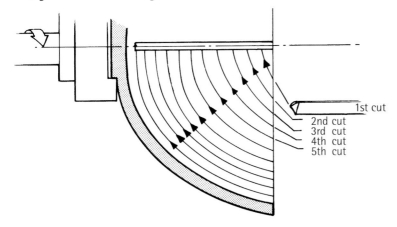

1st cut
2nd cut
3rd cut
4th cut
5th cut

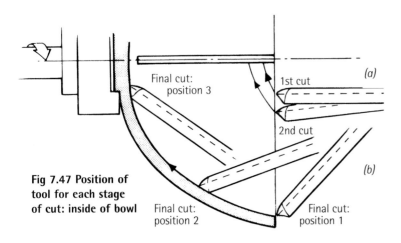

Fig 7.47 Position of tool for each stage of cut: inside of bowl

Final cut: position 3
1st cut
2nd cut
Final cut: position 2
Final cut: position 1
(a)
(b)

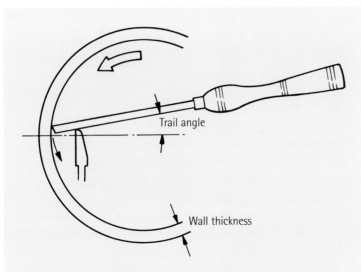

Trail angle

Wall thickness

Fig 7.48 Scraping: inside of bowl. (1) The scraper must trail and be kept dead flat on the rest (Law 6). (2) Adjust the rest height so that the scraper cuts slightly above centre. (3) If the tool digs in, the cutting edge will be forced downwards into fresh air
Note: Obviously, to clean up dead centre of the internal shape, the scraper must be cutting on dead centre. This is achieved by increasing the trail angle

offer your depth gauge up to the bowl. When the 2 x 1in touches the rim, you will have gone deep enough.

Fig 7.46 should assist in explaining the order of cutting. Fig 7.47 shows the angle of presentation **(a)** for the commencing cuts and **(b)** for the swinging movements of the gouge from the rim to the centre.

Finishing touches to the inside of the bowl to remove any undulations are carried out with the 1in (25mm) domed scraper. The toolrest must be positioned so it affords maximum support, and at a height that enables the cutting edge of the scraper to engage the wood slightly above centre. Again, if a dig-in is experienced the scraper will be forced downwards into fresh air and not wood (Fig 7.48).

Remember to traverse from the rim towards the centre. Such traversing should be smooth and flowing if a smooth, flowing internal profile is to be arrived at. Keep the scrapers dead flat and limit the overhang to as little as possible by adjusting the toolrest as necessary. On internal surfaces, always ensure that the radius of the tool is slightly 'quicker' than the internal shape, or the tips will almost certainly dig in (Fig 7.49).

The process of soaking the end grain with oil can now be repeated on the inside of the bowl, and the work is completed by skimming with a freshly ground scraper and then, of course, sanding and final oiling.

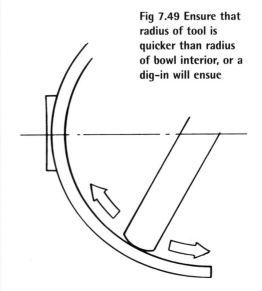

Fig 7.49 Ensure that radius of tool is quicker than radius of bowl interior, or a dig-in will ensue

Fig 7.50 Using the left hand to support the bowl wall when scraping near the rim

I do not recommend trying to make the bowl walls too thin during the learning process. Bowls of this size look and feel right if the finished thickness is about ⅜in (10mm). Even with this thickness, you will need to steady the bowl wall with your fingers to prevent the tools chattering, which would of course impair the finish (Fig 7.50; see also 7.43 and 7.44).

I do recommend that your early bowls be similar to the finished example in Fig 7.51, which has 'slow' flowing shapes and no tight curves. Bevel contact is much easier to maintain and confidence and proficiency should quickly increase. A final word on bevel-rubbing: many turners are over-zealous in their application of the bevel when bowl turning, which results in the tool edge becoming hot. While it is true to say that the bevel must rub behind the cut, a better description might be that it should *glide* along behind the cut.

There is obviously a great deal more to faceplate work than bowl turning, but if the basic techniques are mastered, then the making of such things as bases for standard and table lamps, candlesticks and wall clocks, pot stands, breadboards, platters, etc. will present few problems.

PROJECT

Platter

The design in Fig 7.52 might be better described as a dish – a platter usually being a little flatter in section – but for the purpose of this exercise we will stick to the word 'platter'. It is along traditional lines, from a stock size of 10in diameter by 2in thick (255 x 51mm). The outside shape is based on the classical ogee profile, which allows for the forming of a proportionately sized rim or flange on the top; this provides easy access for the fingers to pick the platter up.

Fig 7.51 The completed bowl in North American tulipwood

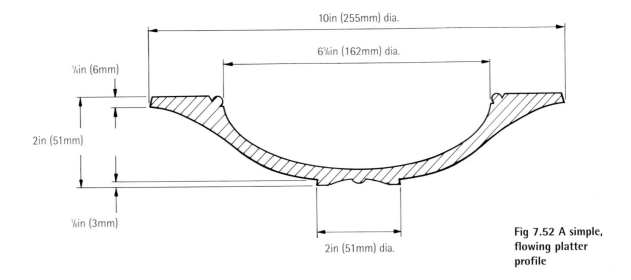

10in (255mm) dia.

6⅜in (162mm) dia.

¼in (6mm)

2in (51mm)

⅛in (3mm)

2in (51mm) dia.

Fig 7.52 A simple, flowing platter profile

As with the bowl described above, the platter will stand on a foot or plinth 2in (51mm) in diameter (10in stock is about the maximum diameter which will be stable when supported on a 2in foot), which this time will be slightly dovetailed to suit the 2in (51mm) jaws of a combination or spigot chuck.

Choice of wood

As suggested for the bowl, above (see page 94). Sycamore has been used throughout for the sequence photographs.

Method

Initial mounting can be done on either a woodscrew chuck or a faceplate, the order of work being very similar to that employed on the bowl. True up the edge of the stock and then the face. Set out the diameter of the foot and size in to a depth of ⅛in (3mm) in the waste wood to the left of your mark. The outside profiling can now commence, making use of the techniques described when making the bowl.

The ogee profile is achieved by locking the arms to the body while pulling the gouge around the convex part of the profile and pushing it to form the concave section near the flange of the platter. Body movements should control the pulling and pushing movements, and after continued practice the action will become second nature. Fig 7.53 shows the bowl gouge being used to refine the nearly completed profile. It is unlikely that early attempts will leave a ripple-free surface, but any slight undulations can be rectified by making use of the square and domed-edged scrapers.

The toe of the ½in (13mm) skew chisel can now be used to undercut the edge of the foot slightly in order to form the dovetailed spigot. Finally, the foot can be slightly dished with the domed scraper to ensure that it sits on its periphery. Alternatively, the profiling of the underside

Fig 7.53 The bowl gouge being used well over on its side in the pull-cut mode

105

Fig 7.54 The completed outside of the platter

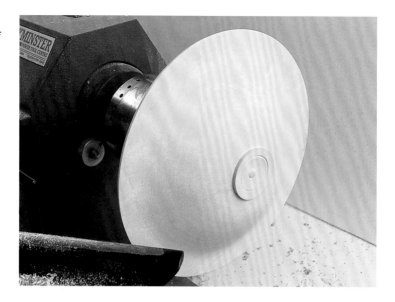

shown in Fig 7.52 can be attempted, and this is not difficult if care is taken.

Now sand and apply your choice of finish. Fig 7.54 shows the completed outside.

The reverse-chucking can now follow, and I make a practice of protecting the polished foot by packing the spigot chuck with a few layers of kitchen roll or toilet paper. Only gentle pressure is required to secure the foot in the chuck. Many turners overdo the tightening and damage the dovetailed portion of the plinth.

With the stock running true (adjust with the hammer if necessary, as before), 'face off' as shown already in Figs 7.20 and 7.21. The next step is to set out the width of the flange so that it looks in proportion. Fig 7.52

gives a suggested flange width, but this can be varied to suit individual preference. Pencil in on the whirling wood the two lines defining the bead and the point of hollowing. Now size in to a depth of about $^{3}/_{16}$in (5mm) to the right of the mark nearest the centre of the stock. A couple more cuts to the same depth, in the waste wood to the right of the first cut, will allow access to form the bead.

Begin forming the outer side of the bead by presenting the $^{1}/_{2}$in skew chisel flat down on the rest and using the long point or toe to form a V-cut about $^{1}/_{8}$in (3mm) deep. Fig 7.55 shows the progress thus far.

By making use of the same tool, the radiused profile of the bead can now be

Fig 7.55 The platter flange set out and sized in

Fig 7.56 The skew chisel used in the scraping mode to form the bead

formed, using the chisel in a scraping mode and with a slight swinging action. It is absolutely vital that the tool is very sharp and only very light cuts are taken. Otherwise, it is likely that the grain will break out on the apex of the bead, particularly on coarse, open-grained woods. Fig 7.56 shows the chisel being so used. At this stage, the short bevel at the edge of the rim can also be formed by drawing the gouge from right to left, with the grain, taking very light cuts.

The internal profiling can now commence, but it is advisable for the flange and bead to be completely tooled and sanded before removing too much of the centre core. This can result in movement in the wood, causing the timber to distort. Going back to tool or sand the edge *after* this has taken place will result in a flange of varying thickness.

As the deepening of the inside continues, it may be advisable also to make use from time to time of the depth gauge shown in Fig 7.33. Remember also to position the toolrest as close as possible, particularly when refining the inside with the domed scraper. After the sanding process, your choice of finish can now be applied to the inside.

Fig 7.57 shows a completed platter in yew-wood.

SUMMARY

1 Ensure that the bowl blank or disc is sound and free from shakes and 'dead' knots.
2 Study the end-grain formation, remembering that it is normal to have the heart side up to avoid the bowl base becoming rounded.
3 Cutting with the grain on the *outside* of a bowl is achieved by working from *small* to *large* diameter.
4 Cutting with the grain on the *inside* of a bowl is achieved by working from *large* to *small* diameter.
5 The best finish is achieved by the gouge being used well over on its side and presented at an angle, with strict bevel-rubbing.
6 Scrapers can be used as 'forming' shapes or as 'improvers'. They lose their edge rapidly and need constant sharpening.

Fig 7.57 A completed platter in yew-wood

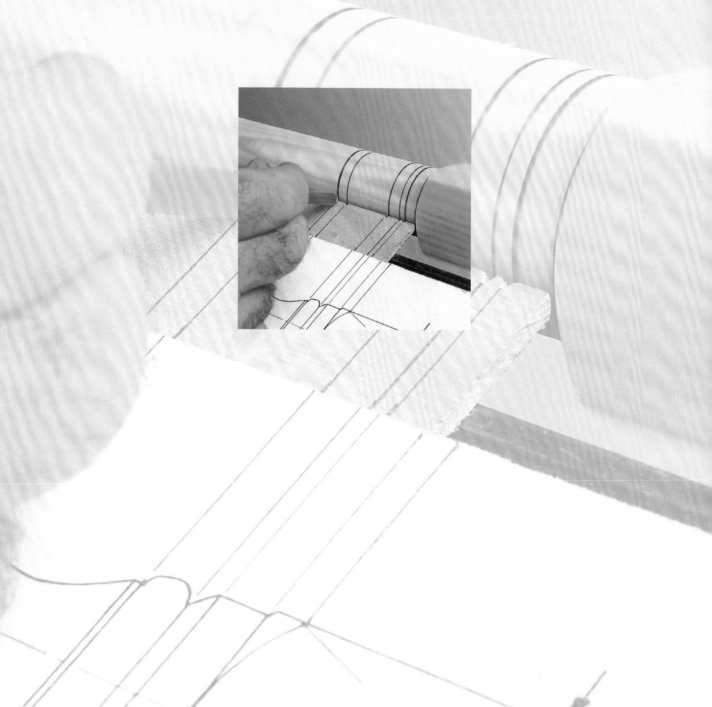

Chapter 8
Copy-Turning

Travelling up and down the country and demonstrating woodturning at various shows is physically exhausting, but extremely satisfying and enjoyable. Certainly, there are few who would question the physical demands on the demonstrator engaged in woodturning some eight or nine hours a day at venues which are always crowded, sometimes claustrophobic and invariably excessively warm. While I am well used to beavering away for such periods of time, it is a different matter to work in these conditions and also give a running commentary, answering a multitude of questions on both lathes and techniques.

Not that I don't enjoy the dialogue with the 'punters', I most certainly do. However, taking into account the prevailing conditions, I have been known to suddenly take off for the nearest bar to partake of Bacchus' treasures. This is neither because I am of immoderate habits nor because someone has posed a question I know not the answer to. It is simply that I must 'oil my larynx' to be able to continue talking!

The advantages of demonstrating are many. First of all it gets me amongst my favourite people, that is workers in wood, who by and large are a happy breed, only too willing to discuss techniques, methods, successes and failures.

Secondly, it is beneficial to me in my capacity as a woodturning instructor; not only because I am able personally to promote my courses, but mainly to identify, through continued dialogue with the enthusiasts, the most common problems they are encountering. I can therefore incorporate the causes and remedies of these problems into my teaching methods and general approach.

Another great advantage, of course, is that it gets you known. I do not think I would have written this book had I not been demonstrating one year for the Coronet Lathe and Tool Company at the *Woodworker* Show at Alexandra Palace.

In Chapter 4, On Sharpening, I mentioned that my research (based on dialogue with the hundreds of aspiring turners with whom I have come into contact) indicated that the greatest single problem in the learning stages is the accurate grinding and sharpening of the tools. This research and collating of facts also reveals that most beginners have great difficulty in making two or more identical items. Time after time I am approached and asked how to go about making a set of matching chair or table legs, spindles for hourglasses, balusters for staircases, etc.

There is no doubt that the ability to copy-turn is a great asset, and once the basic techniques of cutting with the chisels and gouges are mastered, it is not as difficult as it is sometimes made out to be. I am firmly of the opinion that continued practice on simple copy work will inevitably lead to a student making rapid progress. I encourage beginners to practice simple copying exercises virtually from scratch, and certainly everyone who attends my courses is given an exercise that not only involves copying, but also provides practice in most of the techniques required in spindle turning.

I have heard established turners say that making, say, 50 table legs or staircase balusters is 'boring'. I cannot for the life of me understand why! As I said in an earlier chapter, there is something uniquely satisfying about making a well-designed bowl. There is as much satisfaction for me in producing the turnings for a complete staircase, particularly when you have the opportunity of seeing the work in its completed state — that is, fixed and professionally polished.

Copy work certainly demands discipline and a great deal of concentration. I believe these two factors combine to make it the quickest means to improve your skills. The greater part of my output is this type of turning, such as bar, shop and staircase fittings, furniture components, etc. If you are skilful enough and can combine accuracy with speed, then such undertakings can be extremely profitable. Furthermore, the demand for your services will be constant and you may reach the happy state of being able to pick and choose what you want to do.

Such an assertion may sound rather extravagant, particularly in this age of the sophisticated automatic copy lathes which churn out this type of work in thousands. I can assure you it is not. There is still a demand for quality hand-turned work, for don't forget that the majority of the mass-produced items restrict the choice of timber to only two or three species. If the customer wants something different in the way of timber or design, he will seek the services of the hand-turner. Bear in mind also that the 'automatic people' don't want to get involved in comparatively short production runs.

I have said that copy-turning is not as difficult as some would have you believe, and I stick by that statement, assuming you possess the necessary determination, discipline and patience. I will not pretend that combining speed with accuracy is other than difficult, and it only comes with experience and constant everyday practice.

Provided the beginner is prepared to work carefully and methodically, there is no reason why simple copy work should not be attempted very early in his woodturning career. Be reminded, though, that no one has yet found a way of replacing wood which has been cut away in error. I recall a lady onlooker at one of my demonstrations making the remark that woodturning was very similar to the potter working his lump of clay on the wheel. She couldn't have been further from the truth! When things go wrong for the potter, all that is required is for another piece of clay to be stuck to the original and off he goes again. With the turner, removing wood from the wrong place, or too much of it in any part of the design, means that particular piece of wood is destined for the scrap pile, accompanied by a few choice adjectives.

In simplistic terms, copy-turning is merely repeating a predetermined design, ensuring the design features are positioned in identical places and to the same width and diameter. While it is impossible to work to engineering tolerances, a good copy-turner making use of a few simple aids, combined with a good eye, can produce copies that will stand up to close scrutiny. The development of a good eye comes with constant practice, of course, and very often the experienced turner does not have to resort to callipers and the like to determine diameters.

Some may say that copy-turning should not be included in a book aimed primarily at the newcomer to the craft, but I disagree. Beginners should be encouraged to 'have a bash', almost from day one, and personally I consider skills and technique will develop rapidly if the novice concentrates the majority of his time on this type of work.

Accordingly, I have set out three separate copying projects. The first is a fairly simple and straightforward piece of spindle turning combined with faceplate work, which can be developed into a very useful and saleable commodity: a bar stool. The second project, a staircase baluster, will be more of a challenge and also provide the opportunity to explain how to make and use a 'steady'. Finally, I describe the making of identical faceplate turnings, and the project is an attractive plinth or base that can be put to a variety of uses, such as a lamp or candlestick.

PROJECT

Bar stool

These are becoming increasingly popular as more and more people refurbish or create 'live-in' kitchens. Unfortunately, many of the stools I see in the shops are of dubious quality, flimsy in design and rarely produced other than in substandard pine. There is, however, nothing wrong with pine in itself, this species being the choice of many for kitchen units, and I have made a good many stools in good-quality, clean and straight-grained Scots pine.

Probably the most favoured wood for kitchen fittings is oak and, as I was fortunate enough to acquire some short ends of my favourite English variety, I took the opportunity of using some for this particular project.

This is a fairly simple exercise combining faceplate and spindle turning. It also provides a test of repetition turning skills in producing the four 'identical' legs.

Design considerations

The example in Fig 8.1 was copied from a stool I bought for a song at a car-boot sale, and it would be difficult to design anything more traditional. It is sturdy without looking too heavy and clumsy. For stability, the four legs are splayed so that the bottom of each is outside the line of a perpendicular projected from the edge of the seat. For comfort, the edges of the seat are well rounded over and the top is also slightly dished.

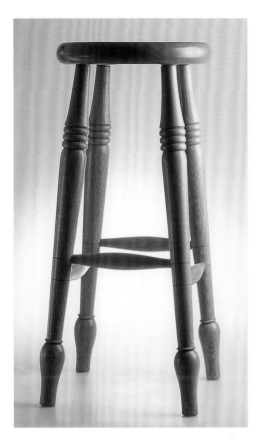

Fig 8.1 The completed bar stool

The height of the stool can be made to suit: what might be comfortable for a tall person will not be ideal for a person much shorter in stature. The measurements given in the illustrations for this project are therefore only a guide, and can be adjusted according to personal preference.

Choice and preparation of stock

In addition to pine and oak, ash, elm and beech are also eminently suitable. Ideally, the top should be in one piece and quarter-sawn to minimize warping. This may not always be possible, however, and there is nothing wrong with edge-jointing two or three narrower boards. (This process is described in all standard books on joinery and cabinetmaking.)

The timber for the legs and stretchers should be chosen with great care, as it is essential that clean, straight-grained pieces are used. The piece of timber used for the top should have one side — the intended underside — planed to a smooth finish. If possible, all the component parts should be cut from the same board to give a good grain and colour match.

Order of work

The underside of the seat is marked out with diagonal lines, and from their intersection an 11¾in (298mm) circle is struck with dividers. The positions of the four holes are then marked in on the diagonal lines at a distance of 4⅜in (111mm) from the centre. All four marks are best reinforced with a pointed awl to ensure positive location for the drill bit. A pilot hole to accommodate the woodscrew chuck is also required on the dead-centre mark, and then the stock can be brought to a circle on the bandsaw.

Boring the seat holes

There are several methods of doing this, and probably the easiest and best is to make use of a pillar drill. If a pillar drill is not available, all the holes can be bored on the lathe with the help of suitable jigs, as described later in Chapter 10.

Fig 8.2 provides constructional details of a jig for use with the pillar drill. It is nothing more than two pieces of MDF (medium-density fibreboard) hinged together, with the lower section drilled and counterbored to enable it to

Fig 8.2 Constructional details of boring jig

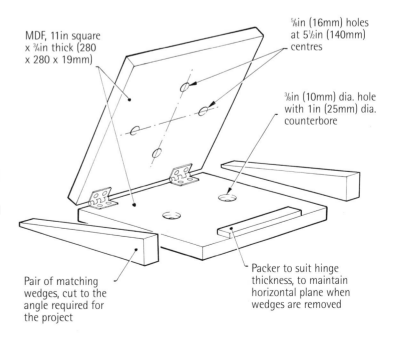

MDF, 11in square x ¾in thick (280 x 280 x 19mm)

⅝in (16mm) holes at 5½in (140mm) centres

⅜in (10mm) dia. hole with 1in (25mm) dia. counterbore

Pair of matching wedges, cut to the angle required for the project

Packer to suit hinge thickness, to maintain horizontal plane when wedges are removed

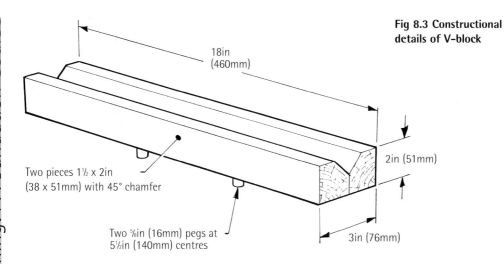

Fig 8.3 Constructional details of V-block

18in (460mm)

2in (51mm)

3in (76mm)

Two pieces 1½ x 2in (38 x 51mm) with 45° chamfer

Two ⅝in (16mm) pegs at 5½in (140mm) centres

be bolted to the pillar-drill table with no part of the bolt heads protruding. This type of jig allows for the insertion of a pair of matching wedges positioned at opposite sides, the angle of the wedges corresponding to the intended splay of the legs. The upper table is also bored with two pairs of holes at right angles to one another, at 5½in (140mm) centres. These will accommodate the ⅝in (16mm) diameter pegs on the underside of the V-block in which the legs — or any round stock — are cradled while being bored.

The V-block, shown in Fig 8.3, is simply two pieces of 1½ x 2in (38 x 51mm), with a 45° chamfer worked on each piece, glued and screwed together. Two pieces of ⅝in (16mm) dowel are sunk in the underside to fit in the corresponding holes in the top platform.

By referring to the half-elevations shown in Fig 8.4, it will be seen that the angle of the wedges for drilling the seat is 7° (90 - 83°) and the angle for the stretchers is 5° (90 - 85°). These can now be set out using a protractor and adjustable bevel, and cut to size on the bandsaw.

In the interests of safety, the seat should be securely clamped to the jig while boring the ⅞in (22mm) diameter holes. (Please note that the clamps have been removed in the photograph for clarity.) I use a sawtooth bit, making sure that the depth stop on the pillar drill is correctly adjusted to prevent boring the holes too deep. To ensure accurate drilling, the diagonal pencil lines on the underside of the seat must be lined up with the centre of the pillar, as shown in Fig 8.5.

Fig 8.4 Half-elevations showing method of determining true angles of legs and stretchers

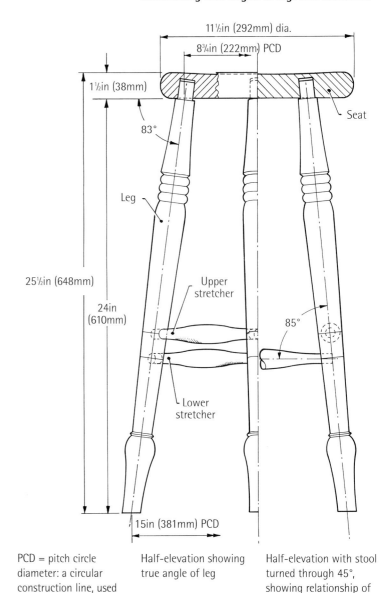

11½in (292mm) dia.

8¾in (222mm) PCD

1½in (38mm)

83°

Leg

Seat

Upper stretcher

85°

25½in (648mm)

24in (610mm)

Lower stretcher

15in (381mm) PCD

PCD = pitch circle diameter: a circular construction line, used for spacing holes or slots

Half-elevation showing true angle of leg

Half-elevation with stool turned through 45°, showing relationship of stretcher to leg

Fig 8.5 Boring jig in use for the seat holes. The tapered 7° wedges can be clearly seen, as can the method of lining up the pencil marks with the central pillar of the drill press

Fig 8.6 Rounding over the seat edges. Note that the gouge is well over on its side (flute facing the direction of cut) and being pulled from small to large diameter

With the four holes bored, the blank can now be mounted on the screw chuck and, with the lathe running at about 1000rpm, both the face and edge can be brought into balance with a ⅜in (10mm) bowl gouge turned well over on its side. This will ensure that only the supported part of the tool edge will be in contact with the whirling wood, thus avoiding any tendency to dig in.

The radius on the edge is formed with the same tool, again used well over on its side and pulled towards you, that is, from small to large diameter, which means cutting with the grain (Fig 8.6). The radius can be refined with a square-ended scraper if necessary.

The slight dishing on the seat top is easily achieved with the bowl gouge, followed by refining cuts with a domed scraper. Complete the seat by sanding down to about 320-grit paper.

Legs

These are prepared from 2in (51mm) stock and cut to their finished length. Careful study of Fig 8.7 will assist in the preparation of a full-size marking stick or 'rod'. These are invaluable in repetition turning, and all the salient profile points, stretcher locations and various

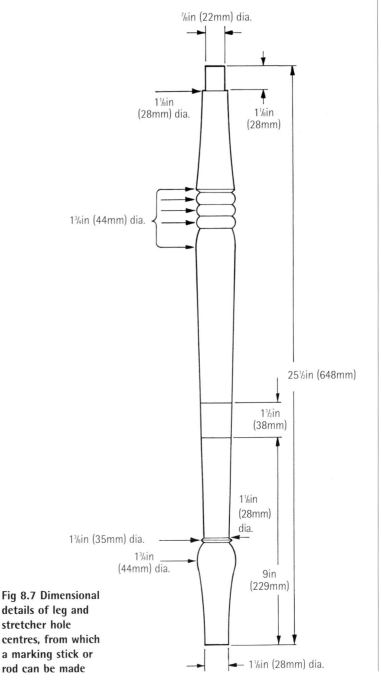

Fig 8.7 Dimensional details of leg and stretcher hole centres, from which a marking stick or rod can be made

⅞in (22mm) dia.

1⅛in (28mm) dia.

1⅛in (28mm)

1¾in (44mm) dia.

25½in (648mm)

1½in (38mm)

1⅛in (28mm) dia.

1⅜in (35mm) dia.

1¾in (44mm) dia.

9in (229mm)

1⅛in (28mm) dia.

Fig 8.8 Typical sizing stick for use when only one set of callipers is available

diameters can be marked on them. The rod can be made from thick card, plywood or thin-section wood.

There are four main diameters to size in to on this particular design, and if you possess only one set of callipers you may well wish to make a sizing stick as shown in Fig 8.8. This can be a piece of scrap wood turned down to a tapered cylinder, with shallow chisel nicks on the appropriate diameters. Using a sizing stick is much quicker and more accurate than using a ruler.

I have several sets of callipers, and my method is to mark the four diameters permanently on the rod and colour-code them to identical-coloured tape stuck to the callipers. This provides for very quick setting up, and also helps to avoid using the wrong set to size in.

Mount the first leg between centres at about 2000rpm and reduce the stock to a parallel cylinder, making use of the calliper set at 1¾in (44mm) to arrive at the thickest diameter. Move the toolrest close to the work and lodge the rod on it, taking care that it is accurately lined up. Now take a pencil and scribe in the salient points on the whirling stock. For accurate location of the pencil I usually use a three-cornered file to make a series of V-grooves on the leading edge of the rod. Fig 8.9 shows the rod in use.

The other three sizing cuts can now be made. The parting tool is used in the one-handed mode and the calliper is held in the other hand. The most important sizing is the ⅞in (22mm) spigot at the top of each leg, which will fit into the corresponding holes on the underside of the seat. These must be a good push fit. It should be noted that I have deliberately left a slight shoulder at the base of the spigot, which prevents the leg being

Fig 8.9 Making use of the marking stick to transfer the salient points on to the turned cylinder

hammered in too far and possibly breaking through the top of the seat.

Profiling can now commence, using the toe of the ½in (13mm) skew chisel to make V-cuts on the marks indicating the three beads near the top of the leg. The same tool can be used (either the toe or the heel) to develop them to the finished half-round profile. Alternatively, a parting tool or a spindle gouge can be used to achieve the same result.

The taper between the beads and the ⅞in (22mm) spigot can then be formed with either a roughing-out gouge, a spindle gouge or, if you are competent enough, a ½in (13mm) skew chisel.

The long taper between the bottom of the three beads and the 1⅜in (35mm) diameter *pointed* bead near the bottom of the leg is best formed with the roughing-out gouge. If this tool is very sharp, it will leave an acceptable finish. You may prefer to finish the taper with a skew chisel, but this tool does not necessarily guarantee a better finish, particularly on some timbers with pronounced interlocking grain. In both cases, it will probably be necessary to steady the workpiece with one hand to prevent whip, and the resultant spiral effect on the

Fig 8.10 Planing the long taper with a skew chisel, using the left hand as a steady

surface of the wood. Fig 8.10 shows a 1in (25mm) skew chisel being used.

The final shaping at the bottom of the leg is completed with the aid of the ½in (13mm) skew and the roughing-out gouge. I always think it advisable to make a slight chamfer at the very bottom of the leg to prevent break-out of the end grain.

The positions of the stretchers can now be marked on the leg. I prefer to use the toe of a skew chisel to make a slight V-cut, which not only assists accurate drill location but also adds to the visual appeal.

The leg can now be sanded, commencing with nothing coarser than 150-grit paper and going through various grades to about 320 grit. A handful of shavings applied to the whirling wood will burnish oak to a pleasing shine, and also highlight any scratches caused by careless sanding.

When satisfied with the finish, position the leg behind the lathe on a couple of V-blocks for reference, and then make the other three legs to match.

Stretchers

These are prepared from 1¼in-square stock (32 x 32mm). To take into account the splay of the legs, the upper stretcher is cut to a length of 8⅞in (225mm), and the lower one to 9⅛in (232mm). I use a ½in (13mm) diameter drive centre, which allows me to cut the ⅝in (16mm) spigots without fouling the metal. The shape of the stretchers is simple, and the whole profile can be fashioned with a roughing-out gouge. It will be seen from Fig 8.11 that the last ¾in (19mm) at each end is turned to a parallel ⅝in (16mm) diameter. This, of course, will be the spigot that fits into the corresponding-size hole to be bored in the legs.

Repeat the sanding process, as described above, on each stretcher.

Upper stretcher

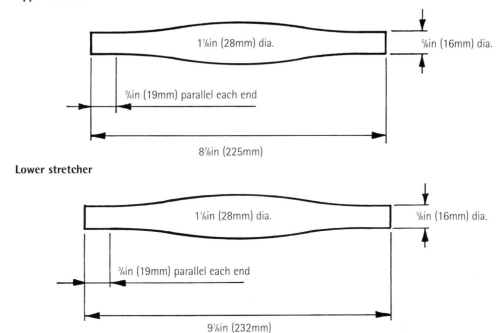

1⅛in (28mm) dia.　　　　⅝in (16mm) dia.

¾in (19mm) parallel each end

8⅞in (225mm)

Lower stretcher

1⅛in (28mm) dia.　　　　⅝in (16mm) dia.

¾in (19mm) parallel each end

9⅛in (232mm)

Fig 8.11 Dimensional details of the stretchers

Boring the stretcher holes

Fig 8.12 shows a cutaway section of a leg and the relationship of the two blind stretcher holes. It will be necessary to fix the drilling jig at 90° to the fixing used when boring the holes in the underside of the seat. It would otherwise not be possible to bore the holes in the required positions, because the central pillar of the drilling machine would prevent it.

The two pegs in the V-block are located in the corresponding holes of the drilling jig, and the two 5° wedges inserted between the hinged tables. It is *vitally important* to arrange each leg to be bored so that the bottom of the leg is to the right when viewed from the front; otherwise the stretchers will leave the legs in the wrong plane! Fig 8.13 shows the correct set-up.

To provide accurate radial boring, the V-cradle must be positioned so that the centre point of the drill bit locates exactly in the centre of the V formed by the chamfers.

Start the process by boring the *lower* stretcher hole in all four legs to the required depth, which is determined by the depth stop on the drill press.

Fig 8.12 Cutaway section of leg, showing the 'blind' stretcher holes

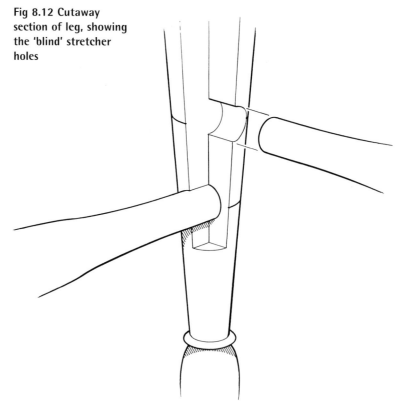

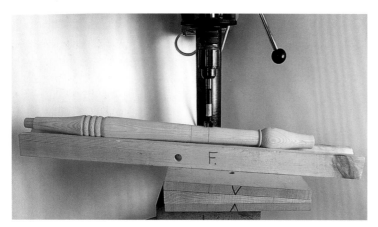

Fig 8.13 Method of boring the *lower* stretcher hole. Note that, with the 5° wedges inserted from the end opposite the hinges, the bottom of the leg *must* be positioned to the right of the operator when viewed from the front

The holes for the upper stretchers can now be commenced, but it is important to understand that we require (for the want of a better expression) two left-hand holes and two right-hand holes. This can be achieved easily by inserting a short length of ⅝in (16mm) dowel in the previously bored lower stretcher hole. Then bore the upper hole in two only of the legs with the dowel facing towards the central pillar of the drill press, and with the drill bit at 90° to the dowel (Fig 8.14). The two opposite-hand holes are

Fig 8.14 Method of boring for the *right-hand* upper stretcher. A ⅝in (16mm) dowel has been inserted in the previously bored lower hole. It must be positioned at 90° to the drill bit and facing towards the central pillar of the drill press

drilled with the dowel facing the operator (Fig 8.15). This all sounds very complicated, but it isn't really, and careful study of Figs 8.13-8.15 should clarify the process.

Assembly

It is advisable to dry-fit all the component parts before glue is applied. I use a PVA glue, smearing each joint with a light application, commencing the assembly by fitting the legs into the seat holes only about ¼in (6mm) deep. By springing the legs open I am able to insert each stretcher in the leg holes so that they 'bottom'. The stool is then turned upside down, the top resting on a clean sheet of thick cardboard, and the legs are carefully hammered home. If the jointing is good there is no need to use clamping devices.

Finishing

You may prefer to apply your choice of finish as each component part is completed on the lathe. A sealed and waxed finish lends itself to this choice, although great care must be taken to avoid getting wax on the joints before the gluing process. An alternative is to use tung oil or Danish oil. It will probably require a minimum of three applications with a 24-hour interval between each coat, but the finish is extremely durable.

I chose to spray the completed project with two coats of sanding base coat, followed by the application of a soft paste wax, and am more than satisfied with the results.

Fig 8.16 The full-size drawing of the rod and sizers used in making a baluster

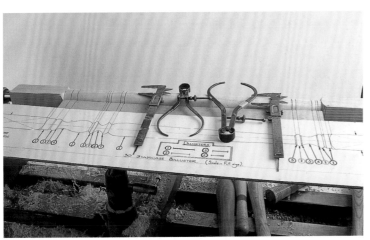

Fig 8.15 Method of boring for the *left-hand* upper stretcher. This time the dowel must face in the opposite direction, towards the operator

PROJECT

Staircase baluster

The design of these is usually determined by the architect or customer. A typical example is the one illustrated, which was made following a drawing supplied by a firm of shopfitters. The drawing was small-scale, so the first task was to reproduce it full-size on some thick card and number the various key diameters.

Again it is necessary to prepare a 'rod' or marking stick. Because square sections are to be left on the balusters at both ends, the rod needs to be made slightly different from the one used for the bar stool. Here, a piece of thick card, the full length of the baluster, was stuck to a piece of thin plywood. The length of the plywood corresponds to the measurement between the square sections, and protrudes to the front of the card by about 1½in (38mm). The reason for this will become obvious later. The salient design features are projected to the front edge, and the key diameters colour-coded on the rod and callipers (Fig 8.16), as was done for the bar stool.

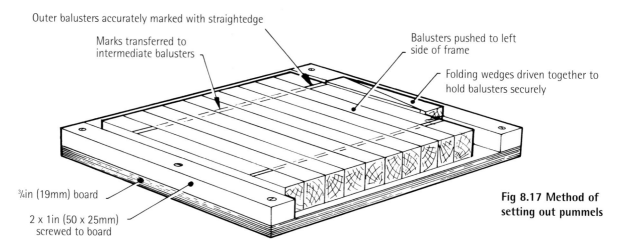

Outer balusters accurately marked with straightedge

Marks transferred to
intermediate balusters

Balusters pushed to left
side of frame

Folding wedges driven together to
hold balusters securely

¾in (19mm) board

2 x 1in (50 x 25mm)
screwed to board

**Fig 8.17 Method of
setting out pummels**

For this particular order, 48 balusters were
required. It is essential in this type of work for
each piece of wood to be accurately centred;
also, the extent of the 'pummels' or square
sections needs to be carefully marked. My
method of speeding up the marking of the
pummels is to lay about ten pieces of stock on
a sheet of plywood or chipboard on to which I
have screwed three pieces of wood to form 90°
angles. The intended balusters are laid out on
the device and secured with a pair of folding
wedges. It is necessary to mark out two of the
balusters initially with pencil and try square,
and these must be positioned one at each end.
The intermediate pieces are marked by laying a
straightedge across these marks and pencilling
all the way across (Fig 8.17).

Marking the centres on every spindle using
the method of drawing diagonal lines would be
time-consuming and extremely tedious. There are
several quicker, still accurate, methods. Perhaps
the easiest is to mount a piece of wood on the
screw chuck, turn it to a cylinder and then form a

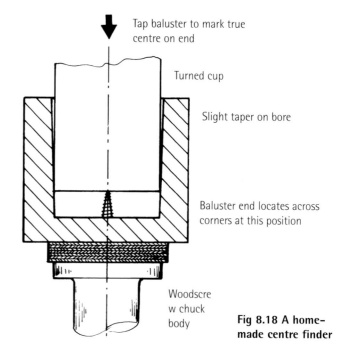

Tap baluster to mark true
centre on end

Turned cup

Slight taper on bore

Baluster end locates across
corners at this position

Woodscrew chuck
body

**Fig 8.18 A home-
made centre finder**

Fig 8.19 The home-made centre finder in use

tapered hole in the 'open end' large enough to
take the square section of the baluster. The hole
must be deep enough for the tip of the
woodscrew to be exposed so that it can prick the
end of the inserted baluster. When forming the
tapered hole with the parting tool, care must be
taken not to foul the screw. As the required
depth is neared, leave a narrow cone of wood in
the centre whilst removing the remainder of the
waste wood to the required depth. The cone can
be removed by unscrewing the stock from the
chuck and cutting it away with a gouge. Fig 8.18
gives details of how the centre-finder is made
and Fig 8.19 shows it in use.

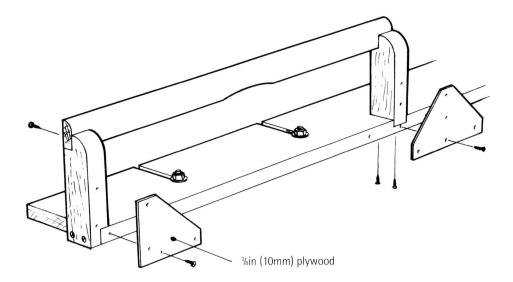

Fig 8.20 A home-made wooden toolrest

⅜in (10mm) plywood

Turnings of this length and section — the example is 30in long, 1⅝in square (762 x 41 x 41mm) — can present problems even for the experienced turner. The greatest of these problems is 'whip'. Additionally, unless you have a toolrest which spans the length of the work, you will be forever moving the toolrest about, which is both time-consuming and frustrating. If a metal toolrest as used in the photographs is not available, the problem can be overcome by making a wooden toolrest that bolts to the bench. This device is adjustable because of the slots in the base. The piece forming the actual rest is interchangeable for different rest lengths if necessary. Fig 8.20 provides details of the construction.

The problems associated with long, slender turnings are that the tools tend to deflect the wood from its true axial path, and that in many cases the wood starts to whip even without the application of the tools. If this is not prevented in some way, the wood will bounce off the tools and most likely grab and dig in. The surface of the timber will also take on a shallow spiral effect and will not be turned truly round. There are several things that can be done to minimize these problems:

1 Reduce the speed of the lathe.
2 Slacken off the tailstock pressure as much as possible.
3 Leave the smallest diameters in the design till the end.
4 Break the design down into sections and join afterwards. Turnings with square sections,

Fig 8.21 A typical metal steady, made for the Woodfast lathe

like balusters and newel posts, lend themselves to this.
5 Make use of a back stay or 'steady'.
6 Use one of your hands in the 'supporting technique' (see pages 60–1).
7 Take fine cuts with sharp tools used in strict bevel-rubbing mode. Scraping methods mean that there is more resistance to the tool and the workpiece will be deflected a great deal more. This inevitably leads to a dig-in. Be aware that blunt tools, particularly the skew chisel, can also produce this spiralling effect, even when the work is not slender.

There are many types of 'steadies' available, and some lathe manufacturers supply them. Fig 8.21 shows a typical steady for the Woodfast lathe.

Fig 8.22 A home-made steady

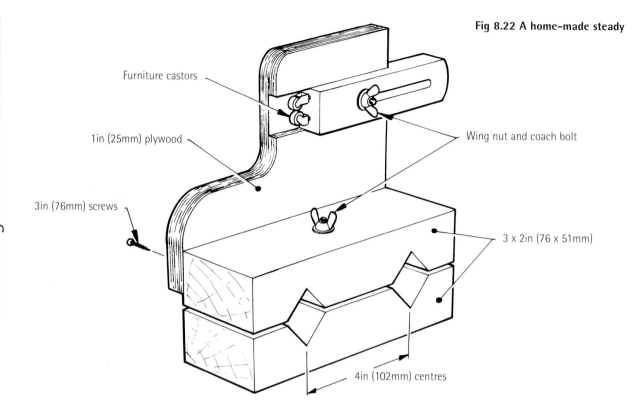

Furniture castors

1in (25mm) plywood

3in (76mm) screws

Wing nut and coach bolt

3 x 2in (76 x 51mm)

4in (102mm) centres

An alternative is to make your own. These can take various forms and you will need to design one to suit your particular lathe. The example shown in Fig 8.22 is suitable for lathes with twin bed bars and it is not difficult to construct. It is important that any steady is easy to move from side to side, and with this in mind the two pieces with the V-notches are clamped to the bed with a bolt and wing nut. Wing nuts are also used on the two bolts securing the slotted cross piece to the upright. The slot in the cross piece is cut out by boring a series of holes and squaring out with a carpenter's chisel. This slot allows for movement back and forth to suit varying diameters of stock. The castors need to be tightly embedded, and accordingly the holes for the shanks must be slightly undersize. It is *vital* that the castors are positioned so that a centre line drawn between them is exactly in line with the centre of the wood.

There are disadvantages with all types of mechanical steadies: they tend to be noisy; the resultant friction can char the workpiece (it is not uncommon for the workpiece to start smoking); and more importantly, as far as the professional turner is concerned, they most certainly slow down the rate of output.

Because of the disadvantages mentioned, the professional turner will do his utmost to manage without a mechanical steady and rely purely on the supporting technique. To be able to do so requires a great deal of practice, but perseverance and determination will be rewarded.

To make use of any steady, it is first of all necessary to turn the stock (or part of it) to a cylinder. The steady is then positioned in the most advantageous place, usually somewhere near to the middle of the length of wood. Having prepared your stock ready to be turned, mount a piece in the lathe and set the speed between 1000 and 1500rpm. I normally arrange for the thickest part of the baluster to be nearest to the headstock, because I prefer to steady with my left hand and work from left to right. The pencilled lines indicating the pummels should be clearly seen on the whirling wood, and the first step is to cut these with the toe of the ½in (13mm) skew chisel. Start with light cuts taking out small chips, repeating the process from either side of the inside line until the cut is continuous round the wood and to the desired depth. The action of the skew to produce a radiused shoulder is, if you recall, one of rolling and lifting. The area between the

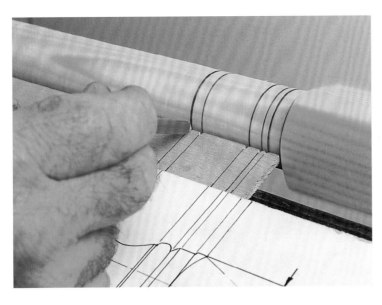

Fig 8.23 The rod being used to mark salient points on the baluster

pummels is then reduced to a cylinder with a roughing-out gouge, rolling it well over on its side when cutting adjacent to the square sections to avoid fouling the whirling corners.

The rod and pencil can now be used, lathe running, to mark the salient design features. It will be obvious now why the plywood should be cut to the length of the turned section, for otherwise it would foul the square pummels (Fig 8.23).

If you intend making use of a steady, now is the time to position it to your best advantage

Fig 8.24 The baluster after the sizing in has been completed

— with the lathe not running, of course. Making use of the previously prepared sizers and a ¼in (6mm) parting tool, cut in the key diameters at the appropriate places. When these have been completed the workpiece will be as shown in Fig 8.24.

The beads and coves are then cut with chisels and gouges, and the long taper can be fashioned with the roughing-out gouge. Remember that this tool, if very sharp, will produce an acceptable finish on many kinds of wood if it is angled to induce a paring action and the bevel pushed boldly on to the surface of the wood. Fig 8.25 shows a skew chisel being used to make a planing cut from left to right (downhill) along the tapered section.

Fig 8.25 A skew chisel being used to make a planing cut on the tapered section

Fig 8.26 The completed baluster, still mounted on the lathe. It can now be set up on a pair of V–blocks behind the lathe to serve as a master copy

The necessary sanding can now be done, and a handful of shavings can be used to burnish up the surface. The completed baluster is shown in Fig 8.26.

With continued practice at this type of turning, not only will your skills improve rapidly, but you will develop a good eye that will eventually eliminate the need to do other than a very little sizing in.

PROJECT

A plinth

Most people associate copy-turning with turning between centres only. It is true that the bulk of my copy work falls under this heading, but nevertheless, a good deal of faceplate work also needs to be copied. As an introduction to the methods I use, I shall describe the making of an attractive plinth or base which can be put to a variety of uses.

As always, the first step is to make a full-size drawing on a piece of card which can later be stuck to a piece of plywood. Project the salient points to both the edge and the side of the plywood and again make the V-notches for pencil location (Fig 8.27).

The disc, which should be slightly oversize both in thickness and diameter, is first of all turned to a true cylinder with the ³⁄₈in (10mm) bowl gouge (lathe speed about 1000rpm). The rod and pencil are now used to mark the desired thickness (Fig 8.28). After positioning

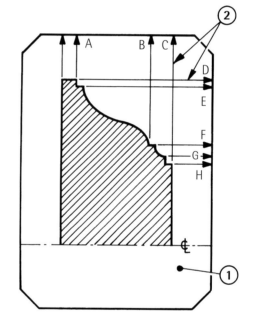

Fig 8.27 Preparing the rod.

1 Produce a full–size half-template

2 Produce projection lines A, B, C, D, E, F, G, H

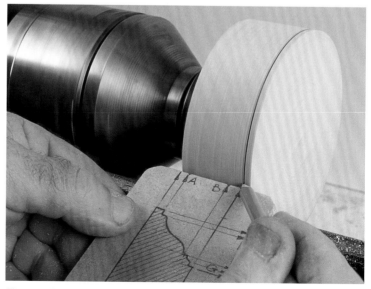

Fig 8.28 Rod and pencil being used to mark the thickness of the plinth

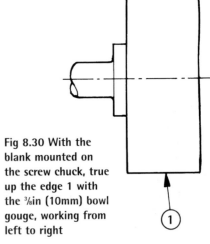

Fig 8.29 The rod being used to mark out the face of the plinth

Fig 8.30 With the blank mounted on the screw chuck, true up the edge 1 with the ⅜in (10mm) bowl gouge, working from left to right

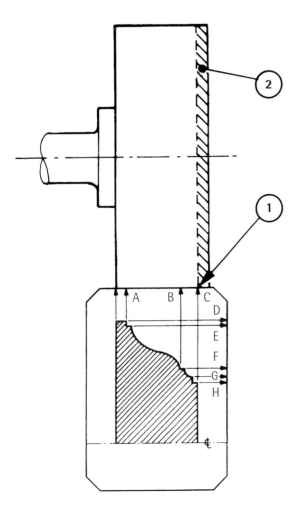

Fig 8.31
1 The rod is offered up to the whirling disc and the finished thickness C is pencilled in
2 Remove the waste wood with the bowl gouge and square-ended scraper

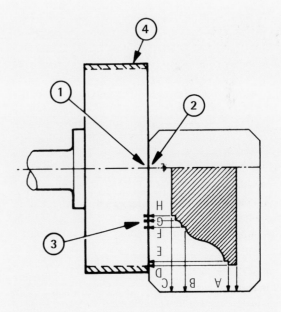

Fig 8.32 1 Mark the exact centre on the face of the plinth
2 Line up the centre of the rod with the centre mark on the wood
3 Pencil in intermediate points E, F, G, H
4 Pencil in the finished diameter D and remove the waste wood with the bowl gouge, working from left to right

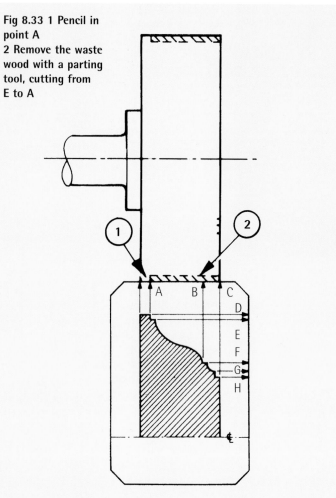

Fig 8.33 1 Pencil in point A
2 Remove the waste wood with a parting tool, cutting from E to A

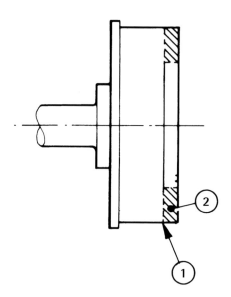

Fig 8.34 1 Pencil in point B
2 Remove the waste wood with a parting tool, cutting from F to B

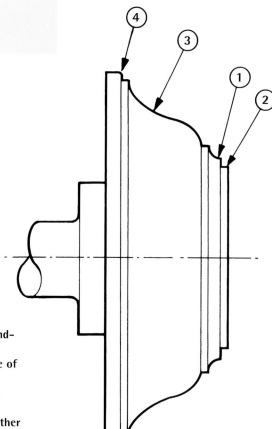

Fig 8.35 1 The cove is shaped with either a small gouge or a small round-nose scraper
2 The outer fillet is cut with the toe of the skew chisel
3 The ogee section is formed with a small gouge and scrapers
4 The small radius is formed with either gouge or scraper

Fig 8.36 The completed plinth

the toolrest across the face of the disc, the waste can be removed with the bowl gouge and square-ended scraper.

The face of the disc can now be marked out using the rod and pencil (Fig 8.29). The sequence of cutting as shown in Figs 8.30 to 8.35 can now be undertaken, making use of the bowl gouge, parting tool and scrapers. Fig 8.36 shows the completed plinth.

All the above projects are fairly straightforward, but the reader will have learned something about the methods used and the simple appliances which can be made to assist. (There are other methods of copying, of course, and all kinds of other gadgets that may assist.)

SUMMARY

1 Students should attempt simple copy-turning, virtually from day one.
2 Planning and setting out are vital stages in the process.
3 Always make a full-size drawing of the project, from which the rod is prepared.
4 Speed is not important in the learning process, but accuracy and concentration are essential.
5 Home-made wooden toolrests to span the full length of a project are simple to make and avoid the irritation of constantly moving the short rests from side to side.
6 The 'steadying' of long, slender turnings can be achieved either by using the supporting technique or by means of a mechanical steady.

Chapter 9
Sanding and Finishing

It is said that the finish can make or mar any woodworking project, and woodturning is no exception. It is also true to say that no matter how well any finish is applied, it will not disguise poor workmanship and the lack of care that has gone before. A good finish or polish applied to any piece of poor-quality turnery will not improve the appearance. In fact, it will have the opposite effect – that is, it will only serve to highlight the shortcomings of the turner. It follows, therefore, that both the turning and the finishing techniques must be of a high standard if the maker's reputation is to remain 'untarnished'.

Equally important is the *durability* of your chosen finish or polish. You will certainly not have customers coming back for more if you make use of a finish that will not stand up to its intended use and becomes tatty after only a short while.

The need for a finish

Very few woodworking projects of any kind are left in their natural state, and there are usually several reasons why an appropriate finish must be applied:

1 To enhance the beauty of the wood by bringing out the grain and colour.
2 To protect the surface from dust, grime, fingermarks, etc.
3 To seal the surface. This helps to limit the amount of moisture absorbed.
4 To enable domestic artefacts to be wiped with damp cloths or even washed.
5 To change the natural colour of the wood by staining.

In short, the object of applying a finish to woodwork is to seal, protect and enhance its natural beauty.

However, as emphasized above, a good finish applied to poor work is no better than a poor finish applied to a piece of exquisite turning. The success or otherwise of a piece of completed turnery depends on *every* step from preparation to finish.

What are the steps?

Most of these steps have already been dealt with. I have stressed the need to make use of quality tools that have been carefully and accurately ground to the 'acceptable degree of sharpness'. I have urged you to discipline yourself to *practise, practise, practise* in the forming of the basic profiles using cutting techniques, wherever possible, to leave the best possible surface finish straight off the tools.

Without such preparation you will need to spend a disproportionate amount of time sanding your work to get a reasonable surface to apply the finish or polish. Too much sanding destroys the 'crispness' of a piece, so it must be your aim to minimize this step towards your goal.

In most cases, however, it is inevitable that a certain amount of sanding will have to be done (this amount being inversely proportional to the ability of the turner) to remove surface blemishes. It should not be used to *shape* the wood, but merely to improve the surface.

Sanding is a boring, tedious chore and I loathe it. Nevertheless, you must discipline yourself to go patiently through the correct sequence of procedures if the best results are to be achieved.

You will discover faceplate work will require considerably more sanding than spindle turning, and side grain sands much more easily than end grain.

Experience will teach you that sanding can sometimes make the surface more uneven than it was before. For example, knots, being harder than the surrounding wood, will tend to become 'raised'. Timbers in which there is a pronounced difference in density between the quick-growing spring growth and slower-forming summer growth will sand unevenly. The darker rings (the hardest and densest) will also become raised. As an experiment, turn a small bowl in Columbian pine and sand it with some 100-grit paper. You will only have to run your fingers over the surface to realize how uneven and 'rippled' the surfaces of such timbers can become.

Unnecessary sanding should obviously be avoided. For example, I turn a good many newel posts and balusters in Scots pine which I know will be painted. If the timber is of good quality, I am able to avoid any sanding at all, the finish from the tool being more than satisfactory for a painted finish. Similar work in hemlock, which usually has little 'life' in it, gets a quick application of 100-grit paper, again good enough for paint application. Such work carried out in oak or mahogany, or any timber where a 'clear finish' is to be applied, demands a much more sympathetic approach, and several grades of paper may be needed to achieve the desired finish.

Before we come to the sanding stage, the first step is to examine your piece of turnery closely for any defects such as worm, insect or nail holes, slight cracks or shakes. These will need to be 'stopped', and there are many proprietary brands of 'stopping' on the market. This needs to be pressed well into the defect (use a waste piece of wood, not a tool blade), and it is as well to leave it slightly proud of the surface to take account of any shrinkage in the drying process. Most of these products are fairly slow-drying and it may be necessary to leave the piece overnight before commencing the sanding.

Many different shades of stopping are available, but even so, on special projects it is advisable to test for colour-matching on a waste piece of identical wood. Mixing two colours together sometimes gives a better match.

Types of abrasive material

Although we invariably use the term 'sanding', modern woodturners rarely use either sand- or glasspaper. These have been superseded by garnet paper, aluminium oxide and silicone carbide papers. All are quite suitable, and the latter is made up of waterproof backing and glue, being more commonly known as 'wet-and-dry' paper.

Abrasives are graded by numbers: the higher the number, the finer the paper. I normally make use of four grades of paper in my complete finishing process. For between-centres turning, I rarely use anything coarser than 150 grit, other than on turnings to be painted. The sanding is completed by then making use of 220 grit, which on some timbers is the only

grade I use. After the application of sealer or polish, I generally use 320 grit to 'cut it back'. (**NB**: Any liquid applied to timber has the effect of raising the grain, this effect varying from timber to timber. The term 'cutting back' merely means sanding very lightly with a fine abrasive to restore the original smoothness.)

On faceplate turnings, I generally start the sanding process with 100 grit (if I am hand-sanding), and then go on to the finer 150 and 220 grits to obtain the desired finish. The 320 grit is used as described above.

The selection of grit size for the initial sanding is important, and only experience and knowledge of timber will provide an adequate guide. Too fine a paper may not remove the blemishes, but too coarse a paper will inflict more damage than was originally on the surface. For example, I turn a good deal of mahogany for cabinetmaking projects and I know making use of anything coarser than 220 grit will mean that circular scratches will be visible when the project is polished.

It must be appreciated that nearly all sanding is *across* the grain, and the depth of the circular scratches is increased as grit size is increased. To avoid these unsightly scratches, my advice is to use nothing coarser than the grit sizes I have mentioned. Wherever possible, it is advisable, before going to the next finer grade of paper, to stop the lathe and sand *along* the grain. It does help!

For best results, before proceeding to the finer papers, all the scratch marks from the initial sanding should have been obliterated by the intermediate sanding.

Methods of sanding

In the interests of safety, the toolrest must be removed. Prepare the paper by tearing it neatly into four equal parts and then fold each piece into three. This provides three sanding faces and helps to prevent the frictional heat becoming too uncomfortable for the supporting fingers.

Where the lathe has a good range of speeds (and it is not a major operation to change them), I normally 'drop down a cog' from the turning speed. I find it more efficient, and the

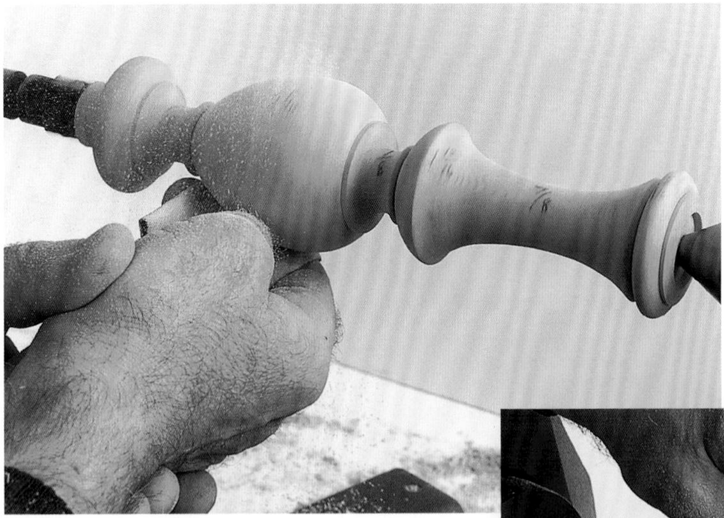

Fig 9.1 Sanding in the 'safe position'. Note that the toolrest has been removed

Fig 9.2 Making use of a spindle gouge to sand a cove

frictional heat transmitted to the supporting fingers is certainly reduced.

For the majority of the sanding, the paper can be held between the fingers and the thumb and additional support can be given by the other hand clasping the wrist.

Wherever possible, sand *underneath* the whirling wood, because in the event of the paper or fingers 'grabbing', the centrifugal force throws both clear of trouble. (You can see now why the toolrest must be removed; Fig 9.1.)

For sanding coves, I wrap the paper round an appropriately sized spindle gouge to ensure the desired profile is maintained (Fig 9.2). V-cuts and fillets are sanded with the edges of the paper, but great care is needed so as not to destroy the crisp intersections.

On long cylinders or flowing shapes, do not dwell in one position. Keep the paper on the move and traversing in both directions to prevent scratching and the build-up of frictional heat. A trick used by some turners to prevent the fingers becoming uncomfortably hot is to use a piece of thin leather between the fingers and the paper.

A technique I employ for top-quality cabinet turnings is to wipe the whole of the turning with a damp cloth. This raises the grain and will need 'cutting back' when dry with 320-grade paper. This process is sometimes repeated several times, and is always done when the work is to be stained (mahogany and oak are often stained). Otherwise the application of the stain would raise the grain and subsequent cutting-back might well expose bare wood. Make sure clean water is used, particularly on mahogany.

On the safety aspect, be extremely careful where squares or pummels form part of the workpiece. Contact with these while sanding can lead to a severe rap on the fingers. In fact, such features are often referred to as 'knuckle knockers' in the trade.

Directing our attention now to the sanding of faceplate turnings, it will soon be evident that this is even more loathsome than sanding spindle turning. Why? Because, as mentioned earlier, end grain is much more difficult to sand satisfactorily than side grain, and therefore more sanding needs to be done, particularly if toolwork is less than perfect.

Because of my loathing of sanding, I always do my utmost to achieve the best possible finish on bowls and any type of faceplate work before I start the sanding. Here are a couple of tips to help towards that better finish. Stop the lathe and examine the bowl for rough patches of end grain. Some timbers are notorious for this, but it can be improved as follows:

1 Soak the rough patches with sanding sealer. I prefer the cellulose-based variety and I always thin it down with cellulose thinners (about 50-50) for this purpose. Danish oil can also be used, providing it is compatible with the intended finishing product. The reason why I prefer the sanding sealer is that I use it as a basecoat for *every* finish I use, be it wax, friction polish, pre-catalysed lacquer or Danish oil.

The soaking of the end grain has the effect of softening the fibres, and a newly sharpened scraper – I personally use a small spindle gouge, but this is not recommended for the beginner – should remove the trouble and leave a nice, smooth surface. Some timbers even resist this method, and you may have to resort to:

2 Repeating the soaking process, but this time using some kind of tool to scrape the affected area locally; that means without the lathe running. You can use either your normal turning scraper or a cabinetmaker's scraper. Sometimes I make use of a piece of broken glass, but be very careful if you do!

The bowl can now be sanded, starting with 100-grit paper. (I must confess that on really stubborn end grain I sometimes resort to 80-grit.) The safe area to sand faceplate work is in the quadrant between 6 and 9 o'clock. It is also advisable to have the fingers pointing downwards so they cannot be bent backwards against the joints, which can be very painful (Fig 9.3).

Initially, the paper will fetch off a considerable amount of dust, but gradually this diminishes to a point where virtually no dust at all is evident. This is the time to stop

Fig 9.3 Sanding in the safe area – faceplate work

and go to the next grade of paper, repeating this process until the desired surface finish is arrived at.

Finally, and on all categories of turning, I always burnish the surface with a handful of shavings, which makes the piece more pleasing to the eye.

Power sanding

Many bowl turners now use this system, which consists of foam-backed abrasive disc pads mounted in an electric drill. The abrasive discs are interchangeable by means of the Velcro system, and are available in grit sizes ranging from 60 to 400 grit. As the lathe and drill are rotating in opposite directions, frictional heat is minimized, as are the chances of inflicting those irritating scratch marks which are always likely when hand-sanding. This method is obviously much quicker than hand-sanding, and flowing-shaped bowls can be completely sanded without resorting to hand methods. Obviously, very small, ornamental or detailed bowls cannot be power-sanded, but the saving on time on many bowls is tremendous.

You will need considerable practice before you become proficient in its use, but it is worth persevering. In the interests of safety, do not try

Fig 9.4 Power-sanding the outside of the bowl

to use other than the bottom half of the disc, and sand in the quadrant described above for hand-sanding methods. Fig 9.4 shows the outside of a bowl being sanded with this method.

Be warned, however, because you may think you are in the Sahara Desert with a sandstorm raging. The dust cloud can be considerable.

The perils of dust

Power sanding conveniently leads me to the problems and perils associated with dust, which is the scourge of woodturners. Mention was made in Chapter 1, Trees and Wood, that the dust from some species, particularly the tropical hardwoods, can be harmful. I think it true to say that while some timbers are more likely to give trouble than others, dust from any source

will do nothing to improve your health. Everything possible should therefore be done to minimize exposure to and inhalation of fine dust. The least that can be done is to wear a face mask when sanding. These are available from most hardware shops and are inexpensive.

Much better protection will be given by a battery-powered respirator. These provide a constant supply of clean air through the inbuilt filters, and are deceptively lightweight and comfortable to wear. Additionally, the flip-up visor protects the eyes and face from flying debris such as loose bark and flying splinters. They are not cheap, but even so I consider it a small price to pay for such vital protection to lungs and eyes particularly. Fig 9.5 shows examples of the inexpensive dust mask and the powered respirator.

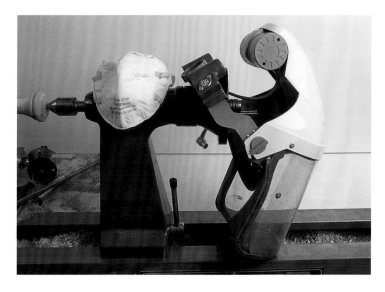

Fig 9.5 Typical examples of an inexpensive disposable face mask (left) and a modern powered respirator

Fig 9.6 Method of using a dust extractor on a piece of spindle turning so as to ensure optimum dust collection

If the turner intends to specialize in bowl work, I believe a portable dust extractor is an absolute must, but even these have their limitations. While they will efficiently collect dust from a localized area, such as when sanding a bowl, they are not so effective in collecting dust on spindle work over about 15in (380mm) long. To overcome this problem I hold the hose in one hand and sand with the other, keeping the hands close together to ensure optimum dust collection. This method is very tiring, but it is the most efficient way I know (Fig 9.6).

Staining

Many turners do not stain their turned objects at all, relying on the natural colour and beauty of the wood to speak for itself. I too avoid staining wherever possible, but some timbers – and mahogany is a perfect example – look better for it. On this and similar timbers, the colour of the wood can vary tremendously even from different parts of the same bole. The colour can be brought to a better degree of uniformity by making use of stain.

Bear in mind that staining can only make the wood a *darker* shade than the original colour, it cannot lighten it. Faceplate turnings do not take kindly to staining, as the end grain absorbs more stain than the side grain and therefore tends to go much darker in colour.

Any areas of torn grain are also likely to stain darker than the surrounding wood, which means that the preparation must be perfect.

There are many types of stain available, and I use an industrial cellulose-based stain which is easy to apply and dries evenly. It can either be applied with a rag or sprayed on, with good results from both methods.

Sealing

As stated earlier, I use a cellulose sanding sealer as a base coat for every finish I use. It seals the grain and prevents dust, fingermarks, smudges, etc. from soiling the wood. It also provides for uniform absorbency of the final finishing or polishing application. Like any liquid it will raise the grain of most timbers, but this is easily cut back to the original smooth finish with some 320-grit paper or wire wool.

Sealer can also be applied either with rag or brush. I prefer to use a good-quality varnish brush, which makes it easy to get into the nooks and crannies. The powder additive mixed in the sealer during manufacture provides for easy cutting back, and the application of two coats of sealer is not a bad finish in itself.

When applying sealer, polish, oil, etc. to a piece of wood that is mounted in the lathe, it is as well to cover the lathe bed with a dust sheet or newspaper to prevent the substance soiling the bed. It can set very hard, and movement of the toolrest and tailstock can become very difficult.

Polishing or finishing

Beginners to the craft can be forgiven if they are perplexed by the problem of choosing the most suitable finish from the bewildering variety available. Finishing woodwork of any kind is a subject and trade on its own and whole books are devoted to it. All I can hope to do is provide a summary of the finishes I consider to be the most suitable for woodturning projects.

The first piece of advice I can offer is to keep the finish as simple as possible. If you use a cellulose sanding sealer as a base coat, as I recommend, on top of this you can choose a type of finish suitable for each particular project.

Choice of finish

In deciding what kind of finish to apply, the following points must be considered:

1 Is the piece of turning intended to contain food? If so, you are restricted to a finish that does not smell or taste and is non-toxic.
2 Will the finished product be likely to be washed or wiped with a damp cloth?
3 How much handling is the object likely to get?
4 Do you require a glossy, satin or matt finish?
5 For drinking vessels, special treatment is required.

Products I use

Danish oil
I use this for turnings that come under **1** and **2** above, such as salad bowls, platters, cheese and breadboards, decorative bowls, etc. It can be applied (lathe stationary) with either rag or brush. Immediately after application I sand it in with some 320-grit wet-and-dry and then burnish it with a handful of shavings (lathe running). Successive coats can be applied at 24-hour intervals, which will produce a pleasing satin finish that will not peel, crack or chip. It is also heat- and water-resistant.

Wax
I prefer to use pure carnauba wax on extremely dense timbers, and a mixture of this and beeswax for less dense timbers. Choose a fast lathe speed and melt the wax on to the whirling wood, but take care not to overload. It can be immediately burnished up to a high gloss by using a clean rag. There are also some excellent proprietary brands of wax available, such as Bri-Wax, Chestnut, Liberon, Mr Jamiesons, Rustins and Sorby, and these come either coloured or clear. Wax finishes are suitable for articles that are not likely to be handled too much and which are intended for ornamental purposes.

Friction polish
The advantage of this type of polish is that it is simple to apply and an extremely glossy shine can be achieved in a couple of minutes.

Products such as Speedaneeze and Crafteeze are tried and trusted polishes, but because they are not particularly durable, again they are more suited to ornamental turnings which are unlikely to be continually handled.

Apply it while the wood is stationary; I think a more even coat can be applied this way. Then start the lathe and, using the same rag, apply an even pressure along the span of your turning until the desired shine is achieved. If you wear spectacles, make sure you are standing to one side when you start the lathe up. The centrifugal force sends a fine shower of polish flying in your direction and this can set very hard on the lenses and take some moving.

Fig 9.7 shows a collection of oils, waxes and friction polish.

> **WARNING:** Using rags to apply any type of finish to wood whirling round on the lathe can be dangerous, particularly on natural bark edges. If the rag 'grabs', fingers can be seriously injured. An alternative and safer method is to make use of kitchen roll or a proprietary brand of 'rag' such as that manufactured by Liberon, which is guaranteed to tear rather than trap the retaining fingers. Rags that have been soaked in finishing oil, cellulose polish, etc. are a potential fire risk (spontaneous combustion). After use, they should be kept in an airtight jar until they can be disposed of safely.

Fig 9.7 A small selection of the many suitable finishing products now available

Rustins Plastic Coating

This is ideal for drinking vessels and, although it is quite expensive and the finishing process can take some considerable time, it is worth both the expense and the effort involved. It produces a tough, mirror-like finish that is heat- and solvent-resistant. The bare wood can be stained (use the same brand) before applying the coating with either brush or spray gun. Several coats may be necessary, and full instructions are included with the product.

Pre-catalysed lacquers

These are really industrial finishes and intended to be sprayed on to the work. They provide a tough and durable surface. Although best results are achieved by spraying, they can be brushed on if they are thinned down. I use them quite frequently for polishing standard lamps, reproduction tables, etc., but then I have a spray booth providing ideal facilities.

There are numerous other types of polish, many of which are no doubt equally suitable, but I can only comment on those I have personally used. My advice is to keep the polishing process as limited and simple as possible.

DIY
Sanding Table

Such an attachment for the lathe is extremely useful for sanding the bottoms of boxes and the underneath sections of lids, plinths, bowls, etc. It is very simple to construct and the components required are a faceplate, a few discs of ¾in (19mm) plywood (on which to stick the various grades of abrasive paper), a plywood platform, and a turned stem. One end of the stem is joined to the platform and the other end is turned to a diameter that will provide a good fit in the toolrest holder on your lathe.

Fig 9.8 shows how the sanding plate is constructed and Fig 9.9 shows constructional details of the sanding table, together with a Picador protractor mitre fence. This accessory is invaluable for such jobs as truing up the edges of laminated or built-up work and sanding mitre joints. The top of the platform will require routing out to a depth and width suitable to accommodate the mitre fence, as shown in the drawing.

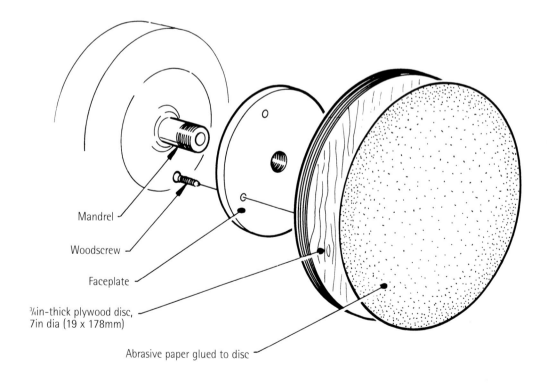

Mandrel

Woodscrew

Faceplate

¾in-thick plywood disc,
7in dia (19 x 178mm)

Abrasive paper glued to disc

**Fig 9.8
Constructional
details of the
sanding plate**

**Fig 9.9
Constructional
details of the
sanding table**

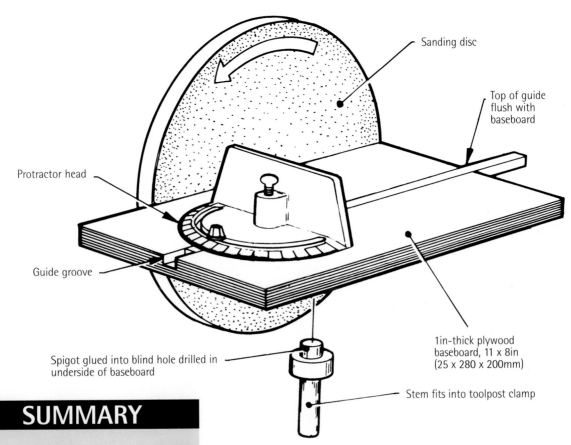

Sanding disc

Top of guide
flush with
baseboard

Protractor head

Guide groove

Spigot glued into blind hole drilled in
underside of baseboard

1in-thick plywood
baseboard, 11 x 8in
(25 x 280 x 200mm)

Stem fits into toolpost clamp

SUMMARY

1 The success or otherwise of any finish is
totally dependent on every step which leads
up to it being carried out to the very best of
your ability.

2 Sanding is boring, dusty and tedious, and
must be kept to a minimum by aiming for
the best possible finish straight off the tool.

3 In normal circumstances, grit sizes 100,
150, 220 and 320 should be adequate to
achieve the most satisfactory surface for
applying the finish.

4 Always remove the toolrest when sanding,
and wherever possible sand in the 'safe' areas
of the workpiece.

5 Always wear a dust mask or respirator, and
if possible use a dust extractor.

6 The choice of finish must be influenced to
a great extent by the intended use of the
turned piece.

7 Ensure that the final polish or finish is
compatible with any base coat that has been
applied to the piece.

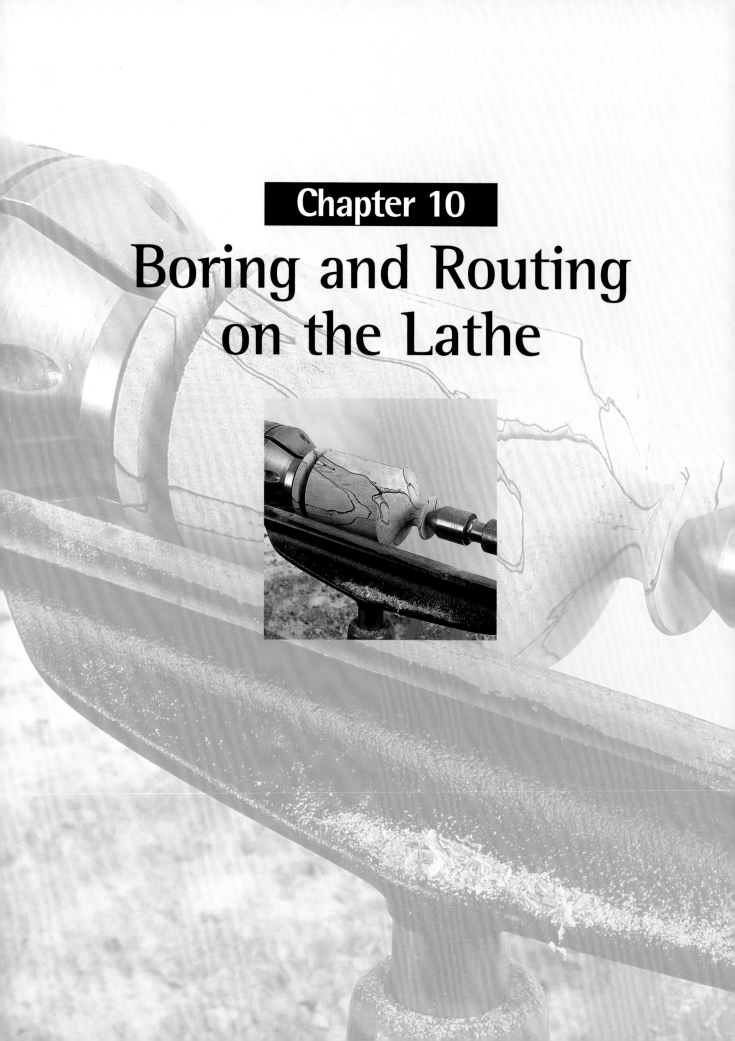

Chapter 10

Boring and Routing on the Lathe

oring holes in turned projects plays an important part in my everyday commercial turning, and this chapter describes the various types of boring bits and drills which I consider suitable for such work. Sharpening techniques and optimum speeds for boring are described, together with the use of simple jigs.

Additionally, I show how that most useful of power tools, the hand-held router, can be put to good effect for fluting and reeding sections of turned work in conjunction with simple jigs that fit on the lathe.

Finally, several projects embracing the use of boring tools are included.

Types of drill bit
(See Fig 10.1)

Engineers' twist drills

These are available in very small sizes and are suitable for drilling holes in both wood and metal. I personally do not use sizes exceeding ¼in (6mm) diameter for wood boring because I consider that larger holes can be made more efficiently with some of the bits described later. Nevertheless, twist drills are particularly useful for boring small holes in such projects as

condiment sets, and for small inlay work. They are normally sold in high-speed steel and are perhaps best purchased in sets contained in revolving drum holders; these are easily stored and inexpensive.

Sharpening

Traditionally, this type of drill was always sharpened on the grindstone by offering the drill up to the face of the grindstone so as to maintain the original angle. A rolling action is then required to maintain the existing profile, this process being repeated on both cutting edges.

It is easy to destroy the original profiles, and this will render the bit ineffective. Due to the difficulties involved, it may be an advantage to make use of one of several types of sharpening jigs available on the market which are specially made for this type of bit. They are not expensive and make sharpening quick, simple and accurate.

Fig 10.1 Drills and accessories suitable for boring on the lathe. *Below, left to right:* **engineer's twist drill, flatbit, lip and spur bit, sawtooth machine bit, Ridgway power expansive bit, Jacobs chuck (mounted on arbor) and key.** *Above:* **standard-lamp shell auger**

Suggested speeds for boring

Best results will be obtained with this type of bit if the lathe is set to run at its fastest speed. These bits may be used in the hand-held electric drill to bore holes in wood mounted on the lathe (not running, of course), in conjunction with various types of drilling jigs, when undertaking inlay work; the fast speed of the electric drill will not harm the bit.

Useful tip

As there is no pronounced point on this type of bit, they have a tendency to skid, particularly on other than flat surfaces. This of course means that the hole will not be accurately located, but the problem can be prevented by making a small hole with a pointed awl to give the bit a start.

Flatbits

These were originally intended to be used in portable electric drills, but they are also suitable for boring in the lathe. The long point facilitates accurate location even when drilling at an angle, although for many boring operations connected with woodturning the point is too long and needs to be shortened to prevent bursting through the bottom of intended blind holes. As the wood is bored with a scraping action, the bits will require frequent sharpening, but they produce a reasonably clean hole and are not expensive.

Flatbits also lend themselves to modification, such as being ground to a taper shape for boring out the insides of thimbles, etc. For special jobs where only a shallow hole is required, it is an advantage to cut down the length of the shaft to provide maximum stability and prevent flexing. They are available in sizes ranging from ¼in to 1½in (6–38mm).

Sharpening

The bit should be secured in a vice and a fine knife-edged file should be used to lightly touch up the forward cutting edges, taking care to maintain the original angle and to make an equal number of strokes on both sides, otherwise the cutters will become unbalanced and will not perform satisfactorily. If the point needs to be shortened, it is essential that centricity be maintained by sharpening both sides equally, counting the number of strokes

with the file. The same principle applies if it is decided to put a taper on the bit.

Suggested speeds for boring

As mentioned above, these bits were originally designed for use in electric drills, and consequently all sizes can be used with the lathe adjusted to its fastest speed.

Useful tip

Whether this type of bit is used in the headstock or tailstock, I always ensure that the nose or tip is located in the centre mark of the wood before I start the lathe. In the interests of safety, I consider it best to stop the lathe before withdrawing the bit from the completed hole.

Lip-and-spur bits

These are also known as **brad-point drills** and **dowel bits**, and are available in sizes ranging from ¼in to 1in (6-25mm). The brad point allows for very accurate location and also prevents skid. They perform well in both side and end grain and are particularly suited to deep-hole boring. The angled chipping bevel produces clean, accurate holes *if* the bit is entered slowly and evenly to allow the spurs to score the circumference of the hole. They are not too expensive and, apart from the sawtooth machine bits, they are probably the most useful bits to purchase.

Sharpening

Use a fine flat file to sharpen the cutters and the spurs, again ensuring an equal number of strokes is used on each so that both are kept at the same height. The brad point will only occasionally need filing, but take care to maintain centricity.

Suggested speeds for boring

Bit size	Speed (rpm)
Up to ½in (13mm)	Approx. 1500
Over ½in	Approx. 1000

Sawtooth machine bits

These are without doubt the best and most useful to the woodturner. They also happen to be the most expensive but, as in most cases with tools and equipment, you get what you pay for. Wherever possible I prefer to make use of them, as they will bore holes quickly, cleanly and accurately in end and side grain. Their efficient action requires little power, and if well maintained they are a joy to use. They are available in sizes ranging from ⅜in to 4in (10–102mm) and they all come with a ½in (13mm) shank.

Sharpening

Secure the bit in a vice and sharpen as follows:

1 The teeth should be sharpened with a small three-cornered file, each tooth receiving the same number of strokes to maintain the equal height.
2 The cutters or lifters should be sharpened with a narrow flat file, working it through the throat of the cutter, never from the top. Take the utmost care to maintain the original angle and straight edges.
3 The brad point can be sharpened occasionally with a flat file, but it is essential that centricity is maintained.

Suggested speeds for boring

The general rule is: the larger the hole to be bored, the lower the speed of the lathe, although it is appreciated that most lathes will not have the range of speeds to run at the exact rpm recommended.

Sawtooth bit size	Speed (rpm)
⅜–⅞in (10–22mm)	1000
1–2in (25–51mm)	500
Over 2in	Slowest speed available

William Ridgway power expansive bits

These are designed to produce flat, clean-bottomed holes in wood, laminates and plastic. They are available in medium and heavy duty, the latter being the type shown in the photograph. The smaller of the two allows holes to be bored ranging from ⅞in to 2in (22–51mm), while the larger one has a range of 1⅜ to 3⅛in (35–79mm). There is no doubt that they provide a cost-effective alternative to buying a large number of the bits listed above.

Sharpening

A flat file is used to lightly sharpen the inside of the spurs and the cutters or lifters from underneath, again taking care to maintain original angles.

Suggested speeds for expansive bits

The same as for the sawtooth bits.

Standard-lamp shell auger

This is the only tool designed purely for long-hole boring in the lathe on such projects as table and standard lamps. Its special shape has been designed to cut into end grain easily, its central lip ensuring that long holes can be accurately bored to receive the electric cable. The auger is normally 30in (760mm) long and is available in three sizes, but I use only the ⁵⁄₁₆in (8mm) size. It is employed in conjunction with a jig that fits in the toolrest holder; alternatively, lathes having a hollow tailstock can make use of a special hollow cup centre which allows the auger to pass through.

Sharpening

I have had my long-hole-boring auger for many years and have never yet had occasion to sharpen it. When not in use, I hang it up and the business end is protected with a piece of wood, drilled out to receive the auger with a push fit. I understand resharpening is an exact science, for it is very easy to destroy the original profiles, and the consequences are that the auger will no longer bore accurately. If sharpening is attempted, great care must be taken not to alter the profile. A few light strokes with a fine file should be sufficient.

Suggested speed for boring

The manufacturers recommend a speed of between 750 and 1000 rpm to be ideal.

Jacobs chuck, arbor and key

With the exception of the lamp-standard shell auger (which is the only hand-held boring tool), all types of bits, when used in connection with woodturning projects, are normally held in a Jacobs chuck (Fig 10.1, right). As mentioned in

Fig 10.2 Boring jig no. 1 (general-purpose jig)

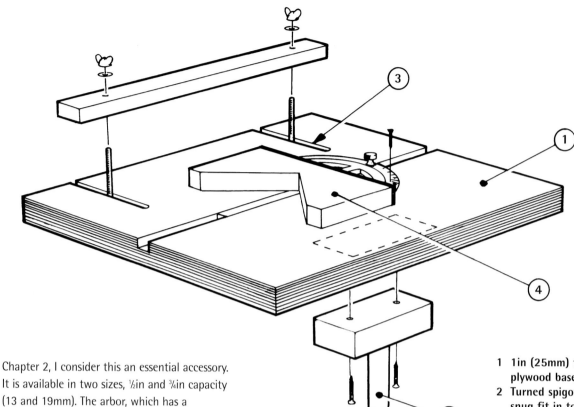

Chapter 2, I consider this an essential accessory. It is available in two sizes, ½in and ¾in capacity (13 and 19mm). The arbor, which has a machined Morse taper, is separate from the actual chuck. The appropriate size to fit your own lathe must be obtained, facilitating use in both the headstock and tailstock. In addition to being used for boring operations, it can of course be employed as an alternative to the woodscrew chuck, if a spigot is turned on one end of the workpiece to fit the chuck.

Home-made jigs for boring

Simple jigs can assist boring operations by way of speed and accuracy. Most turners have dozens of jigs scattered about their workshops, not only for boring, but for all kinds of jobs. The most important demands on any jig are accuracy and speed of setting up. They need not look like works of art – some of mine look very crude, but they fulfil their purpose.

General boring jig

The type of jig shown in Fig 10.2, which again incorporates the Picador mitre fence, is extremely useful in many operations where the

drill bit is held in the chuck secured to the headstock, enabling the wood to be fed on to it manually and without assistance from the tailstock. Boring with the aid of the tailstock is an extremely slow method compared with manual feeding. (However, holes to be bored to a depth exceeding about 1½in (38mm) are more accurately made by the support and advancement of the tailstock.)

Construction of the jig is fairly simple, and similar in concept to the sanding table described in the previous chapter. One end of the turned stem is joined to the platform and the other end is turned to a diameter that will provide a good fit into the toolrest holder.

As mentioned in Chapter 8, Copy-Turning, it is sometimes advisable to break down the design of long, slender turnings into shorter sections to prevent 'whip'. Turnings with square sections incorporated into the design, like balusters, lend themselves particularly well to this treatment. The square sections need to

1 1in (25mm) thick plywood base
2 Turned spigot for snug fit in toolrest holder
3 ¼in (6mm) slots to facilitate sideways movement of the hardwood fence
4 Wooden V-block screwed to Picador mitre fence; the fence slides in the housing formed in the platform top

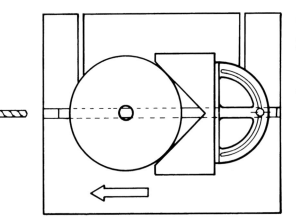

Fig 10.3 Plan view of jig no. 1, showing the V-block being used to bore a flex hole in the edge of a table-lamp base

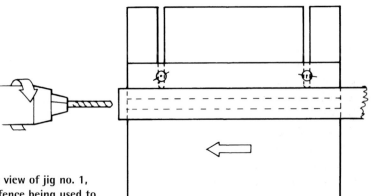

Fig 10.4 Additional plan view of jig no. 1, showing the adjustable fence being used to bore a mortise in the end grain of a piece of square-section stock. The stock is advanced manually without assistance from the tailstock

be cut to length, centred and then bored to take a tenon formed on both ends of the turned section.

To set up the jig, I mount between centres a piece of wood of the same section as the piece to be bored, and adjust accordingly the height of the jig. The wooden fence is then pressed up to the workpiece and secured by nipping the two wing nuts. The depth of the hole can be gauged either by sticking some masking tape on the drill bit or by a pencil mark on the fence. The boring can then begin, but remember to adjust the speed of the lathe according to the type and size of bit being used.

The same jig can also be used to bore the edges of discs such as table-lamp bases. A piece of wood with a 45° V is prepared and screwed to the Picador mitre fence, enabling it to be slid back and forth in the matching housing cut in the platform top. When setting up, care must be taken to ensure that the centre of the V is dead in line with the tip of the drill and the jig is parallel to the lathe bed.

Fig 10.3 shows the jig set up to bore a radial hole in the edge of a disc, and Fig 10.4 shows it set up to bore a hole in the end grain of a piece of square-section stock.

Jig for angled and round-section boring

Another extremely useful jig is shown in Fig 10.5. This will facilitate the boring of holes at an angle (the underside of stool tops, for example), and of course holes at right angles to the surface of the wood, efficiently and quickly.

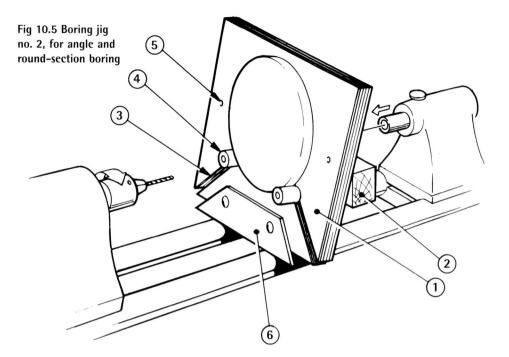

Fig 10.5 Boring jig no. 2, for angle and round-section boring

1 **1in (25mm) thick plywood backboard**

2 **2 x 2in (50 x 50mm) hardwood, full width of backboard and hinged to it, bored centrally with a hole that is a dead fit on the tailstock barrel**

3 **45° slots to allow for the adjustment of the button supports**

4 **Button supports, adjusted and secured with bolts and wing nuts**

5 **Location holes for V-block attachment**

6 **'Gravitating' support block secured with bolts and wing nuts (NB: To facilitate the up-and-down movement, the bolts run in two 90° slots cut in the base of the backboard)**

The design consists of a main platform of 1in (25mm) plywood which is hinged to a piece of 2 x 2in (50 x 50mm) hardwood. Into the centre of this hadrwood piece, a hole is bored which must be exactly the same size as the tailstock barrel and about ¾in (19mm) deep. This will ensure that the jig is accurately located every time it is used. The bottom of the platform should just clear the bed bars when it is suspended on the tailstock barrel. The long angled slots allow for the two turned 'button' supports (secured with bolts and wing nuts) to

be adjusted according to the diameter of the disc to be bored. Button supports of different diameters can be made, to allow for a greater range of diameters to be bored.

When boring angles, the bottom of the platform is obviously swung away from the lathe bed. To keep the jig at the required angle and prevent sideways movement, the adjustable support on the bottom edge of the jig will automatically gravitate and settle on the lathe bed bars. It is then secured in position by tightening the two wing nuts (Fig 10.6).

Fig 10.6 Jig no. 2 being used to bore the underneath of a stool top

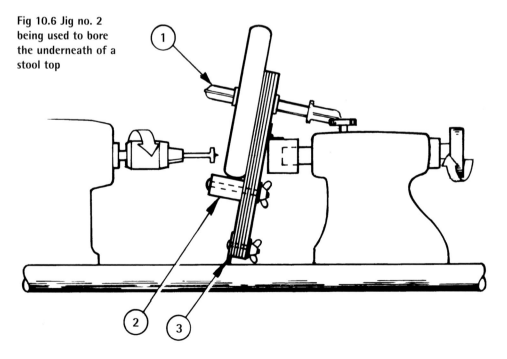

1 **G-cramp (C-clamp) secures the stool top to the jig**

2 **Button supports ensure that the three holes are bored concentrically**

3 **The bottom support block has gravitated and settled on the bed bars. This provides stability and maintains the same angle of splay when the wing nuts are nipped**

Fig 10.7 Jig no. 2: elevation showing the V-block attachment being used to bore a 90° hole in a piece of round-section stock

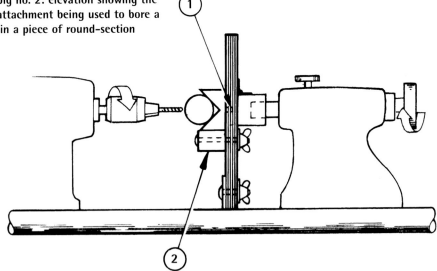

1 The two dowels in the back of the V-block locate in the two holes in the backboard. It is vital that these two holes are precisely located so that the centre of the V-block is dead in line with the lathe centres
2 The two button supports provide extra stability

Fig 10.8 Jig no. 2: plan view showing method of boring angled holes

1 11° wedge fits between the backboard and the V-block
2 The V-block is secured to the wedge with a 11/4in (32mm) x no. 8 woodscrew
3 The V-block is hinged to the backboard. The button supports should also be used to stabilize the V-block

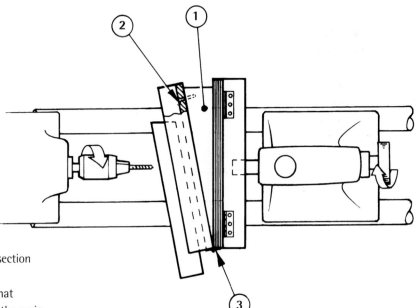

The same jig also allows for round-section stock to be bored by making a V-block incorporating two ¼in (6mm) dowels that locate in corresponding holes bored in the main backboard. The centre of the V must be exactly in line with the lathe centres, or the resulting holes will not be radially true. Fig 10.7 shows how the V-block is constructed and located.

Finally, the V-block principle can be used to bore holes at an angle in stool and chair legs to receive cross pieces or stretchers. For this it is necessary to prepare another V-block of identical proportions to the first, but minus the two locating dowels.

To set the jig up, first of all fix the *dowelled* V-block to the jig. This will establish true centre height. Now bring up both button supports so that they just touch the V-block, and secure them. Remove the block and replace it with the *undowelled* version, which is hinged to the

backboard. It only takes a couple of minutes to screw the hinge on and it does make things easier. A wedge, cut to the required angle (typically about 11°), is located behind the V-block and secured to it by means of a 1¼in (32mm) x no. 8 woodscrew. Fig 10.8 shows constructional details.

Jigs for inlay work or decorative turnery

As your turning skills improve, you will probably want to experiment with inlay work or, as it is sometimes called, decorative turnery. Extremely attractive pieces can be produced by using

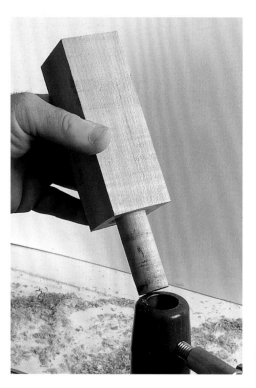

Fig 10.9 The drilled guide prepared for the toolrest holder

Fig 10.10 Locating dead-centre height on the guide

plain timbers and inlaying them with contrasting-coloured wood.

So as to space the inlays equally around the circumference of any given circle, it is necessary to make use of a device called a **dividing head** (sometimes refered to as an *indexing plate*). Many modern lathes have this capability built in, as have many modern chucks. Additionally, it is possible to buy a simple dividing head from several outlets, and they can be adapted to fit any make of lathe.

Generally, there are 24 divisions on the head and it is locked in position by means of a spring-loaded pin. Any equal division of 24 can thus be utilized to inlay, drill, flute, reed, etc. On the Woodfast lathe used for the photographs in this book, the largest pulley in the headstock is drilled with 24 equally spaced holes which are engaged by a spring-loaded pin passing through the headstock casting and activated by a comfortable knurled knob. This device can be seen clearly in Fig 10.19.

In order to ensure that the holes are bored radially (on dead centre), it is necessary to make a guide for the chosen drill size. This is simply a piece of square-section stock with a round tenon or spigot turned on one end to fit into the toolrest holder with a good tight fit (Fig 10.9). Ensure that the square shoulder is pushed right down on to the toolrest holder, as this will

give accurate location every time the guide is used. By making use of the chosen drill bit and a Jacobs chuck secured in either tailstock or headstock, dead centre can be marked on the guide, and then a hole of the required diameter (⅜in (10mm) in the example shown) bored all the way through (Fig 10.10).

Routing on the lathe

The hand-held router can be used to good effect on the lathe, particularly for reeding and fluting table legs, standard-lamp components, Adam fireplace surrounds, four-poster bed supports, etc. Fig 10.11a and b shows sections of reeded and fluted profiles respectively. Again it is necessary to use the dividing head to space the reeds or flutes equally.

If the reeding or fluting is to be done on a parallel or tapered cylinder, perhaps the simplest means to achieve it is to make a box-like jig for the router to sit in, so it can traverse the full length of the workpiece in the rebates worked in the two guides.

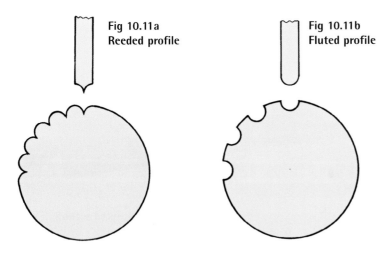

**Fig 10.11a
Reeded profile**

**Fig 10.11b
Fluted profile**

Different-size boxes can be made up to suit the work in hand, and Fig 10.12a and b gives details of a jig constructed for a Coronet No. 3 lathe with round bed bars; this was not difficult to make. Such jigs may be adapted to suit most types of lathe; the most important requirement (to ensure radial cutting) is for the router guides or rebates to be positioned so that the centre of the cutter is in alignment with the lathe centres.

If the turning is tapered in its length, the box can be packed up at one end to compensate. Alternatively, the box can be cut on the required taper. In the case of slender turnings it may be necessary to pack the workpiece with wedges to prevent it flexing under the power of the router.

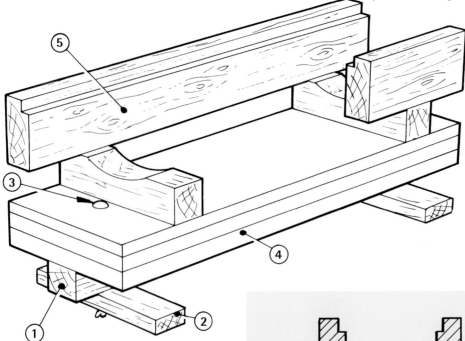

Fig 10.12a Constructional details of the routing jig

1 This full-length piece of wood needs to be a snug fit between the bed bars and deep enough to allow the cross pieces **2** to tighten on to the bed bars by means of the bolts and wing nuts **3**
4 The 'body' of the jig can be made up of several thicknesses of chipboard
5 The rebates in the two full-length guides (one is cut away for clarity in the drawing) should be formed to ensure that the router slides freely between them

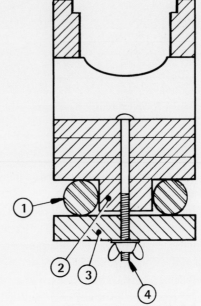

Fig 10.12b Section through routing jig

The bed bars **1** are 1½in (38mm) in diameter and the spacer **2** is fractionally less in thickness. This means that the two cross pieces **3** tighten on to the bed bars by means of the bolt and wing nut **4**

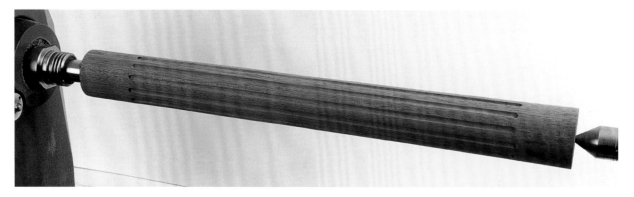

Fig 10.13 The completed fluted section

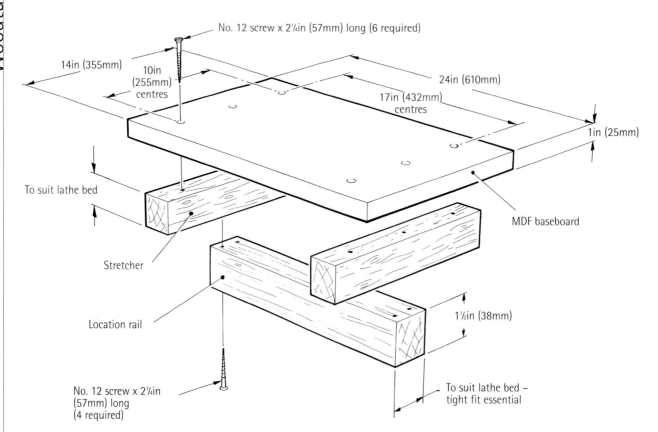

No. 12 screw x 2¼in (57mm) long (6 required)

14in (355mm)

10in (255mm) centres

24in (610mm)

17in (432mm) centres

1in (25mm)

To suit lathe bed

MDF baseboard

Stretcher

1½in (38mm)

Location rail

No. 12 screw x 2¼in (57mm) long (4 required)

To suit lathe bed – tight fit essential

Fig 10.14 A typical router baseboard

Fig 10.13 shows a completed standard-lamp component fluted in this manner.

The trade turner is often required to reed or flute curved profiles, and for this a different set-up is needed. Instead of working over the top of the workpiece, the router is used from the side on a baseboard constructed so as to enable repeated positive and accurate location on the lathe. Fig 10.14 shows a jig constructed to suit the Woodfast lathe. The height of the baseboard is governed by the depth of the two stretchers, and it must be sufficiently high to enable the cutters to cut on centre.

Some kind of router carrier is obviously required, and Fig 10.15 provides constructional details of one such. The centre height of the wooden carrier must be calculated to suit the lathe being used.

Fig 10.15 Example of home-made router carrier

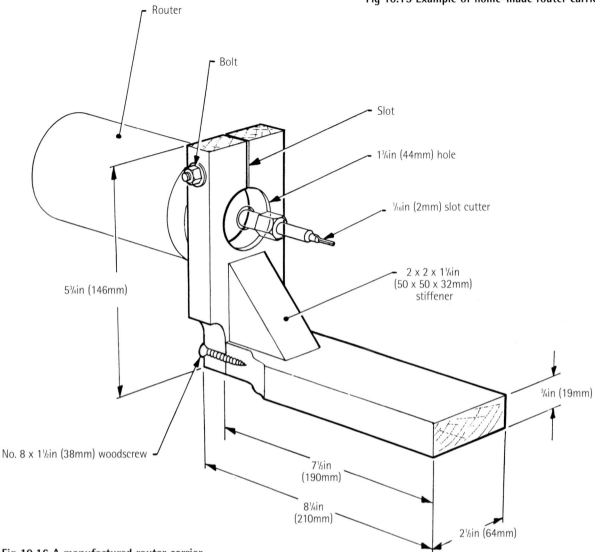

Router

Bolt

Slot

1¾in (44mm) hole

¹⁄₁₆in (2mm) slot cutter

2 x 2 x 1¼in
(50 x 50 x 32mm)
stiffener

5¾in (146mm)

¾in (19mm)

No. 8 x 1½in (38mm) woodscrew

7½in
(190mm)

8¼in
(210mm)

2½in (64mm)

Fig 10.16 A manufactured router carrier

I prefer to use a purpose-made metal carrier as shown in Fig 10.16, which I bought at one of the woodworking shows. It will be seen that the router can be moved up and down considerably, and this makes it suitable for most types of lathe centre.

With the router being used in this mode to follow curved profiles, it will quickly become apparent that to achieve an even depth of cut, some kind of depth stop must be incorporated. I simply make use of a ¾in (19mm) cube of close-grained wood, centrally bored to be a good push fit over the router cutter, which is allowed to protrude the desired amount. This wooden collar needs to be rounded on its leading edge to allow access to profile intersections. The rounding can be achieved by

147

mounting the cube of wood on a spigot turned on any scrap piece of wood and shaping carefully with very light cuts. Fig 10.17 shows a close-up of the wooden collar, and Fig 10.18 shows the router being used on a curved profile.

With a little experience and know-how, the router can be put to use on the lathe for many other projects, such as slot-mortising, or dovetailing and dowelling tripod legs to table columns.

Fig 10.17 Close-up of the wooden collar depth gauge

Fig 10.18 Fluting a curved profile

PROJECT

Inlaid nut bowl

This project makes use of the jig for inlay work described on pages 143–4. In this example a 5 x 2in (127 x 51mm) disc of oak was used, and inlaid with six ⅜in (10mm) diameter sycamore plugs. After turning the outside of the bowl using the methods described in Chapter 7, position the boring guide and secure the dividing head with the locking pin. The depth of the hole needs to be regulated, and this can be achieved by sticking some masking tape on the drill at the appropriate place. After boring the first hole, relocate the locking pin at the required interval (4 spaces in this case) and repeat the process until all six holes have been bored. Fig 10.19 shows the boring operation; the in-built dividing head and locating pin can also be clearly seen.

The next step is to prepare the sycamore inlays, and these can be turned between centres in batches of six. The grain must be arranged so that it runs along the face of the inlay; it is not desirable for end grain to be exposed on the finished project. It is vital that the sizing is accurate, or the inlays will not fit satisfactorily. They can then be cross-cut to about ¼in (6mm) long.

A quicker and much better method is to make use of a plug cutter; these are available in several sizes. They are quite expensive, but are very efficient and accurate. Fig 10.20 shows the plug cutter in use.

The inlays are glued in, and after they have been allowed to set, the turning, sanding and polishing of the outside of the bowl can be done. Complete the project by reverse-chucking and hollowing out the inside. Fig 10.21 shows the finished article.

This method can be used to build up intricate patterns of inlay. This example is only intended as an introduction.

Fig 10.19 Boring the holes for the inlays. The inbuilt dividing head and locking device are clearly visible

Fig 10.20 The plug cutter in use

Fig 10.21 The completed inlaid bowl

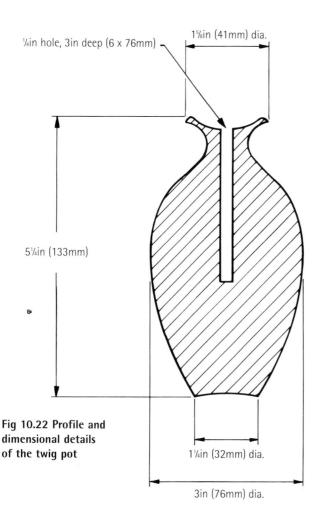

¼in hole, 3in deep (6 x 76mm)

1⅝in (41mm) dia.

5¼in (133mm)

**Fig 10.22 Profile and
dimensional details
of the twig pot**

1¼in (32mm) dia.

3in (76mm) dia.

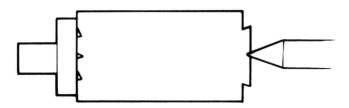

Fig 10.23 Preparing the dovetailed spigot to fit the O'Donnell jaws

Fig 10.24 Initial sizing and profiling of the neck completed

Twig pot

All 'early learning' projects should be fairly simple and not require any great outlay on material. Additionally, such projects should be proven good sellers so that some of the substantial expenditure for the lathe, tools and accessories can be recouped. Twig or grass pots fall into this category. The boring process is basic and the project also provides further excellent practice with the gouges in forming nice flowing profiles.

Design

I have gone for the popular bottle shape in this particular design, but there are limitless shapes and profiles that would be suitable for such a project. I try to avoid being over-fussy with detail, although some bland timbers will stand discreet detail. Fig 10.22 provides details of the bottle profile and dimensions.

Choice of wood

Limb or branch wood from such species as yew, laburnum, cherry, sumach, lilac, etc. are all readily available from prunings, and very often free of charge. The timber should preferably be fairly dry, but for practice purposes green wood is ideal. My choice of wood for this project was spalted beech, which can show spectacular fungal patterns.

Method

By reference to the drawing, the wood can be cut to length and mounted on the lathe, initially between centres. Because I intended to make use of the compression mode of the 2in (51mm) O'Donnell jaws to drive the piece, I cut the stock to a length of 6in (152mm). (The O'Donnell jaws are an optional accessory for the APTC scroll chuck, available in three useful sizes and capable of being used in both compression and expanding modes.) Fig 10.23 shows how the stock is prepared for the 2in spigot jaws. If a woodscrew chuck is to be used (and this is fine), allow an extra ¾in (19mm); Fig 6.48 on page 78 shows the suggested method of preparing the stock for the woodscrew chuck.

Fig 10.25 Boring the hole

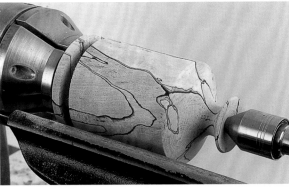

Fig 10.26 The overall length has been sized in with tailstock support

With the wood firmly secured, reduce the stock to the largest diameter of 3in (76mm) with a sharp roughing-out gouge. Size in the diameter of the top (1⅝in (41mm)) at the open end. Use a ⅜in (10mm) spindle gouge to shape the flowing profile of the adjacent cove, cutting from large to small diameter from both sides until the final diameter of ¾in (19mm) is arrived at. Fig 10.24 shows the project thus far.

Position the toolrest across the face of the pot and face off the end grain with a ¼in (6mm) spindle gouge. Now prick dead centre with the toe of the skew chisel to facilitate an accurate location for the hole boring. (Both these techniques were described in Chapter 6, Figs 6.49 and 6.46 respectively.)

The 3in deep by ¼in diameter (76 x 6mm) hole can be bored by making use of a ¼in spindle gouge (also described fully in Chapter 6, Fig 6.53) or by means of a Jacobs chuck and ¼in drill bit inserted in the tailstock (Fig 10.25).

Continue by using the gouge to dish the end grain slightly, and also to form the small chamfer where the end grain and outside profile merge. The overall length can now be pencilled in and a couple of parting cuts made to the left of the mark (in the waste wood) down to the base diameter of 1¼in (32mm). This will allow access for the gouge to be swung unimpeded to the bottom of the curve. Fig 10.26 shows the work completed to this stage; note that the tailstock has been brought up to provide added support.

The final profiling can now be achieved with the ⅜in (10mm) gouge, aiming for nice flowing curves. Fig 10.27 shows the turning completed.

All that now remains is to sand and polish, and part off with a newly sharpened parting tool. Ideally the base should be slightly concaved and sanded to a fine finish. Fig 10.28 shows a similar pot in spalted beech, completed and polished.

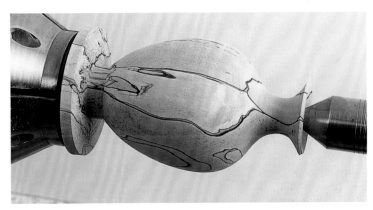

Fig 10.27 Profiling completed prior to sanding and polishing

Fig 10.28 A completed and polished pot in spalted beech

PROJECT

Pepper mill

Design

In this case the design is based on a 7in (178mm) mechanism marketed by Craft Supplies Ltd, and Fig 10.29, showing the component parts and how they are assembled, is reproduced by courtesy of this company.

A variety of shapes can be made, but I prefer to keep the profiles of the body fairly simple, avoiding too much adornment. I always ensure that the largest diameter on the finished turning is at the base, or the project will look top-heavy and out of proportion.

Choice of wood

Teak, oak, walnut and sycamore are all suitable.

Method

Draw out the project full size (Fig 10.30). Mount the stock on the screw chuck and reduce it to a cylinder (Fig 10.31).

Fix the Jacobs chuck with a ⅞in (22mm) bit to the tailstock. Reduce the lathe speed to between 500 and 1000 rpm. Wind in the tailstock to bore the hole to a depth just over half-way up the body. To prevent the drill bit binding, it is advisable to withdraw it from time to time to remove the waste. It should also be noted that the traverse on most tailstocks is insufficient to bore the full-depth hole on one winding. It is therefore necessary to stop the lathe and reposition the tailstock further in towards the headstock when the hole has been part-bored (Fig 10.32).

The rebate to take the bottom retaining plate is formed with either a parting tool or the toe of the ½in (13mm) skew chisel, used scraper-fashion. Remember that the stock is only supported on a single woodscrew, so do not try to remove too much wood at a time. Light cuts and patience are the order of the day. It will be found that a ⅞in hole will not quite accommodate the female part of the mechanism, so this needs to be enlarged slightly with the skew (Fig 10.33).

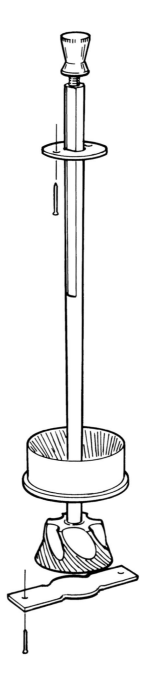

Fig 10.29 Pepper mill mechanism (minus the top retaining plate, which is not required if this method is adopted)

The capstan, the parting cuts and the spigot are set out at the headstock end, following which the main body is parted off. Ensure that the spigot is a good fit in the partly bored main body. The body is now reversed, jammed on to the spigot, and the main bore completed (Fig 10.34).

Remove the body and part the spigot off to about ¼in (6mm) in length. A shallow recess now needs to be made (with the parting tool) in the face of the spigot to house the driving plate. This recess allows the driving plate to finish flush with the surface of the wood, and looks much more

Fig 10.30 Dimensions of a typical pepper mill

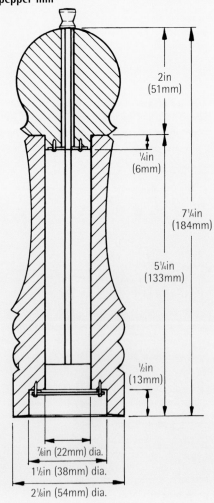

2in (51mm)

¼in (6mm)

7¼in (184mm)

5¼in (133mm)

½in (13mm)

⅞in (22mm) dia.

1½in (38mm) dia.

2⅛in (54mm) dia.

Fig 10.31 Mount the stock on the woodscrew chuck; bring up the tailstock for support and reduce it to a cylinder

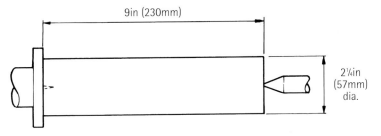

9in (230mm)

2¼in (57mm) dia.

Fig 10.32 Fix the Jacobs chuck in the tailstock and bore the ⅞in (22mm) hole just over half-way up the body

Fig 10.33

1 Use a parting tool or the toe of the ½in (13mm) skew to form the rebate to take the bottom retaining plate. Also, very slightly open the ⅞in (22mm) bore to house the female part of the mechanism

2 Set out the parting cut and the spigot (which must be a good push fit in the ⅞in main bore) and then part it off

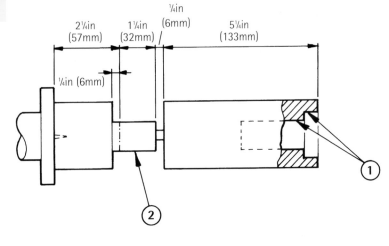

2¼in (57mm)

1¼in (32mm)

¼in (6mm)

5¼in (133mm)

¼in (6mm)

① ②

Fig 10.34 Reverse the body on to the spigot and complete the main bore

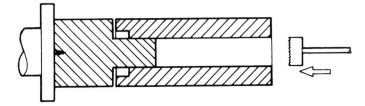

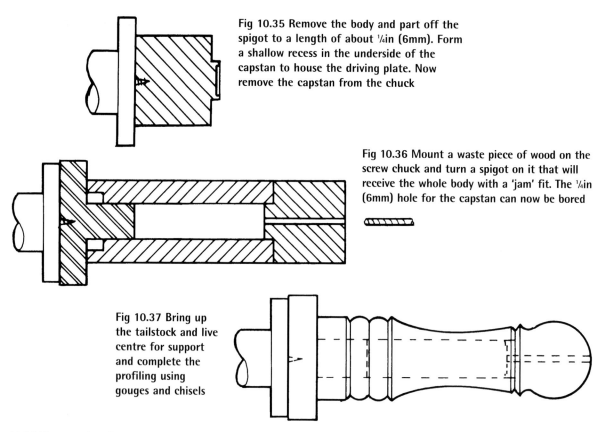

Fig 10.35 Remove the body and part off the spigot to a length of about ¼in (6mm). Form a shallow recess in the underside of the capstan to house the driving plate. Now remove the capstan from the chuck

Fig 10.36 Mount a waste piece of wood on the screw chuck and turn a spigot on it that will receive the whole body with a 'jam' fit. The ¼in (6mm) hole for the capstan can now be bored

Fig 10.37 Bring up the tailstock and live centre for support and complete the profiling using gouges and chisels

Fig 10.38 The completed pepper mill

professional than simply tacking it in position (Fig 10.35).

Remove the capstan from the woodscrew chuck and replace it with a piece of waste wood about 2½in (64mm) square and of about the same length. On this a ⅞in (22mm) spigot is required, which will receive the base of the mill on a good push fit. The ¼in (6mm) hole can now be bored in the capstan (using a Jacobs chuck held in the tailstock) to take the spindle mechanism (Fig 10.36).

The tailstock and live centre is brought up to give support, and the profiling with gouges and chisels can be completed in preparation for sanding and polishing (Fig 10.37).

The final step is to lightly sand the inside of the top of the main bore so that the spigot on the capstan can turn freely. With this spigot left on the underside of the capstan, there is no need for a top retaining plate to be fitted. Fig 10.38 shows the finished project.

There are other and much quicker ways of making pepper mills, but this method requires minimal equipment. Some of the others involve several sizes of expensive drills and chucking equipment.

Fig 10.39 Profile and dimensional details of the table lamp

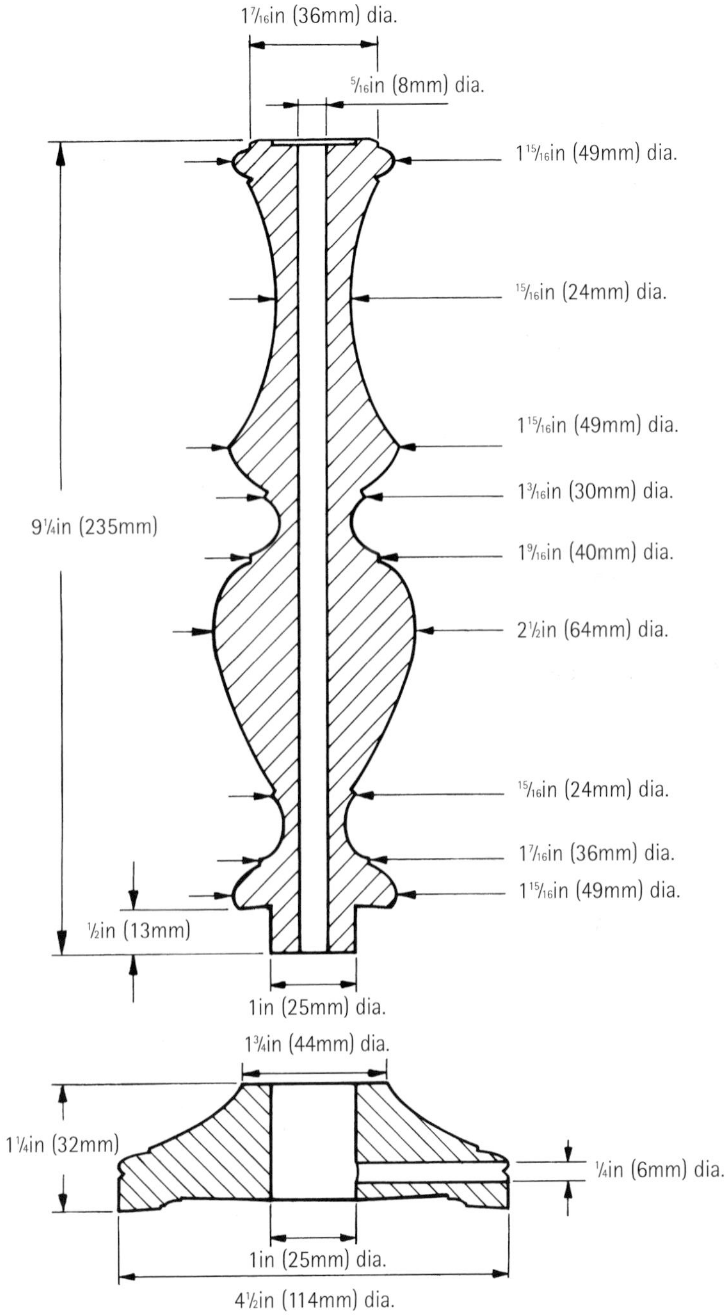

PROJECT

Table lamp

This project is an exercise in both spindle and headstock turning, and provides the opportunity to explain methods of boring long holes and the equipment required to do it.

Design

I have designed the lamp with traditional profiles so that continued practice in producing flowing curves with the gouges and chisels can be undertaken. Fig 10.39 shows the profile and dimensional details.

Choice of wood

This is down to personal preference, and consideration should be given to matching up with existing furniture and fittings, but any suitable hardwood can be used. For photographic convenience, Scots pine has been used in the sequence photographs.

Method

Making the pillar

By referring to the drawing, the wood for the pillar can be dimensioned and turned to a cylinder between centres. Then commence the long-hole-boring operation. This can be achieved in one of two ways:

1 If the tailstock barrel is hollow, a ring centre can be inserted to allow the long auger to pass through.
2 Where the tailstock barrel is not hollow, a jig supplied by the manufacturer can be fitted into the toolrest holder.

Method 1 is used in this example.

Fig 10.40 shows a typical auger, hollow ring centre, centre finder, counterbore tool, and the brass fixing plate to which the lampholder is fixed. With the hollow ring centre fitted in the tailstock, the centre finder is passed through the tailstock and located in the existing mark on the workpiece. Now the tailstock can be tightened to provide sufficient

drive. It is advisable to apply a dab of wax on the hollow ring centre to prevent burning.

After removing the centre finder, use the auger to bore about half-way down the workpiece, going forward about 2in (50mm) at a time and then withdrawing to remove the debris; otherwise it may well bind and run off centre. It makes for smoother boring if the tip

1⁷⁄₁₆in (36mm) dia.

⁵⁄₁₆in (8mm) dia.

1¹⁵⁄₁₆in (49mm) dia.

¹⁵⁄₁₆in (24mm) dia.

1¹⁵⁄₁₆in (49mm) dia.

1³⁄₁₆in (30mm) dia.

1⁹⁄₁₆in (40mm) dia.

2½in (64mm) dia.

¹⁵⁄₁₆in (24mm) dia.

1⁷⁄₁₆in (36mm) dia.

1¹⁵⁄₁₆in (49mm) dia.

9¼in (235mm)

½in (13mm)

1in (25mm) dia.

1¾in (44mm) dia.

1¼in (32mm)

¼in (6mm) dia.

1in (25mm) dia.

4½in (114mm) dia.

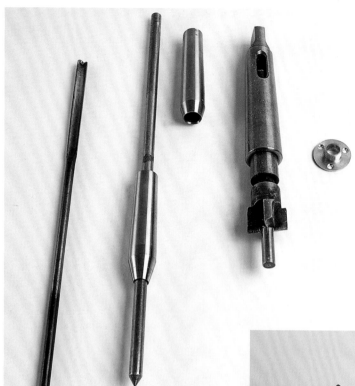

Fig 10.40 *Left to right:* **auger, centre finder (installed in a hollow ring centre), hollow ring centre, counterbore tool, brass lamp fitting**

of the auger is occasionally dipped in wax. Fig 10.41 shows the auger in use.

Replace the drive centre in the headstock with the counterbore tool. This accessory serves three purposes: (1) the peg fits snugly into the part-bored hole so as to maintain centricity; (2) the spurs at the bottom of the peg will impart sufficient drive when tailstock pressure is applied to enable the boring to be completed by repeating the procedure described above for using the auger and centre finder; (3) as its

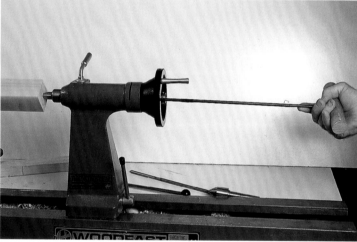

Fig 10.41
The auger in use

name suggests, it can be used to bore a hole the size of the spurs (in this case, a 1in (25mm) hole), which is very useful in joining long lengths together. Complete the operation from the tailstock end.

Fig 10.42 shows a piece of wood that has been bored and counterbored, and then sawn down the centre so as to clarify the operation.

Replace the hollow ring centre with the revolving centre and true up the workpiece. As with the bar stool and staircase baluster described in Chapter 8, a marking stick can be prepared for the lamp pillar so as to simplify the setting-out procedure. The key diameters are again colour-coded and callipers set from them. Fig 10.43 shows the prepared marking stick with the colour-coded diameters clearly visible.

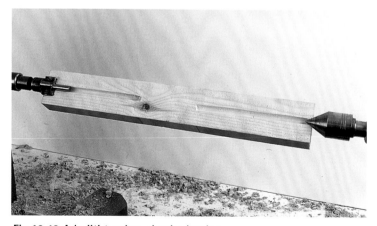

Fig 10.42 A 'split' turning, clearly showing the method of boring and counterboring

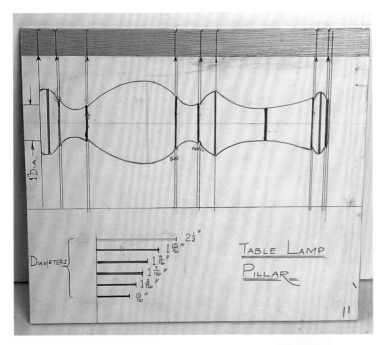

Fig 10.43 The prepared marking stick, showing the colour-coded diameters

Fig 10.44 Making use of the marking stick to pencil in the salient design features on the whirling wood

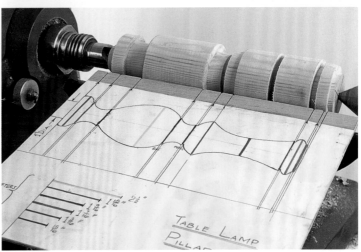

After reducing the stock to the largest diameter (colour-coded yellow in this example), the marking stick can be carefully placed on the toolrest and the design features pencilled in on the whirling wood (Fig 10.44). The sizing operation can now start with the 1in (25mm) tenon at the bottom of the pillar. This forms the joint with the base, and must be accurately sized to fit the corresponding 1in hole to be bored in the base. Note that this tenon is 'stubbed' so as to be short of the ¼in (6mm) hole drilled in the base through which the electrical cable will be passed. The other five sizings can now be done, taking care that the callipers have been accurately set and used in the correct locations. Fig 10.45 shows the sizing in completed, with the marking stick held in close to clarify the procedure.

The profiling can now start. The majority of this can be done with the ⅜in (10mm) spindle gouge. It will be necessary to use the toe of a skew chisel to form the V-cuts, and a parting tool to tidy up the fillets or flats. Aim for nice flowing curves and crisp intersections. Fig 10.46 shows the final refining of the pillar with the spindle gouge.

The counterbore tool can now be used to form the shallow recess at the top end of the pillar to house the brass fixing plate to which the lampholder is screwed. A safe way of counterboring is to set the lathe speed at

Fig 10.45 Sizing in completed, with the marking stick held in close to clarify the procedure

Fig 10.47 Counterboring the recess for the lampholder fitting

Fig 10.48 The 1in (25mm) softwood spigot prepared to 'jam-fit' the base

Fig 10.46 Final refining with the spindle gouge

about 500rpm. With the lathe stationary, grip the workpiece with one hand and start the lathe with the other. Now gently wind the tailstock forward until the desired depth has been reached. In the interests of safety, *always remove the toolrest*, and *never* attempt this operation on square-section stock. Fig 10.47 shows the recess being counterbored.

The pillar can now be carefully sanded, going through 180, 220 and 320 grits, and your choice of finish applied.

Making the base

Again by referring to the drawing, the stock for the base can now be prepared and cut to a disc. A 1in-diameter (25mm) hole is then bored through on centre. Next, make a push-fit chuck for the lamp base. Proceed by mounting a piece of softwood on the screw chuck, then, after reducing it to a cylinder, turn a 1in-diameter spigot to receive the base on a good push fit (Fig 10.48).

By using the methods described in the Plinth project (pages 122–5), a full-size half-template can be made from Fig 10.39, to simplify setting out the required diameter, thickness and design features (Fig 10.49).

The disc is first turned to a true cylinder with the ⅜in (10mm) bowl gouge, using a lathe speed of about 1000rpm. Now pencil in the finished thickness and tool off to this mark, with the rest repositioned across the face of the disc.

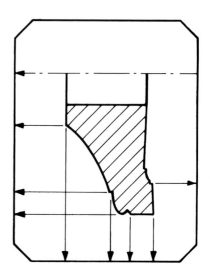

Fig 10.49 The half-template used for setting out the base

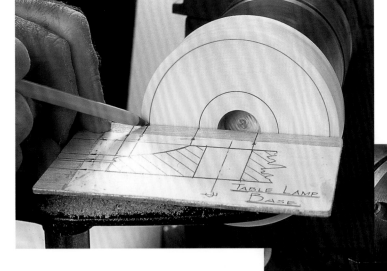

Fig 10.50 The template in use

Fig 10.51 Drilling the ¼in (6mm) flex hole with a hand brace

Continue by offering up the template to the face of the whirling wood and pencilling in the design features and diameter. Because there is a 1in hole in the centre of the base, a line has been projected on the template ½in (13mm) to the right of the centre mark to facilitate accurate lining up. Fig 10.50 shows the template in use.

Profiling can then be completed with gouges and scrapers, as described for the Plinth project in Chapter 8 (pages 122–5). Before sanding, a ¼in (6mm) hole needs to be bored through the edge of the base so as to merge with the 1in hole to receive the electrical cable. This can be done either with a power drill or with a hand brace (Fig 10.51). If your lathe mandrel is not fitted with a locking device, you may need someone to hold the disc in order to prevent it from spinning while the hole is being drilled.

Sand and polish, then complete the turning by reverse-chucking in the 1in spigot, which enables the underneath to be profiled as in Fig 10.39.

Assembly
After ensuring that the tenon is a good fit in the base, it can be glued up and the lathe used to cramp it together while the glue sets.

The final operation is to fix the brass lampholder fitting with small brass screws. Fig 10.52 shows a completed and polished lamp in walnut.

Fig 10.52 A completed and polished lamp in walnut

Fig 10.53 Three completed pens, with a commercially made presentation case

PROJECT

A wooden twist pen

For the final project in the book I shall describe the making of a wooden twist pen. These have become popular in recent years both with the hobbyist and with the professional production turner. To meet this demand, many of the leading stockists of woodturning accessories have added to their catalogues a variety of kits which include all the hardware needed to make a quality pen.

Prior to a recent teaching and demonstration visit to Utah, I had only once attempted to make a pen, which ended in failure because of indequate equipment; I really could not understand the apparent fascination which pen making had for many turners, particularly in America. This changed, however, after my host in Utah, Dale Nish (the internationally known woodturner and author, and proprietor of Craft Supplies USA), suggested that to while away some of my spare time I might make use of his home workshop and have a crack at making some.

With all the necessary equipment and parts to hand, and with some guidance and pointers from Dale, I successfully completed several quality twist pens. Having handled and used them, it was easy to understand the fascination. What a difference they are from the cheap and nasty mass-produced ballpoint pens which are strewn about almost anywhere you look. A well made, handcrafted pen reeks of individuality, and there is something uniquely satisfying about using one. What is more, they are fun to make, they sell very well and become personal and coveted possessions. They make a wonderful gift for any special occasion, and needless to say I have made quite a number since returning from America.

Design

This is very much influenced by the type of kit you decide to buy. I have gone for a basic straight-barrelled design, as this affords the beginner the opportunity to get accustomed to the special equipment and the drilling operation without worrying too much about elaborate design. Kits from reputable outlets include instructions for making, and it is important to read them carefully.

Fig 10.53 shows three completed pens of the chosen design in different woods, one enclosed in a presentation box which is also readily available.

Choice of wood

I suggest that exotic hardwoods with striking colour be used. Expensive species such as cocobolo, kingwood, tulipwood, bucote, stripy ebony, etc. – which we all tend to shy away from for cost reasons – can be obtained as prepared pen blanks at a very reasonable cost. The more striking the wood, the more the interest that will be shown in your finished product.

Experienced pen makers often use highly figured burrs and spalted wood; these can be exquisite, and are much sought-after. My advice to the inexperienced, however, is to ignore them until a fair degree of confidence and efficiency has been attained. This is because the more curly and interlocking the grain, the more difficult it is to reduce the wall successfully to the required thickness of 1/25in (1mm). Additionally, such timbers are notoriously difficult to drill accurately.

Method

It is very important in pen making to work in an orderly, well-organized manner. Many of the components are small and round, and tend to roll off the bench on to the floor and get lost in the shavings. I make use of a Black & Decker Workmate fitted with an auxiliary top on which to lay out the tools, glue and accessories in an orderly manner. For the pen mechanisms and fittings, I prefer to make use of a plastic box with compartments, which can be bought from most DIY stores.

As a means of storing the wooden blanks in matching pairs after they have been drilled through, I have devised a stacking board which is simply a piece of 3/8in-thick (10mm) MDF nailed to a softwood baseboard. Equally spaced holes have been drilled in the MDF to receive 1/8in (3mm) brass rod (1/8in wooden dowel would do fine) on a good push fit.

This device allows the matched blanks to be stored horizontally. This is important, particularly after the brass tubes have been stuck inside the wooden blanks. Leaving a space between the blanks prevents them accidentally bonding together. Fig 10.54 shows the auxiliary table laid out in an organized manner with the component parts, tools and accessories.

If you have not purchased ready-made blanks, they can be prepared from offcuts of exotic species on the bandsaw. Although the diameter of the finished pen blank will be a bare 3/8in (10mm), it is advisable to cut them about 5/8in (16mm) square to allow for the drill bit wandering off centre. This is not uncommon when drilling down the end grain, and the extra material allows concentricity to be maintained around the hole as the stock is reduced to the required diameter.

If my method of drilling is to be adopted, it is important for the blanks to be accurately dimensioned to the suggested thickness, and also cut dead square on each end to a length of not less than 4 3/8in (111mm).

The next step is to cross-cut the blanks into two equal halves. Because it is desirable to preserve the grain match on each blank, it is advisable *before* they are so cut to draw a bold line about 1in long in the centre of each, enabling the grain to be reorientated correctly. Each piece will now be slightly over 2 1/8in (54mm) long, and it is a good idea to use either masking tape or elastic bands to store them in matching pairs prior to the drilling operation. Fig 10.55 shows several pen blanks in various stages of preparation.

Fig 10.54 The auxiliary table, with all the pen-making accessories to hand

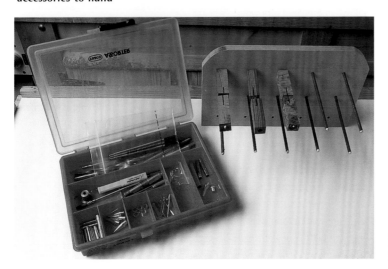

Fig 10.55 Pen blanks in different stages of preparation

Drilling the blanks

The blanks can now be drilled out to receive the brass tubes, and for this kit a 7mm ($\frac{9}{32}$in) brad-point drill is required. There are several methods of drilling. With care it can be done on the lathe by securing the bit in a Jacobs chuck attached to the headstock, and advancing the tailstock to force the blank on to the drill. Please note that this method requires each half of the stock to be cut about ¼in (6mm) over length, as the hole needs to be stopped short of the revolving centre to avoid ruining the drill. A piece of masking tape stuck to the drill bit will determine the depth of the hole, and the drilled blank can then be cut to length, leaving the hole all the way through.

Whichever method is used, it is important that the drilling is started at the 'grain match' end to preserve alignment, and that the blank is frequently withdrawn to clear the debris; otherwise the bit will overheat, and most likely wander off centre. Drilling speed is not critical, but I have found that approximately 1500rpm is suitable for most timbers. Fig 10.56 shows a blank being drilled out on the lathe.

A quicker and more accurate method of drilling is to make use of the pillar drill, incorporating a simple jig clamped to the table. The jig is simply a piece of MDF with two intersecting 45° angle cuts, which provides a positive location and register for each blank and prevents it twisting. It is necessary for only one blank to be centred and punched. This allows the jig to be precisely located before clamping.

Providing the blanks have all been accurately dimensioned and the ends cut square, they can all be quickly positioned and drilled with little effort. Finger pressure applied through another short piece of MDF with a similar cutout is adequate for drilling a small-diameter hole such as this, but for larger holes it is *dangerous* unless the wood is securely clamped. Please note that a 100% success rate should not be expected with any method of drilling, but to minimize failures it is essential that a sharp bit is used and fed slowly and evenly down the full depth of the blank. After drilling, each matching pair can be stored on the stacking board. Fig 10.57 shows the drilling jig in use.

Fig 10.56 Using the lathe to drill a blank

The gluing operation

There are several types of glue that are suitable for gluing in the brass tubes, but I prefer the gap-filling cyanoacrylate (superglue). Even with this, it is advisable to coat the inside of the drilled hole in the wood blank as well as the outside of the brass tube. To provide a good 'key' for the glue, it is suggested that the outsides of the brass tubes be thoroughly cleaned with white spirit (mineral spirit) or thinners, followed by light abrading with 120-grit paper. This ensures a good bond. Fig 10.58 shows the glue being smeared on to the inside of the hole direct from the container, and Fig 10.59 shows the outside of the brass tube being similarly treated. To prevent glue contaminating my fingers, I inserted a nail punch in the end of the tube so that my hand was well away from the area to be glued.

Fig 10.57 The drilling jig in use

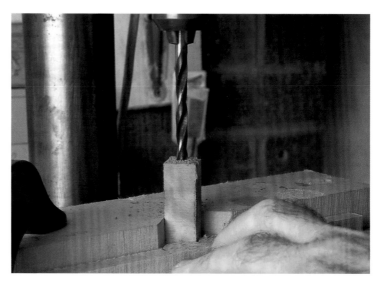

Fig 10.58 (left) Applying glue to the inside of the hole direct from the container

Fig 10.59 (above) Smearing the glue on to the outside of a tube. Note the nail punch inserted into the tube to prevent glue contamination of the fingers

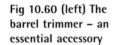

Fig 10.60 (left) The barrel trimmer – an essential accessory

Each tube should be inserted into the 'grain-match' ends with a twisting motion to encourage even distribution, and pressed in flush to the end of the blank. Speed of assembly is vital, as the glue cures very quickly. After the gluing process, each matching pair can again be placed on the stacking board until the glue is thoroughly cured.

> CAUTION: Superglue cannot distinguish between wood and human flesh, so extreme care must be taken to avoid contact with the fingers – emergency hospital treatment may be required to unstick them.

Trimming the barrel

Before the blanks can be mounted on a mandrel for turning, it is necessary for each end to be trimmed absolutely flush and square to the end of the brass tube. It is also vital to clean any glue overspill from the inside of the tube. Fortunately, there is a special tool called a barrel trimmer (Fig 10.60) which performs both tasks simultaneously. This tool is fixed in the chuck of a power drill (or a carpenter's brace) and fed into the tube until the wood is trimmed down to the tube. Each end is treated in the same manner. For this operation it is essential that the blank is held firmly in some kind of vice. Fig 10.61 shows the barrel trimmer in use. Take great care to remove only the slightest amount of brass tube, as the finished

Fig 10.61 The barrel trimmer in use

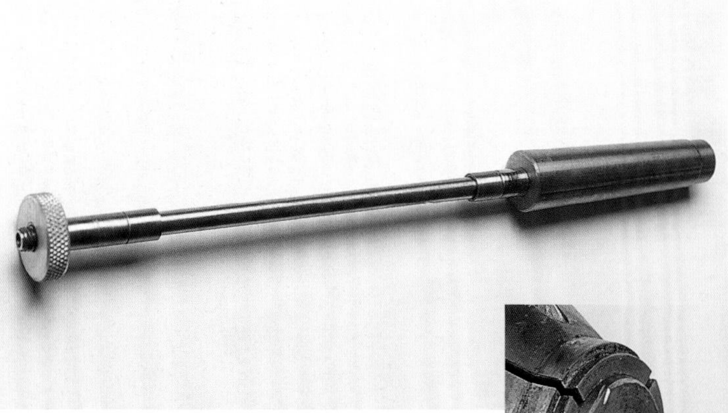

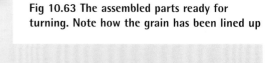

Fig 10.62 A quality double mandrel

Fig 10.63 The assembled parts ready for turning. Note how the grain has been lined up

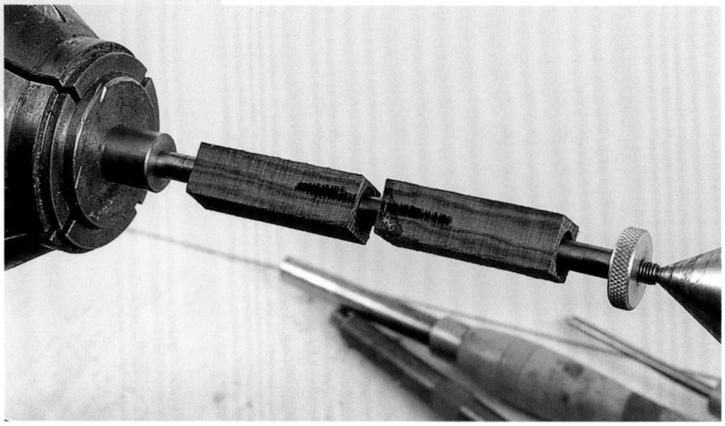

Fig 10.64 Roughing down with a small gouge

lengths are quite critical. If too much is removed, the pen mechanism will not function efficiently.

The final process before mounting the blanks on the lathe is to create a new 'grain match' reference on the inside of the tubes, because the marks on the wood will shortly be turned away. This can be done with a fine marker pen, although I usually use a pointed awl to scratch a mark on the insides.

Lathe mounting systems

There are several types of mandrel available for pen makers, some intended to be used in a Jacobs chuck and some with a machined Morse taper to fit in the headstock mandrel. Fig 10.62 shows the type I prefer. This is a double mandrel allowing both barrels to be turned simultaneously, and comes complete with bushings and brass tightening nut. The purpose of the bushings is to provide an accurate diameter register for the wood to be turned down to, and they should be positioned at both ends and at the centre.

It must be stressed that the diameter of the mandrel must be exactly the same as the inside of the brass tubes. Any sloppiness will result in disaster. Most mandrels are centrally drilled at one end so that the revolving centre – a must for pen turning – can be accurately located, thus maintaining true running.

The turning operation

Insert the mandrel into the headstock and assemble the component parts in order: that is, a bush followed by a wood blank, then the centre bush followed by the second blank and

third bush. Finally, after ensuring that the components have been correctly assembled and grain-matched, apply moderate pressure to the locking nut and to the tailstock. Fig 10.63 shows the components correctly assembled and ready for turning.

Many wood lathes have a top speed of around 2000rpm, and this is adequate, although a faster speed is preferable with such small diameters. Personally, I use only one tool for the whole turning process, which is a ½in (13mm) skew chisel; but I suggest that, until a fair degree of skill and confidence has been acquired, the bulk of the waste wood is removed with a small roughing-out gouge.

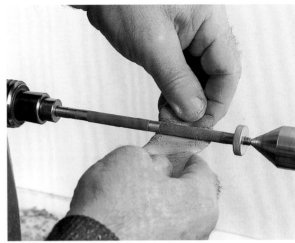

Fig 10.65 (left) Making refining cuts with a skew chisel

Fig 10.66 (above) Sanding to a fine finish

The rules of cutting wood correctly must be strictly observed, and tools must be very sharp.

Such small sections, particularly in exotic hardwoods, will not tolerate scraping methods. Proceed carefully with the gouge until most of the excess wood is removed, and then complete the sizing down to a diameter marginally thicker than the bushes, using the ½in skew chisel. It is a good idea to test the flatness of the surface with a straightedge – I use a cut-off steel rule, but a short piece of hardwood would serve the same purpose. Then refine if necessary. Fig 10.64 shows the bulk of the material being removed with the roughing gouge, and Fig 10.65 shows the refining cuts being taken with the skew chisel.

Sanding

Excessive sanding speeds will generate too much heat and may result in the now veneer-thin walls splitting. Slow the lathe speed down to about 750rpm and gently sand through the grades (180 to 600 grit for a really fine finish) and down to the exact outside diameter of the three bushings. It is good practice, with the lathe stationary, to sand along the grain with the two last grit sizes to obtain that super finish (Fig 10.66).

Polishing

Pens, of necessity, are handled a great deal, and perspiration can result in unsuitable finishes being quickly removed, leaving a less than desirable appearance. Personally, I spray mine with a tough melamine gloss lacquer, but very few woodturners have access to spray equipment.

Polishing on the lathe will provide an acceptable and fairly durable finish if care is taken and the following suggested procedure adopted. First of all, apply a coat of cellulose sanding sealer with a rag or a small brush. Ensure that the sealer has been well diluted with thinners (about 50-50) to improve penetration into the wood. Allow it to dry for a few minutes and then cut it back with the finest abrasive paper you have, *along the grain, with the lathe stationary*. Continue by applying a coat of good-quality friction polish, buffing up to a good gloss with the lathe running. Finally, by pressing a stick of carnauba wax to the whirling wood and buffing up with a clean rag, you should finish up with a fairly durable and pleasing finish. Fig 10.67 shows the final burnishing being done.

Fig 10.67 Final burnishing with a soft rag

Fig 10.68 Simple device for laying out the component parts in order

Fig 10.69 Using an ordinary woodworking vice to press the writing tip into a non-grain-match end

Fig 10.70 Pressing in the pen mechanism, brass end first

Final assembly

All the work that has been done to this stage can be ruined if some suitable means of assembling the pen is not used. Some kind of vice is required, and it is vital that the jaws are lined with a fairly soft material such as copper or MDF so as not to damage the fittings. I use a standard woodworking vice with the jaws suitably lined with MDF.

Lay out the component parts in order of fitting on the simple device shown in Fig 10.68. This is made from two pieces of softwood, 1½ x ⅝in (38 x 16mm). A shallow chamfer is worked on each piece, and then they are glued together to form a V-section in the middle. Remember to grain-match the parts.

Assemble in the following order:

Press the writing tip into the non-grain-match end of one of the tubes (Fig 10.69).

Insert the twist mechanism, brass end first, into the other end of the same tube. It should be squeezed in up to the ring-like indentation

Fig 10.71 Squeezing the pen cap and clip into the other non-grain-match end

Fig 10.72 The completed pen

mark on the chrome part of the mechanism. At this stage, remove it from the vice, insert the ink cartridge and screw it fully home. If the tip does not extend far enough, remove the cartridge and squeeze the mechanism a little further into the tube (Fig 10.70). Now slip on the centre ring.

Insert the cap and clip a little way into the non-grain-match end of the other tube and squeeze together (Fig 10.71).

Hand-squeeze the two sections together and align the grain with the tip of the refill fully retracted. Fig 10.72 shows the completed pen.

If you have made a good job of the pen, you will undoubtedly want to make many more and perhaps make presents of them to your friends and associates. It might be a good idea to present one to your doctor; it might encourage him to write in a more legible style!

SUMMARY

1 As with all woodworking tools, drill bits must be maintained in good condition. To prevent damage to the cutters, some kind of drill stand is essential for storage.

2 When sharpening, it is imperative that the original profile is maintained and the cutters are filed to the same height.

3 Before the lathe is started, ensure the speed has been fixed to suit the type and size of drill bit being used.

4 Boring jigs can be made up, and with a little thought and ingenuity most boring problems can be overcome.

5 When boring deep holes, retract the bit from time to time to remove the waste, otherwise it will bind and overheat.

6 For routing, a dividing head is an absolute must. It is essential that it is accurately made.

7 Many hollowware projects can be speeded up by boring away a great deal of the waste wood.

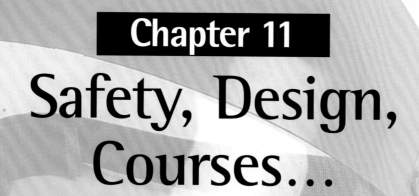

Chapter 11
Safety, Design, Courses…

Safety in the workshop

Safety is *the most important aspect of this book*, and I considered long and hard whether it ought to be the subject of the first chapter. The reason for this not being so is that a good many of the safe working practices and measures described would not necessarily mean a great deal to the newcomer to the craft if they were merely included as a list without the relevant potentially dangerous operations, equipment and tools first being described.

While the woodturning lathe is arguably the safest of all woodworking machines, there have been instances of serious injury being caused to the operator. In my opinion, the reasons for this can be put down to one of three things:

1 Ignorance of the correct techniques – incorrect methods are nearly always dangerous – and safety measures.
2 Taking unnecessary risks, even when experienced. Most professional turners take 'acceptable' or 'calculated' risks to speed up production, but even so the chances of injury are increased, particularly when combined with no. 3 below.
3 Tiredness or lack of concentration. The well-known saying 'familiarity breeds contempt' is particularly relevant to all wood machinists. It must be remembered that all machines can 'bite', and most accidents occur through lack of concentration and towards the end of the working day when tiredness has set in. My advice is to stop when you feel tired, or if your mind is so engrossed in something else that it prevents you from applying maximum concentration.

The object of this section is to refresh the reader's memory on what has gone before relating to safety, and also to include one or two more points which have not been touched on. Remember, many of the following points are basically the application of common sense.

Safety rules

Ensure the electrics are safe – that is, the machine is properly earthed and installed in accordance with the maker's instructions. If a secondhand lathe is acquired, obtain the services of a qualified electrician to check it over. It will be money well spent.

- Rubber plugs should be fitted to all woodworking machines.
- Examine the electric cable from time to time to make sure it is in good order.
- Always isolate the lathe from the mains when changing speeds or applying the 'test of tightness'.
- Ensure that the lathe is securely bolted down to a good solid bench, in the case of a bench model, and occasionally check the tightness of the nuts.
- Sensible dress must be worn. Loose, dangling sleeves must be avoided at all costs. Good strong footwear is also very important. Tools are sometimes dropped or roll off the bench, and can cause nasty wounds if you are shod in trainers or similar footwear.
- Use a purpose-built grindstone that is properly enclosed and designed to run at the correct speed. Occasionally check the soundness of the stone as described in Chapter 4, On Sharpening. Some form of eye protection must always be worn when using the grindstone.
- Study the Laws of Woodturning (pages 45–53) as frequently as possible. Breaking any one of them can be dangerous.
- Always examine the wood for faults, such as dead knots, splits, shakes, etc. If any of these are evident, discard the timber and find some sound stock.
- Ensure that all the locking handles have been tightened and the work spins freely before switching on the power.
- Always stand to one side and out of the 'firing line' when starting the machine.
- Make sure that there is not less than ¾in (20mm) of toolrest protruding by the end of the wood on which you are working.
- In the early learning stage, it is advisable to stop the lathe when making adjustments to the toolrest.
- Minimize the downward leverage on the tools by keeping the rest as close as possible to the workpiece.
- Always remove the toolrest when sanding. Wherever possible, sanding must be done in the 'safe' position.

- Some kind of protection against dust is essential. Make use of a dust mask or respirator, and/or an extractor unit.
- Keep a fire extinguisher in the workshop and do not smoke or allow anyone else to smoke in the shop.
- Wear a face shield when turning natural-edge bowls.

The above list is by no means exhaustive. Very often, safety boils down to just using your common sense, being patient and not taking risks.

Design

As your turning skills improve, you will automatically develop a good eye for shape and proportion (in other words, design), and now is the time to really use your eyes and observe the work of others.

There is no shortage of sources that will stimulate and generate design ideas. Visits to stately homes, museums, galleries, antique shops and craft centres can be a constant inspiration. Many books are devoted purely to the art of good design, architecture, classical Greek and Roman profiles, the 'Golden Ratio', etc. Most of the woodworking magazines regularly publish articles including designs for turning projects. The sources of design are endless and if the student is sufficiently enthusiastic and motivated to produce things of beauty, experience will enable him to tell when a project looks right.

Woodturning courses

Since being pioneered by the late Peter Child, woodturning courses have sprung up everywhere, and certainly a good tutor can impart sufficient knowledge to a novice on a two-day course (the most popular duration) to allow him to develop his skills in a safe and confident manner.

These courses are not cheap, and if I was paying out good money to go on such a course, I would want to know the answers to the following questions:

1 How many other students will be on the course? My own view is that two is the optimum number. I previously did courses for a wood-machine retailer where four people per course was the norm. I do not recall any complaints, but I felt I could have given better value for money if only two students had participated. In my capacity as a teacher at the local college of further education, I have had as many as sixteen students sharing four lathes. Progress can be made, but inevitably it is slow.

2 How many lathes are available and what make are they? There is no substitute for 'hands-on' experience (preceded of course by explanation and demonstration), so ensure that there is one lathe per student.

3 How much time is actually allocated to 'hands on'? While it is inevitable that a certain amount of theory, explanation and demonstration is necessary, the amount of time spent on these must not be disproportionate to the hands-on time allowed. In my opinion at least 80 per cent of the course time should be so allocated.

4 Is the instructor articulate and able to explain things in a simple and easily understood manner? (Being a good woodturner does not necessarily mean you are a good teacher.) If possible, arrange a visit to the instructor's workshop. This will give you the opportunity to assess him and determine whether or not his personality is compatible with yours. Two days is a very long time to spend with someone you cannot take a liking to.

5 Is his workshop well organized, tidy and comfortable? (The state of a workshop will provide many clues as to the instructor's attitudes, enthusiasm and teaching skills.) If the course is during the colder months, is there any heating in the place? There is nothing worse for the concentration than being cold.

6 Is there a course syllabus and are there any course notes? Personally I would want to know exactly what topics are covered. I appreciate that the pace of every course needs to be adjusted to the receptivity and aptitude of the student, but this is no excuse for a 'let's see how we go' approach, with little or no planning. Inevitably some students will be a little slower than others, but would this mean that the whole of the syllabus would not be covered? I would expect to be supplied with some fairly comprehensive

course notes. No one can be expected to remember more than about 25 per cent of all he is told, therefore notes are an extremely useful means of revising everything that has been explained on the course.

Looking at it from the instructor's point of view, I do feel that many people expect too much from a two-day course of instruction. If the student has learned the basics, as outlined in this book, then I am more than satisfied that he or she will have created a solid *foundation* on which to build with confidence and optimism. Remember, no one can impart that indefinable *feel* into your hands – this can only come with constant educated practice.

Ways forward

Learning the craft of woodturning is a gradual process. As with any form of learning there will inevitably be setbacks and occasions when you may well think you are not making the progress you should. Do not be downhearted, because everyone goes through such stages. There are ways forward, however, that can revitalize and perhaps inspire the student to 'keep right on to the end of the road'. Accordingly, I offer the following ideas to provide a much needed boost, which we all require from time to time.

Evening classes

Some local authorities run woodturning classes. Despite the fact that it is more than likely you will be sharing a lathe with two or three others, much can be learned by listening and looking. A bonus is that many close friendships are forged, and normally there exists an excellent camaraderie, each student swapping ideas and so on, to the benefit of all.

Demonstrations

These are featured at all the major woodworking shows, and most of the demonstrators are only too willing to give advice and help out with any problem you might be encountering. Don't be afraid to ask. I for one certainly welcome any query, and it is more than likely that a good many of the onlookers are experiencing similar problems. Some of the larger suppliers of woodturning equipment and accessories, such as Craft Supplies Ltd, also run regular demonstrations, and they are well worth a visit.

The Association of Woodturners of Great Britain

This association was formed at an international seminar at Loughborough in August 1987. It is organized and administered *by* woodturners *for* woodturners and membership is open to anyone interested in the craft, be they novice or professional.

The advantages of belonging to this association are many. Its aims and objectives can do nothing but improve the standing of the craft in the eyes of the public. The setting up of local 'chapters' provides opportunities for meeting other members living in the area, so as to exchange ideas on techniques, developments and projects. Seminars and exhibitions are also organized, and internationally known turners are invited. Attending such gatherings can be a rewarding and stimulating experience, providing the chance to rub shoulders with the acclaimed. The Association also publishes a newsletter from time to time, updating the membership on all that is happening in the world of woodturning.

Appeal

By now you will have gathered that I am a self-confessed 'wood nut'. Those of you just starting out on your woodturning venture will, I am almost certain, also develop a love for the material. The decimation of the world's rainforests and the destruction of trees by natural disasters such as the hurricane that swept across southern England in 1987 cause much alarm. I think it is incumbent on all of us to do our little bit to ensure that future generations of woodworkers can enjoy all the species of trees that we do.

Do you realize that by donating a small sum to the Woodland Trust, Kempton Way, Grantham, Lincs, NG31 6LL, you can have a broadleaved tree planted where the need is greatest? What is more, your name will be included in the official *Book of Commemoration*. Please think about it, but not for too long – remember that some trees take 100 years to mature!

About the Author

Keith Rowley was born and bred in a coal-mining community in south-east Derbyshire where most of his friends, on leaving school, went to work in the mines. His father, a miner too, was determined that Keith would not follow in his footsteps, and insisted he should learn a trade.

Keith therefore went to work for 'the company' in the joiners' shop, and 'served his time', gaining a wide range of woodworking skills from first-fixing carpentry to fine cabinetmaking. His mentor, whom Keith describes as the most complete all-round woodworker he has known, was also an accomplished woodturner, passing on to Keith his wealth of knowledge and practical skills.

With the demise of the coal industry in the late 1950s, and by then being a married man with family responsibilities, Keith opted for a more secure occupation and joined the Nottingham City Police, spending most of his service in the Criminal Investigation Department.

He took early retirement from the force in 1982 and from then continued woodturning on a professional basis, combining his commercial turnery with private courses of instruction. In his own words, Keith derived as much pleasure from 'making the shavings fly' as he did all those years ago as a young apprentice.

He was in great demand as a demonstrator and teacher at home and overseas, and was a regular demonstrator on the Myford trade stand at the national shows. He was a registered turner with the Worshipful Company of Turners, and considered it a great honour when he was appointed as Midlands area Assessor by this prestigious organization.

Keith was always willing to share his knowledge and experience with others, and this was what prompted him to write the first edition of this book and, in 1996, *Keith Rowley's Woodturning Projects*. They have both proved hugely successful.

Sadly, Keith died in June, 2005. Although greatly missed, his life-long wealth of woodturning experience is captured in his books and DVD to be enjoyed for years to come.

Metric Conversion Table

inches to millimetres

inches	mm	inches	mm	inches	mm
1/8	3	9	229	30	762
1/4	6	10	254	31	787
3/8	10	11	279	32	813
1/2	13	12	305	33	838
5/8	16	13	330	34	864
3/4	19	14	356	35	889
7/8	22	15	381	36	914
1	25	16	406	37	940
1 1/4	32	17	432	38	965
1 1/2	38	18	457	39	991
1 3/4	44	19	483	40	1016
2	51	20	508	41	1041
2 1/2	64	21	533	42	1067
3	76	22	559	43	1092
3 1/2	89	23	584	44	1118
4	102	24	610	45	1143
4 1/2	114	25	635	46	1168
5	127	26	660	47	1194
6	152	27	686	48	1219
7	178	28	711	49	1245
8	203	29	737	50	1270

Index